VOYAGE
GASTRONOMIQUE

VOYAGE GASTRONOMIQUE

A Culinary Autobiography

by

Lillian Langseth-Christensen

A Martin Dale Book

HAWTHORN BOOKS, INC.

PUBLISHERS / *New York*

Contents

PART I

PART II

PART I

1

Food Memories Around the World

Le voyage autour de ma chambre, that rather dated turn-of-the-century-ish phrase, was held to mean a charming (once dashing, now sedentary) gentleman, sitting in his velvet smoking jacket in his book- and memorabilia-lined study, in his advancing years. His memories jumped fondly from a Benares brass tray to an alabaster model of the leaning tower of Pisa, to the books and souvenirs of a lifetime of happy voyaging. He smoked—in my mind—a meerschaum pipe and placed his feet on a beaded Victorian footstool.

Being past any physical effort, he then took his *voyage autour de ma chambre* and recalled through a pink haze of memory his more active discoveries and conquests in remote places—like Rome.

I do not have a beaded footstool and I do not smoke and I am not all that old, but the fact remains that certain things depart and only memories can take their place. My memories from earliest childhood are not of the stones and sculptures, the museums and collections of far places—they are of food, food, food.

I was not a greedy child nor even a hungry one. I remember a rare illness in France—my head ached and there were acute pangs in my interior. I was shy, but finally had to confess to my governess that I was too *krank* to accompany my parents on the day's planned excursion—to a restaurant. They were concerned and, as the symptoms became worse, consulted with the *portier* about the hotel's physician. M. le Docteur was called—from his luncheon—and, being a Frenchman

* NOTE: Recipes are given in the second part of this book for dishes that appear in boldface in the text.

with his own half-eaten lunch awaiting him, was able to make a brilliant and instant diagnosis, "*L'enfant* is 'ungree." That particular malady never affected me again until recently. Now I am always hungry.

Our voyages were gastronomical because food was my parents' passion and preoccupation, and my brother Edward and I grew up at a time when the children of Austrian parents accompanied them through thick and thin—thick and thin soups and batters and sauces in our case. Our young American friends went off to camp or country houses or to the seashore and had themselves happy freckly summers in socks and sandals, with unwashed faces and blades of sweet juicy grass between their teeth. Of all the things American children did, the chewing of grass and straws was, in Father's opinion, the final indignity. The unforgivable insult to the palate, the unhealthy atrocity. Anything on a lower level than superb food and wine that went into the mouth, namely grass, reeds, straws, wooden picks, chewing gum, lollipops, ice-cream cones, popcorn, and other dreams of delight, was forbidden to us. While our friends were growing into carefree adults in overalls and sneakers (an eight-letter word we were never allowed to mention, since every good Austrian parent—and we had two—knew what rubber would do to the soles of children's feet) or even bare feet, we were dragged from Lucullan meal to Lucullan meal accompanied by measured sips of famous vintages.

During those happier days my father kept various cars in strategic places and traveled only with a chauffeur who preceded him to get the car out and running before we arrived. "We" were our parents, Edward and I, and our governess. Any possible hardships of traveling with children were on the governess's shoulders and she was a past master at—in fact a graduate of the school of—imposing silence. Knowing how to raise children who never made a sound was their profession. I can just see the conscientious mother writing the departing governess a reference—"And we never heard the children during the six years of Fräulein Bratenwetterkamp's sojourn with us." Our last and longest-lasting governess (eight years) was a bilingual Fräulein Chaudière who had advantageously come into the world in Alsace-Lorraine, where she had learned to speak both French and German. We had our Mademoiselle and Fräulein rolled into one, which made traveling much more convenient. The chauffeurs were Edward Lawrence and Lawrence Cluen, who changed overnight into Gostike Kotti. One of my chums in New York called him Gostinky, within adult hearing, and that was the end of the chum. For one dizzy period—the Edward Lawrence days—our governess was also a wife, Mrs. Lawrence to be exact. That meant (I now understand why) that we had much less governess underfoot (and were consequently noisier) than we were later on during the days of Lawrence Cluen and Fräulein Chaudière, who were not on the same social plane, let alone married to each other.

Since Edward Lawrence could not possibly be called by his given name—we already had an Edward who took precedence—he was called Lawrence. When Lawrence Cluen took his place he was still called Lawrence and so for many years I was convinced that all uniformed chauffeurs behind steering wheels of cars were Lawrences. (The poor men had to wear leather puttees even in the hottest weather.)

Lawrence Cluen gave way to stolid Gostike Kotti because Lawrence once refused to slow down when my father told him to. I was there on the jump seat at the time, and since I loved Lawrence wildly, I complicated the scene with floods of tears. In those days gentlemen drove their cars from the back seat by means of a flexible rubber tube encased in silk braid. The tube ended in a black hard-rubber trumpet that curved toward the Lawrences' right ears. A slight upward motion to the left told the owner behind the glass plate that his Lawrence was attending. The tube started in an ivory, silver, gold, or bone mouthpiece buried in a discreet silk tassel and clamped to my father's side of the back seat. Lawrence was at the moment giving the Delaunay Belleville the gas (we have all learned to drive cars since then and know that feeding them gas under given circumstances is essential) because he was trying to get the mighty dark-green elephant up and over the Falzarego Pass. With four adults, two children, and a vast luggage trunk fitted with suitcases like a chest of drawers, and with lovely round black leather hatboxes built into the two spare tires in the fender wells and a good four feet of Vuitton luggage on the roof of the car held in place by a sort of brass balcony rail, he was probably saving our lives. The car, naked and unoccupied, must have weighed a ton. With all of us and what was considered proper luggage and extra petrol disposed here and there in dangerous places, it is a wonder we were able to pass over any pass. I remember my father took up his end of the communication tube, shook aside the tassel, pressed the signal button and said, "More slowly, Lawrence." Lawrence apparently stepped on the gas and we made it. Later, Lawrence was shown, cap in hand, into Father's presence and somehow, in my mind, then turned into Gostike Kotti. My last impression was of his large, never previously displayed red pompadour.

Gostike Kotti was older and fatter and always took the low roads. Father brought him to America and was as fond of him as their relationship permitted. Gostike was something of a gastronome himself and was able to contribute a minor bistro here and there to the itinerary. I think he retired when the space between Gostike and the steering wheel became too narrow for comfort.

Planning these voyages, which I now take in memory around my room, jumping from an old menu from Pforte's restaurant in Hamburg to a lovely old hand-blown green Carlsbad Becher Bitter bottle, was my father's major occupation during the short periods between voyages. These were incidentally the times during which we went to schools. The routes were not laid out from Notre Dame to Chartres to Rheims and the Kölner Dom, or from *châteaux* to *Schlösser*; they followed the shortest line from one great chef to the next, from one restaurant and hotel to the next, and during the summers, from one great vineyard to the next. We saw the cathedrals in passing as others saw restaurants on their way from cathedral to cathedral.

We didn't just arrive, wash up, and eat a good dinner. Letters were exchanged, certain things were earmarked for us in advance. Wines were held in reserve. My father was not one to be told the last portion of *fraises des bois* had just been served when *fraises des bois* was what he had driven down dusty roads to eat. Upon arrival we were allowed a few minutes' grace and then a discreet knock brought the *maître* or the owner with menu and wine list and reports. Everything was either in order or certain minor modifications had to be discussed. There was never at any time any question of consultation with anyone else. Mother may have longed for a cup of soup and a rest. She may have had a craving for a Blue Trout or a simple **Chicken Rossini.** What she got and we got and we all ate was exactly what my loving, thoughtful, considerate father had spent days planning for us—and incidentally exactly what he wanted to eat.

I didn't sympathize with Mother. She wore cloche hats because he liked cloche hats and ate **Tournedos Rossini** when she wanted **Sole Valérie.** She was what her friends and family considered a spoiled and fortunate woman. But we were different—we spent short periods of our life with friends who munched on peanut-butter sandwiches and ate Hershey bars. I think I liked vanilla ice cream sodas, hot dogs, and milk-chocolate almond bars more than anything else in the food world. But what we were fed and what we were shown and what we were forcefully exposed to was what, in the end, has made up my memories.

Memory Training

 Y EARLIEST MEMORIES were based entirely on hearsay, but they were nonetheless vivid. Mother had apparently read a German book on memory training for children and applied the method to us.

The point was to keep all events alive in the child's mind by constant repetition—and we all know what repetition will do for even the dullest event. Either Mother or Fräulein would turn to us at regular intervals each day and say brightly, "Do you remember when we went down the Rhine on the *Lorelei* and you fell off your chair just as we were passing the Bishop of Bingen's Mäuse Turm while Father was eating **Saumon Rothschild** and drinking Oppenheimer Goldberg Auslese?" This was calculated to implant geographic, historic, gastronomic, and vinaceous interests. And then there would be gales of laughter so that all memories, no matter how embarrassing, would appear to be connected with enjoyment. The memory-training method depended heavily on the happiness that must be associated with each event. After a few weeks of listening to repetitious details that particular episode was indelibly engraved on our minds and I go through life burdened with a picture of a red plush stool with tassels, red salmon, and the Bishop of Bingen, also in red.

We lived on hilarious memories, by suggestion, of events we actually could not remember at all I have often wished they had applied the same method to recollections of Napoleon's or George Washington's childhood instead of ours. It would have improved my history marks later on.

The "Do You Remember" game was never relaxed. It was practiced on our walks, in the car, at nursery meals and especially at bedtime. At an hour when our friends were being regaled by another stirring chapter out of the *Adventures of Uncle Wiggly,* our bedtime stories were, "Do you remember when you pulled the label off Father's wine bottle and stuck it back into the half-empty bottle? It was Berncastler Doktor 1908." Not a really memorable year except for the label.

Since our parents were preoccupied with everything to do with food and entertaining, they tended to fasten on food events in developing our methodical memories. We were constantly asked to remember how Father had left a dinner party (which we did not, of course, attend) because his hostess had the butler place the emptied **Abricots Créole** plates on the dining-room hearth for the cocker spaniel to lick clean. It took me years to discover that Father had departed so suddenly because he saw the spaniel doing such a perfect job of licking the plates that he wondered whether they just *might* be returned to the cupboard without being washed. And that made him wonder further about the previous night's dessert.

Our forced memories were supported by faded yellow snapshots, albums of picture postcards and other visual aids. After The Method had been used for several years, we could take our oaths on our entire infancy—we even contributed some flowery details out of our own subconscious. And so we relived our memories each day, and our lives became a good six to eight years longer than other people's lives—and full of trivialities that would have been better forgotten.

Whether good or bad, I go through life with something called total-food-and-wine recall, partial general recall and no recall whatever in arithmetic. There must have been madness in Mother's method because I can remember a Squab Saint Charles larded with smoked tongue and filled with a liver-stuffed hard-cooked egg, with a faint flavor of lemon rind in the sauce, and it was good. I remember Otto Baumgarten's Mushrooms Voisin, enormous mushrooms filled high with chestnut purée and served with a truffle sauce. You'll say it was redundant, but it wasn't—and I didn't need any "Do you remember" proddings to remember the dish perfectly. Whenever I see some of those two-to-a-portion mushrooms along with a jar of truffles, I remember it concretely. And mushrooms always remind me of Pforte's Gräfin Loni Tarts (miniature tart shells full of herbed oysters and mushrooms, under a hat of cheese soufflé). The food memories conjure up the circumstances. I invariably remember what we wore and what we said when we ate **Pêches Ninette,** but I cannot for the life of me remember what became of a man called Alfred Landon, who once wanted to be president . . . probably because we didn't eat peaches with him.

Edward had a rather eventless infancy, so his "do-you-remember's" were more relaxed than mine. They started with a marble he swallowed when he was four and remembered in any case. Mine always began with "Do you remember when we lost you in London," but having been six months old, I didn't—but I do now, in every detail, including Nurse Scott who finally ended, with me and my folding pram, at Scotland Yard.

Later Mother read another book entitled, *We Forget Because We Must*, and felt no compunction whatever about forgetting everything, including the Game, but it came too late for me.

Father had a numerical memory which saved him from looking up telephone or house numbers and made life very hard on us. He knew the year Goethe wrote *Werther*, the license number of the car that passed us on the hill, and the size of Dryden's vocabulary. But he had a child (me) who, on a memorable occasion, could not remember the date of the French Revolution.

This sort of inexcusable ignorance was usually rewarded with a punishment of silence. We were not spoken to for a period commensurate with the offense. The French Revolution rated two weeks' silence, but just before we went into it, Father's last words addressed to me were, "You cannot possibly be a child of mine."

I was used to being turned into a foundling whenever I didn't reflect Father's whims and tastes. "That's no child of mine," he would hiss—meaning me. The disclaimer was based on my making a horrible face every time I had to drink my nip of wine or eat anything perfumed with liqueurs. Edward adored his wine and was obviously his father's son. I can see now that I was a sad disappointment to Father, a man who traveled only to taste and buy wines and ate only to enhance each course with the proper vintage. If Mother and we had not accompanied him on his wine-tasting trips, she would have been a wine widow and we would have been wine orphans—a very sad state.

The scenes that were kept alive for us were the very ones we would have forgotten had we had any choice in the matter. "Do you remember when you lost your underdrawers in Zermatt," was not my favorite recollection, nor did I care to know what Father did when the waiter sneezed on my strawberries (he would not let me eat them and there weren't any others). They especially wanted us to remember a crossing on the *Imperator* when we both had whooping cough—an inconvenience that was not allowed to interfere with Father's plans. The Hamburg-Amerika Line apparently set a back deck aside and quarantined us with Fräulein and an officer, who had had *Keuchhusten*, acted as a sort of intermediary. They reminded me that I had shhh-ed them when they came into my room in London one evening because I was charmed with a small mouse at the foot of my bed. I was supposed to remember that Father had two nurses and a male nurse when he had typhoid in New York so that he could be carried down to check his wine-cellar temperatures every day.

We lived, when we were not in hotels or on steamers, in a house in New York and in Grandmother's house in Austria. The Austrian house was old with deep vaulted cellars that stayed, miraculously, at a proper wine temperature all year around. In New York the cellar was a disaster, what Father called *his cross*. Besides the coal bins and trunk room and wine cellar, it contained a huge coal-burning furnace, which was stoked by an Italian furnace-man called Mike. The temperature of the house (not that it mattered, the cellar was the important thing) depended on the utterly Neapolitan non-thermostatic temperature of Mike. It was apt to be heated in July when he was angry, neglected in December when he was homesick. He swept the sidewalk, cleared the snow, and put up with Father. In defense of Mike I can only remember that he always had a good word for the Sheffield Farms milk-wagon horse, which made our piece of sidewalk its feeding station and sprinkled it with oats.

When the house was barely warm enough for us, the wines were suffering. When the wines were happy, we were freezing upstairs. The wine cellar was finally insulated and ventilated separately, but we still had to light what were called our open fires. They consisted of hideous asbestos replicas of logs with perforations, known as gas logs. In our rooms they were further adorned with marshmallow drippings and the charred remains of a well-hidden and never-found Easter egg.

My artificially induced memories include the enormous Vienna Opera tenor Leo Slezak, who supposedly placed me on a chair on top of a table so that I would be high enough to have a look at him. I apparently gave him one look and burst into tears. The memory, largely colored by Fräulein's rendition, went further to include a kiss which brought forth more tears. I have a genuine memory of Leo Slezak ten years later when I was just beginning my art-school life in Vienna. I took Mother, my last tie with home and law and order, to the railroad station and on the way back I stopped on the Graben to buy myself the two things I wanted most in the world, a lipstick and a white ivory toothbrush inlaid with ebony polka dots.

I was not aware at that time that there were ladies known as Lights of Love, and, no wonder, neither was Webster, but I think now that if there could possibly have been such a thing as a tart's toothbrush . . . I bought it that day. As I walked home down the Kärntner Strasse I saw the huge sun-obscuring bulk of Leo Slezak come hatless and coatless, with silk necktie flying, toward me down the street, with every Viennese eye fondly upon him. Although he could not possibly have recognized me, I still remembered my poor show on the table and chair and hurried past. About half a block later there was Slezak, loudly shouting "*Sëu!*" (Viennese dialect for "Hey, you!") and running after me brandishing my tart's toothbrush over his head for everyone to see. All Vienna seemed to be rooted to the spot with delight. He handed it to me and said at the top of his voice and pointing to his cheek, "*Bussie*" ("kiss").

I grabbed my brush and ran. I still have it and a photograph of Leo Slezak, curly-haired and grinning. I told his son Walter Slezak about it when he was in New York delighting audiences with the famous Slezak humor.

My memories of events that took place before I was even aware of what was going on around me, were a combination of suggestion and the snapshots and pictures which were always being taken, but some of them rest on the fact that they were repeated and became actual experiences within my memory. I do not remember any of the European trips until the summer of 1914, but I can recall 1911 as though it were yesterday.

3

Do You Remember 1911?

OF COURSE WE didn't remember 1911, but we heard about it and toasted it so often in subsequent years that we thought we remembered every vineyard and every blown-out tire. Father felt that anyone who was fortunate enough to be alive in 1911 should remember it, and so it was drummed into us, with the help of an album of deplorable snapshots, until the whole summer stood out in our minds as a crystal-clear memory. Later, whenever we were given a nip of 1911 wines we were not only expected to recognize it, we were supposed to put on.expressions of deepest piety. As the beauty and fame of the vintage increased, my awe became so great that I recently brought Father's last four bottles of 1911er to Austria—with the sort of *Pietäts Gefühl* (reverent feeling) that Father always said I lacked.

We opened three bottles during the last thirty years, one every ten years until 1971. At sixty the wines were just beginning to show their age, and the remaining bottles are going to stay as they are— unopened. One of them was never meant for immortality, but I cherish it because of its name, Erdener Treppchen 1911. It always sounded like a little earthen stairway to me and I visualized steep stone steps in a sunny vineyard overhanging a river. Actually Erden is a small town on the Moselle with almost perpendicular vineyards that have nothing to do with anything earthen at all. Father thought of that wine as an unserious *Spielerei* (plaything) in his cellar, a little something he had come across to put into an *Erdbeer Bowle* (Strawberry Bowl) for uneducated palates. A modest wine to chuckle over with one of his cronies.

Informal entertaining was rare with Father, but once or twice a year, when Clarence Whitehill or Friedrich Schorr were not about to be Wotan or Gurnemanz or Hans Sachs, they came for a quiet little wine evening. Baritones were apparently better suited to this sort of thing than tenors. I cannot remember a single Siegfried or Lohengrin or Parsifal with whom Father would have shared one of his intimate, anecdotal, lip-smacking wine evenings.

Judging by the faded, yellowed snapshots with which I still relive 1911, Father had a smart Daimler Landaulet that looked like an overgrown baby carriage and a pre-Edward Lawrence chauffeur who looked exactly like a walrus with a tiny black Heidelberg student's cap on its head. There is a whole series of pictures, taken rather monotonously, by Fräulein Hedwig whenever the hot tires blew out. The dry heat that made 1911 the greatest wine year of Father's life also immobilized his car at all the least convenient places. The composition of the pictures was always more or less the same. Father and his walrus in goggles and swathed from chin to ankle in dusters were disposed dejectedly around the car, the walrus, clutching a very long and obviously inadequate tire pump. Mother could be seen on the back seat, under a parasol, Edward sat forlornly on the battery box on the high running board, and I was a lump under a dust bonnet on the back seat next to Mother. Our Fräulein was only a long shadow in the center of the pictures, and the car was festooned with extra tires rather like a tugboat in New York Harbor.

There were several other snapshots taken when the blowouts occurred propitiously near a vineyard, and these pictures show Father, usually with the vintner, in a very different spirit. In one of them he is standing on an impressive terrace overlooking the Rhine, pitcher in hand, pointing forcefully at the vineyards below. His expression can only be described as utterly contented. On another picture he is just parting from a formally attired man, apparently the owner, and while they are not exactly locked in an embrace, their acquaintance had obviously ripened into affection. As the cases of 1911 wines gradually came into the cellar, it became quite clear that Father had improved the arid hours by placing orders and leaving bids along the way. I do not remember 1911, but I do remember that its wines were opened only for *Weinkönner* ("wine knowers and appreciators"), not for people.

Father had the great advantage, in selecting and buying wines, that he always saw the previous vintage and experienced the weather conditions which preceded a great year, so to speak, on his own skin. Mother told me that we continued one of our trips, in spite of as many as four blowouts a day and relays of tires being shipped along our route, because the late summer of 1911 was working itself up to what wine lovers superstitiously hoped would be a second 1811, and Father was determined to see the harvest.

Another picture caught Father in a cellar, at the end of a double row of barrels, touching glasses with an assortment of flourishing mustaches that completely outshone his own. One of the men has such a heavy gold watch chain across his chest that he had to be the owner. As far back as 1900 Baedeker spoke of the many "indications of the lucrative nature of the local industry." Poor Father, marooned in the *Kelleren* of the Rhine and waiting for tire replacements, had nothing whatever to do but taste wines, watch the grapes, and lay his plans. As time went by his cellar became a byword.

The one woman in the cellar picture is of ripe proportions, in a striped shirtwaist, stiff collar, necktie, pince-nez on a black ribbon, and a frightening arrangement on her head. I remember that Father said she owned a hotel and for me she was Mrs. Adlon. A magnifying glass reveals the hat as an enormous pyramid of dangling cherries, further adorned with the wing of a blackbird, a full-blown rose, a buckle, a cloche brim, turned up on one side, and a veil, gathered into a bow at the back. Whoever they were, they had the wit to taste wines between Ober Kassel and Ehrenbreitstein, and if they recognized the symptoms, they were, so to speak, in on the cellar floor for 1911ers.

From all reports, Edward and I ate with Fräulein so that Father and Mother could mull over their wine plans undisturbed, but we were expected to remember the Egg Biscuit Soup, the **Oeufs Mozart,** and the **Kasseler Rippchen** which they ate, finishing with **Pumpernickel Pudding,** and a bottle of Piesporter Goldtropfchen 1904.

One of the pictures was posed in position for departure from the inn Zur Goldene Rebe—Golden Grape—and its angle would indicate that it was taken by the youngest bystander. The hotel staff is standing in a half-circle behind the car, and Father, sitting next to his walrus chauffeur, is waving graciously over his inevitable map; Fräulein and Edward are sitting backward on the jump seats and I am pleased to note that Mother and I are out in the open air. The top is folded back with a pair of vicious brass hinges but everything else that was brass is shrouded in leather bonnets—headlights, side lanterns, tail lantern. The walrus presumably removed the covers before he lit the acetylene lanterns with a wax match.

Our luggage is piled top-heavily on the fenced terrace on the car's permanent roof and an inverted canvas swimming pool is strapped down over it. Mother reminded me later that as the car proceeded, air was caught under the canvas and the vehicle became a lumbering earthbound balloon trying to get rid of its ballast. As speed gathered the canvas made deafening flapping noises.

Whenever we repeated the German Wine Tour after 1919, Father turned right at Ehrenbreitstein to go on to picturesque Bernkastel on the Mosel, where he loved the ruined fortress and the Hotel Römische Kaiser's **Himmel und Erde** (Heaven and Earth) and sugary sweet pretzels, *Brezeln*. I disliked the nips of wine but I loved the countryside—the whole landscape looked like a German fairy tale come true. There were Rapunzel's high tower, the Wrong Prince's castle, and Frau Holler's feather beds. Knights and dragons belonged in the mysterious forests and we saw most of the Grimm brothers' sly foxes and roosters, owls, crows, and donkeys. There were Hansel and Gretel's *Knusperhäuschen* (gingerbread houses) and clustered toy villages at the foot of steep wine hills.

The German wine names are made for children, who fortunately do not lay in wine cellars, Vogelsang (birdsong), Gottesfuss (God's foot) and Ritterpfad (knight's path) were my favorites. I was a little crushed by Jesuitengarten but I loved Sonnenuhr (sundial), Bruderschaft (brotherhood) and, above all, Grosser Herrgott (Almighty God). There was also a Himmelreich (heavenly Kingdom) and the intriguing Doktor (Thanish) of Bernkastel.

There were two summer wine trips, which I remember we took alternately. One circled through France, and the second, which we took in 1911, started in Paris and cut across to Epernay where Father, needless to say, had business and an "underlined" chef at the Hôtel des Châlons. (Father's first note about this modest hotel is dated 1909. My parents seem to have had an unerring nose for chefs—a culinary serendipity that led them to obscure places which they underlined and footnoted long before Michelin endowed them with stars. It is part of France's solid, reliable charm that there is still an excellent chef and an outstanding wine cellar at 6 rue des Berceaux.)

After Epernay, Father had qualms about our education and we were always given a short turn to Rheims Cathedral—which *he* spent at the Maison Pommery. From Rheims to Bar-le-Duc we were dutifully presented with the telescoped life of Jeanne d'Arc and the coronations of the kings. From Bar-le-Duc to Nancy the interest turned to the unique gooseberry and red-and-white currant preserves of haunting flavor, which at home did so much for Marie's partridge, and spiced ham sauce, **Poires Petit Duc,** and various cheeses.

Nancy, from the old Grand Hotel on the Place Stanislas, was the first place—for me—where history looked better in reality than in our school history books. If Stanislas Leszczynski, ex-king of Poland, father-in-law of Louis XV, and last Duke of Lorraine, had to live in exile, it could hardly have been more beautifully situated. And judging by his Triumphal Arch, the Porte Stanislas, the Place Stanislas, the statue of Stanislas, and the rue Stanislas, they treated him well. We attended our history lectures in the Restaurant Stanislas, where we ate **Potée Lorraine** and, of course, *Quiche Lorraine,* the famous macaroons and madeleines, and **Flan aux Oignons** or **Purée Soissonnaise** or **Lentils à la Stanislas.** Lorraine is not wine country, but father was looking forward.

We had another pause for culture at the Château of Lunéville, where Maria Theresa's husband was born, and turned into the low Vosges mountains to Colmar (for the Isenheim Altarpiece only) and then back to Strasbourg. Father didn't take the Alsatian wines seriously, but he always wanted to see what was going on. If the weather was right, an Alsatian wine just *might,* in his estimation, become pleasant. Edward and I loved Strasbourg, the clock with the cock that flaps its wings when it crows at noon, the tall timbered houses, and the storks on the chimney tops. But it was a city of interminable waiting for Father. He didn't buy wines for the cellar, but he bought short-lived wines for the storeroom—there had to be something in which to cook the **Huhn in Riesling** and the **Brown Sauerkraut**—and he laid in every conceivable sort of *eau de vie.*

Besides following our parents through their wine-tasting and buying tours, we listened to them. The wine lover's In-Language, which was spoken on these trips and whenever Father and his wine tongues met, was not to be believed. Their vocabulary went from effusive to indulgent to death-dealing (by the faint-praise method). There was not only a wine language; there were certain wine sounds that applied to appreciation or condemnation. Wine lovers use a sort of specialized smacking of the lips before they emit a prolonged "Ah." They also have a sibilant, almost supersonic sound that comes just after the wine has been rolled around the tongue and a dubious little "Mmm," which heralds the first doubt . . . Is it just a hair past its prime, does it leave just the faintest shadow of a trace of an after-taste? Is it perhaps deceiving us? Then there is the slow smile, the lighting up of the eyes, when paradise, in a bottle, has been found.

There is a set of emphatic sounds to indicate rejection and there is the shrug when tolerance of youth and immaturity are expressed. I often wondered whether wine drinking could possibly give any pleasure to inarticulate, monosyllabic people who could only describe wine as good or bad, sweet or sour. Wines in Germany were *herb* (dry) or *rüstig* (which meant robust as well as nimble). They were *lieblich* (lovable) or *schmiegsam* (clinging, flexibly submissive). They were *fruchtig* and *frisch* (never *fromm, frölich, froh,* or *frei*), and the way they smelled was their *Blume* (flower). German wines were spoken of as though an athlete or a pretty girl were being described, their *Körpers* (bodies) were *männlich* (manly) and *kräftig* (muscular) or *vollrund* (well rounded) or *mollig* (cuddly and cozy).

All the wine lovers were serious; wine drinking was by no means a frivolous occupation. They ate bits of bread and had an inward look as though the wines were speaking to them. They looked wise, solemn, patronizing, and reproachful by turns and they all kept their eyes suspiciously on each other. They evinced deep emotion for great wines and only an indulgent sigh for the young and unfinished ones. Perhaps, in time, they would show promise . . . who knows . . . perhaps they would become *bedeutend* (meaningful) with maturity . . . or perhaps they would be condemned to remain *Begleitweine* (escort wines) for the rest of their unfortunate lives. Pah for them!—and all the meek, modest, unobtrusive, unostentatious, demure, and coy wines . . . what was wanted were wines with a refined body and a yielding, harmonious personality.

In France, where we expected the most romantic comparisons, they spoke of their wines with reserve. They were either agreeable, elegant, or regal. A wine had to be fragrant (*envelopper le nez*) and *noble* at the same time; it had to be both *charmant* and *voluptueux*. They condemned their wines as being *pas assez subtil* or *manquant d'équilibre,* others were entirely *trop vigoureux.* I heard of a wine that had *bonheur,* others were *léger* or *opulent et succulent,* or even *amusant.* French wines either had or didn't have equilibrium, and some were *souple mais nerveux.*

This didn't go on for a few hours, it went on for weeks in France, Alsace, Germany, along the Weinstrasse and La Route des Vins. Father laid in his delicate and robust wines, his prestigious *grands vins* and champagnes and his cooking and *Vin Chaudeau* wines. It wasn't so much that wines were selected to serve with the various dinner courses as that dinners were arranged around the wines. When Father felt like an opulent red wine in New York, Mother had to call Luchow's on 14th Street to send up an imported rack of venison or a hare. Shaffer's Market supplied tender pheasant and **Rehrücken mit Kastanien** (Saddle of Venison with Chestnuts).

Liqueurs were laid in for the ladies, for ghastly concoctions which were the forerunners of today's simplified cocktails, and for perfuming (or saturating) desserts. Brandies had to be selected, fortified wines were shipped back from Spain, Portugal, and London. French wines accompanied red meats and game, desserts and oysters, cheese and some fish. But Father served German Rhine and Moselle wines with birds, fish, veal, and—contrary to some tastes—with lamb. He selected German wines for the festive *Bowlen*—Waldmeister, **May Wine,** Himbeer, and **Pfirsichbowle** (woodruff, strawberry, and peach bowls)—and sparkled them with German Sekt.

As we neared the boundary, Fräulein Hedwig, from her vast repertoire of apt songs for every location, struck up *"Die Wacht am Rhein"* and we crossed into Germany singing. We were still in very minor wine country but in major health country, and Father always took time out at Brenner's Hotel Stephanie in Baden-Baden, with a slow turn through the Schwarzwald, for the good of his health— which the serious purposes of the rest of the trip did much to undermine.

Shopping for Father's Storeroom

$\mathcal{L}$ AYING IN AND maintaining a wine cellar and cultivating a wine tongue was one thing (the most important in life according to Father), but wine without food was impossible and certain purchases had to be made. America produced beautiful beef, turkeys—for which Father could never work up much enthusiasm unless they were disguised as **Dinde à la Provençale** or in the Italian manners as *Filetti di Tacchino Rodolfo*—and lobsters. On the other hand, Americans ate *green* asparagus—one bunch of which Edward and I would have traded, with pleasure, for all of Father's white asparagus—and they actually let their peas grow middle-aged before they picked them.

Mother had a special **Sauce of Eggs and Ham for Cold Asparagus,** and Warm Asparagus with Westphalian Ham was a good as the Asparagus with Crumbs and Orange Butter, but all of them are better now, since we make them with green asparagus, than they ever were with white. (In recent years a chic new brown asparagus has appeared, and we, taking gradually to all of Father's whims and caprices, now drive to Baden and Alsace and Lampenheim to all the hotels which have a special *Spargel Carte* (asparagus menu) in spring. We eat it with smoked salmon, with Swiss or Parmesan cheese with whipped cream (yes, it's true), with poached eggs and Sauce Vinaigrette, with Sauce Maltaise—made with tangerines instead of oranges—with **Sauce Gribiche** and about twenty other ways.

Food purchases in Father's day were usually made in the capitals: Fortnum and Mason in London; Fauchon, Hédiard, and the once great Félix Potin in Paris; at Dallmayr in Munich and to a lesser degree at Meindl in Vienna. Milan had a whole food street to keep Father busy, and other delicacies were shipped from their places of origin. Dijon mustard could be sent from anywhere, but Father felt it had to come from Dijon, as Düsseldorf mustard had to be ordered in Düsseldorf. What present-day housewives collect in a single market-ing cart took Father months of crisscrossing Europe in a car to assemble. Of course Father's way was much pleasanter, although we did not think so at the time.

Between their wine and food purchases, their tastings and test-ings, and constant discussions, it seemed to us that our parents' in-terests were narrow, limited, banal, and handicapping. They never took us to a sports event, race, zoo, or even a movie and wondered why we would even *want* to go to a cinema when there was opera. On these food and wine trips we sat parked in cars outside of caves and cellars, vineyards, markets, and shops. We spent hours in the vestibules of the offices of packers and shippers, and *expéditeurs* in every city in Europe. What we wanted to look at were the pet shops, camera shops, musical-instrument shops, and art-material stores. I wanted nothing more than a window of oil paints (in tubes) and the spectral shadings of pastels in tiered wooden boxes to be per-fectly happy. But instead what did we look at? We peered into the sort of windows that had cans of anchovies in the foreground, bottles of stuffed olives (all facing outward) in the middle distance, yellow cans of olive oil in the wings, and a backdrop of fancy salamis. In Strasbourg Father could stand glued to a window of jars of pâté de foie gras, all exactly alike.

The selection and purchase of this last basic, essential ingredient was complicated by the fact that it came in so many forms. There were blocks, tunnels, parfaits, and pâtés, cans and *terrines*, and fresh goose livers. I remember that we stayed at the old Hôtel Maison Rouge on the Place Kléber (which is now awaiting demolition) and I spent hours on the balcony, watching life go by and longing to climb the lacy cathedral spire. We ate Bäckeofe cookies and *Apfelkrapfen* (apple fritters) and *Bettelmann* (beggar cookies), and sang *"Zu Strassburg, Zu Strassburg, Du Wunderschöne Stadt,"* a song that Fräulein produced from Strasbourg's German period.

When Father was in search of a certain homemade goose-liver pâté near Strasbourg, all for our own good, of course, I remember a visit to an estate where the farmyard was filled with rows of wooden crates that were little larger than the geese whose long necks and heads projected from the tops of each. I hadn't heard the horror tales of force-feeding geese for the sake of enlarging their livers and I took the whole thing to be in preparation for shipment. The geese set up a great chattering and quacking in anticipation of their feeding when a girl with a great bowl of cartridge-shaped *Stopperdeln* (stuffers) came into the courtyard. She fed the geese and stroked their necks with one deft motion. Stuffers resemble the *Schupfnudel* (potato noodles) of Baden, which would indicate that the original purpose was the same. In German a *dumme Gans* is a silly goose, and those silly geese set up a great clamoring for more stuffers. I was told on later trips that the geese were having their livers enlarged on the principle of rich food and no exercise, which set me thinking and I often considered (but never did) urging a walk on Father after he ate a particularly heavy dinner.

Goose livers are being enlarged scientifically now, but when we were children it was done with the long, narrow potato and flour dumplings. We always stayed overnight at the estate and we were served their favorite desserts—stuffers swirled in a pan with butter and bread crumbs and sugar.

Later Mother managed to buy large goose livers in New York and Marie studded them densely with slivered blanched almonds before they were roasted. When they were done they looked exactly like little brown hedgehogs and were called Goose-Liver Porcupines—for the adults they were a great delicacy. I remember that there was consternation at dinner when Karl Braun, the basso of the Metropolitan, helped himself to half a whole goose liver and munched contentedly while several guests got none. For me goose livers were pure torture, since leftovers (when Karl Braun had not been a guest) were sieved with butter, beaten with brandy, and mixed with truffles to be put into jars and stored against the day when they were needed for what is now called a sandwich spread. (As I grew up these sandwiches caused me great embarrassment at school and on such occasions, as opera rehearsals, when sandwich luncheons were brought and shared.)

Before the autumn voyage back to New York, to Father's gustatory exile, there was a last mad scramble to the places where he wanted to shop and ship. We were always supposed to eat *authentically,* and that couldn't be done if the *Lebkuchen* (for crumbs for

Sauce Polonaise—*Gott Bewahre*, not for eating plain) didn't come straight from Nuremberg and the smoked eels didn't come from Hamburg. We children were being brought up to appreciate the finer things in life and Father unselfishly dedicated his summers—and weeks of each winter—to our education.

The start for the voyage back to New York in autumn alternated between Hamburg and the Hamburg-Amerika Line, Bremen and the Norddeutscher Lloyd, Paris and the Compagnie Générale Transatlantique, and London and the Cunard or White Star lines. Once Father tried Holland and the Holland-America Line, but he found the food poor, not to his taste, and that was the end of any further education in the Netherlands. We reached the point of embarkation, whether it was Paris or Hamburg, as circuitously as Father's palate dictated. If there wasn't a last pressing purchase to be made, there was a last meal to be eaten. I remember that we once turned from our route to eat a duck in Rouen and on another occasion we turned back to the Baur au Lac in Zurich for a **Züricher Geschnetzeltes** (Minced Veal), and that led to Lyons, and that led to sailing from Cherbourg instead of Bremerhaven.

Our zigzagging about gradually taught us enough about geography and history to pass our exams, but I continued to get a flying zero in math. Had there been a course in gastronomy we would have brought home A-pluses. I didn't even shine in the cooking classes— part of the manual training course—because our efforts were directed toward making peppermint drops and taffy in between building birdhouses and making paperweights.

The conflict of interests between our parents and ourselves continued wherever we went but seemed to us to reach its height when they did their hardware buying. How two adults could manage to work themselves up over a scale was more than I could see. In Vienna they spent days at Matauschek in the Rauhensteingasse and in Paris we sat behind dusty shelves at Dehillerin while they selected salamanders and larding needles, pots and pastry tubes. It always seemed to me to be an extremely undignified occupation, yet I pursue it now with even more ardor than they ever did.

I used to spend those interminable hours while we were waiting for our parents thinking about what I would do when I was grown up. I determined then that if I ever had any children they would not be dragged in my wake while I bought kitchen gadgets and cans of *petits pois* and jars of brandied peaches. I would take them to buy gold leaf and Japan dryer and puppies and cameras and musical instruments. And now the years have gone by and I remember my resolutions as *I* go to Matauschek in Vienna, Sollingen in Munich for knives, and Fauchon in Paris, and I think of Mother when I cross the street (blind to nearby art and pet shops) to look at hams or a particularly alluring display of rolling pins. Mercifully the pendulum has just begun to swing back and on their last visit our children were wildly enthusiastic about a place they discovered in Munich called Dallmayr.

5

Food for Growing Children

ATHER STOOD IN the way of what would have been our normal gastronomic development—over a period of about twenty years —from simple dishes like Sieved Spinach, **Epinard à la Creme,** to **Tarte d'Epinards Pompadour** (Spinach Tart) by plunging us into *haute cuisine* as soon as we had teeth to eat it with and long before we had a taste for such refinements. I can remember having to eat hazelnut bars, drenched in maraschino, when my friends were happily munching animal crackers. Father frowned upon everything that American children grew up on and smiled on many ghastly concoctions on which he had been raised in Austria. As far as he was concerned, an *Armer Ritter* (a poor knight), which was nothing more than a very superior sort of white wine and milk toast, was far more distinguished, though *arm* (poor), than a bowl of puffed rice. He mistrusted everything that was fried; even an egg had to be gently coddled, and deep-fat frying was never mentioned, let alone eaten. I don't think he ever knew there were such things as doughnuts.

Father went through life expecting young and old to rhapsodize over things like **Risotto con Aragosta, Sauce Périgueux,** which went far to spoil the lovely **Chestnut-Stuffed Mushrooms** for me. I disliked everything that contained alcohol and it seemed as though almost everything did. When Edward and I didn't come to blows over which one of us should get the larger portion of the Cock's Combs in Chablis Father was sadly disappointed. That was when we were five and seven and *höchste Zeit*—high time—as Father measured it, for us to appreciate the better things in life. He considered a vast amount of comfortable living—or rather savoir-vivre—and an endless amount of good eating, under the heading of *savoir-manger,* as our patrimony and that training us along these lines could not start early enough. It was, as I think back, his pleasure. His friend Roswell Easton could hardly wait to teach his son John to cast a perfect fly, but Father would not wait (and didn't) to teach us to savor his Lafite with a sliver of cheese, chosen and aged with just as much care, in its way, as the wine.

We were protected, as far as possible, from such contacts as might deaden the wine tongues and taste buds with which he assumed we were endowed. When we were allowed to eat ice cream— only at other children's birthday parties—we had to let it melt in our mouths before we swallowed it, which made us unpleasantly conspicuous among our friends. Father was convinced that eating or drinking anything cold, especially ice-cold water, would eventually kill us—not however, before it had killed our ability to taste and so our enjoyment of life. But ice-cold water for external use only was quite another thing. He believed implicitly in Father Kneipp's Water Cure, and according to his preachings we were roused at dawn each day, given a cold shower and put back to bed. Our new Fräulein Chaudière always wore an extremely warm quilted wrapper and pink curlers for this operation and we hated her. After twenty years in America, Father persisted in calling a shower a douche. I can still hear him telling Mrs. Frederick Steinway that he always took a most invigorating douche before dinner and urging her to do the same.

Ten years later, when I was studying in Vienna, I sneered at the Pfarrer Kneipp fountain in the Stadtpark on my way to school each day. There was the fat Sebastian Kneipp looking benevolent while buckets of cold water poured down over a chubby and smiling infant. In winter the water froze into long icicles, but the bronze infant smiled on. By then I had caught up on my gastronomic education and enjoyed Viennese cookery and baking six or seven times a day, but during the years when we were deprived of our proper privileges in matters of lollipops and Cracker Jacks we felt extremely sorry for ourselves.

What we really wanted more than anything else was to buy an ordinary everyday candy bar or roasted peanuts from the Italian peddlers in the park. Father condemned all peddlers on the ground that they stored their candy trays under their beds at night. The more successful peddlers who had graduated to fueled pushcarts with roasting peanuts or chestnuts, or popping corn, were condemned on the grounds that they stored their carts *next* to their beds at night. The moment I was old enough to patronize pushcarts I became that unsuitably dressed woman you have seen lunching on a frankfurter and pop alongside of the cart on Third Avenue and Fifty-eighth Street. *Vogue* finally took the whole thing up and turned it into the new chic.

When in New York I now have a second resort in the heart of the financial district, a friendly German woman on the corner of Pine Street with an orange Sabrett umbrella over her cart. I share my downtown lunches with an extremely nice officer of the bank on the corner who eats two frankfurters with sauerkraut and mustard. Uptown I share with some decorators from Mr. Scalamandré's staff.

The peddlers with the trays of candy bars have vanished, but my hunger for less sophisticated sweets lingers on and I make lovely desserts out of chocolate bars. Toblerone is the secret ingredient of **Pommes de Terre Elena Gerhardt, Frozen Hazelnut Soufflé** with a heart of hot chocolate sauce, Honey Chocolate Mousse and Grand Marnier Soufflé with Orange Chocolate Sauce.

On the special occasions when we were allowed to eat chocolates, we were given brandied cherries encased in bitter black chocolate with the cherry stem sticking out of the center top. I remember that life's greatest disappointment was a large box of chocolates shaped and wrapped to simulate miniature Curaçao, Grand Marnier, and Créme de Menthe bottles; I scraped off the foil and got down to the bitter chocolate, and sure enough, they contained Curaçao, Grand Marnier, and Crême de Menthe. There were no lighter moments in our diet unless we were ill or when Father and Mother went out.

Our illnesses were always conducted in the proper Austrian manner. No food while we had a temperature, a convalescent **Griess Auflauf** when the thermometer went down, and a slice of palest Prague ham as we improved. Next came sweet **Griesspudding.** The final recovery was suitably marked with a Squab in Farina Soup. I never hear Bach's *"Dank Gesang Eines Genesenen"* without imagining Johann Sebastian staggering to his clavichord after being cured of a bad whooping cough by eating *Taubchen in Gries Suppe* and Prague Ham with Cumberland Sauce.

When Father and Mother went out for dinner we took turns ordering the menu we wanted. The choice was limited, but Edward showed great imagination and ordered different dinners—within reason —whenever it was his turn. I always dreamt of ordering something really outlandish, but when the time came I reverted and asked for **Marie's Rice Pudding** with Raspberry Sauce—Edward invariably snorted. Marie's Rice Pudding was not one of those runny affairs tasting of too much nutmeg and sprinkled with cinnamon but a dream of rather dry rice full of raisins and slivered almonds. The crust and sides were brown and crisp and the raspberry sauce was full of raspberries. Many years later when I had eaten and found wanting almost all rice puddings, I boiled them down to the Hotel Plaza's rice pudding and the Racket and Tennis Club version. The young Yale men, who came into my life some years later, were always put off when they took me to lunch and I still ordered my infantile rice pudding. The Plaza's was creamy and came in individual oval baking dishes, the Racket Club's rice pudding was even better but less available, but our own Marie's Rice Pudding was the best.

Getting Father and Mother out of the house when they were invited out to dinner, or on Mondays when they went to the opera, was a major undertaking. Father taught us that punctilious punctuality was the politeness of kings, but for himself, with the impoliteness of the peasant, he was pathologically unpunctual. So much so that the Hamburg-Amerika Line once held the *S.S. Imperator* (later the Cunarder *Berengaria*) for him, with his friend Commodore Hans Ruser shaking his fist at him from the top of the bridge. When his office factotum, Mr. John J. Dugan, who was always referred to—even in cables at so much a word—as "that old fool Dugan" got him out of the office on time, and Gostike Kotti brought him home on time, and Mother got him under his cold douche on time, he still managed to be late. When everything was set for him to practice the king's politeness, he would make a splendid emergence from the bathroom— wrapped in a turban of Turkish towels and a magnificent bathrobe— and decide on some activity that would make them at least an hour late. He had to have a manicure, he had to have a cup of *Consommé Montpellier* with old sherry, or *Consommé Ambassadrice* with filled mushroom caps, he had to check the progress of his Stilton cheese, and he had to put hot towels on his face. He reviewed what he would have eaten for dinner if he had not been invited out and he recited—with foreboding—what he would probably be served.

Then he would think about his Rüdesheimer and put in a happy half hour checking cellar temperatures and driving Mother, who would long since be sitting in the car, up its beige quilted walls. I had friends who dreaded their parents' absences, but we could hardly wait. Julian van Cortland once told me he was so overjoyed when his mother went away that he kicked off his shoe with such vigor that it sailed up the stairwell and disappeared behind the ledge at the top of the wainscoting. Most of our houses had paneling which did not always go all the way up to the ceiling. There was a ledge which allowed for displaying plates, and in less discriminating homes with a German background the ledges were used for beer steins with Gambrinus or Bacchus sitting on the lid. The well at the back of the ledge in Mother's dressing room was her jewelry safe-deposit box, and since she could never remember where she had tossed up the little chamois bags, we had many dusty searches. In Julian's house the paneling was furred out from the wall and his shoe disappeared behind it forever. He told me that he spent half his mother's absence in trying to recover it and the other half in dreaming up and discarding plausible explanations for one missing shoe. He finally told her that her dog, which would have fitted into the shoe with room to spare, had eaten it.

We waited until the door was closed behind Father and Mother and the coast was clear before we voiced our relief, but we never kicked off our shoes, not after they came back unexpectedly one evening to find me working a large gob of Mother's *Secret de Bonne Femme* cream into my face and Edward making his famous aerial tour of the house—between rare Worcester and bits of Meissen—without once setting foot on the floor. He was just negotiating the jump from the top of the library bookcase to the newel post in the hall when Father and Mother walked in—livid. They had gone to dine with William Bayard (the elder) and Olga Hale at the proper time and place but one week too early. Father rushed to his library to check his sources and find a precedent. The Hales were, as he described it, in their night clothes and Mr. Hale simply said, "Sorry, see you next week," and closed the door. Father felt strongly that he should have been asked in, at least long enough so that he could have telephoned the garage to have Gostike come back. If the Hales had arrived at Father's house one week before their time, he would probably have said, "That was last week," and put them out of his life. As it was, the dinner (a week later) was apparently good, and I remember going to see the Hales and their two sons in Garmisch-Parten-kirchen in 1922.

The constant danger of having Father and Mother return unex-pectedly kept us on our toes, and the pleasures of sifting through their medicines for secret capsules, studying an illustrated book called *Die Gesunde Frau*—"The Healthy Woman"—(apparently German femi-nine health depended largely on standing in profile to the camera with nothing on and with the stomach well pulled in), and walking about in Mother's high-heeled shoes did not come until after Fräulein had been supplanted by Mme. Blé who turned up her hair and went to bed at nine, regardless.

Grandmamma

WHEN WE WERE UNHAPPY in our peanut-butter-less, candy-bar-less, ice-water-less life, not to mention our missing banana splits and hot dogs, chewing gum and gumdrops (on rare occasions a virginal lemon drop was doled out to us), there was always the promise of better things to come. "Wait, just wait until your grand-mamma gets here" (we could have waited indefinitely), "she will bake you HER **Alt Wiener Apfelstrudel**." In those days I considered an *Apfelstrudel* an overrated apple pie and since it was never served à la mode, it failed in its role as an anticipated pleasure.

In summer it was "To Grandmamma's House We Go" (in Carls-bad), but in winter it was "To Our House Grandmamma Comes" (in New York) with several Innovation trunks, enormous hatboxes and the paraphernalia of the complete opera fiend. Long white gloves and fans had a special wooden box with inlaid silver initials—I still have it—and there were etuis for the various opera glasses, ivory glasses for the light gowns, dark mother-of-pearl for the dark dresses. Lace shawls were rolled in pink tissue paper on a satin-covered spool, and a special tall trunk contained the evening gowns with trains which Grandmamma called her toilettes. Somewhere below her long corset she wore a suspended sporran-like chamois pouch in which she brought her pearls, her diamond pins and rings suitable for her orgy of opera.

Grandmamma came to stay for two months each winter, osten-sibly to see us, but actually to hear Caruso. She was of a generation that had to have a *Schwarm* (something to be crazy about) and her

Schwärmerei was Caruso. Every evening (she even followed the Metropolitan to Philadelphia, and, if necessary, to Atlanta) she took up her long white gloves, her opera glasses, and her train. She patted her really fabulous prematurely white hair, a color to which she firmly maintained it had "turned overnight" (the reasons for the sudden turn were variously attributed to worries over us, neglect, a broken heart; or the deaths of Terry, her overweight black and white collie, or of Pagliacci, her overweight black and tan dachshund; or possibly disagreements with her cook Resi). She patted her pearls and her little cache of sacheted lace handkerchiefs. She always cried at the opera, irrespective of the subject; even when it was the *Barber* or a particularly amusing performance of *Fledermaus,* the tears flowed. She was taken and returned by Gostike Kotti, and Father and Mother rented a car rather than go through her performance at an opera performance. Edward and I went with her only once—to *Gianni Schicchi*—and she wept as copiously as during the *"Liebestod."* When I asked her why, she sobbed, *"Es ist doch die Oper"* (But it's the opera).

When she wasn't at the opera she stood enraptured next to a hideous mahogany gramophone with a great morning-glory-shaped horn. Resting her cheek on her folded hands, with her eyes closed, she looked, though oversized, exactly like that devoted smooth fox terrier of the Victor trademark who listened so ardently for his master's voice. She played *Pagliacci, "La donne è mobile,"* and *"Una furtiva lacrima"* over and over again.

Grandmamma was pure Art Nouveau at its worst. She let the Emilian von Skramliks take away priceless Biedermeier furniture so that she could do herself up in gilded bamboo with emerald-green velvet upholstery printed with large droopy red poppies. The bamboo lent a certain botanical orientalism which she found becoming to her *interessante Blässe* (interesting pallor). Clemenceau and many French friends stayed with her when they made their Carlsbad cures and left behind a little touch of the Parisian Metro entrance atmosphere. Fortunately she could not afford to do the whole house in a cross between Art Nouveau, hysteria, and what Central Europe called the *Jugendstil*—for the *Jugend* magazine which supported and established it—and so there were only two living rooms and an entry done in an enmeshing of organic forms and waving lines which inevitably ended in the flowing hair of a maiden with one—rarely two—breasts revealed. The liquid linearity of sinuous draperies from Liberty's in London merged or were interwoven with hair, water lilies, swans, guitars, or a harp. Grandmamma's dining room remained unchanged and in it we ate Resi's superb specialties, which Grandmamma always referred to as HERS—her **Caruso Torte,** her **Ananas Creole,** her liver pâté, her **Sour Cherry and Plum Soup.** I always enjoyed Resi's soups more than any others, not only for their own sake but for the enormous Meissen soup plates and the extra large soup spoons.

I became more interested in Father and less frightened of him when I learned to pronounce and recognize a mysterious word I had heard applied to him—posthumous. His father had died before he was born. He had been the posthumous child of a beautiful young woman, widowed before she was twenty. Grossmamma spoke, thought, lived, in the first person singular. She was always *"Ich,"* and being very cultivated she was *"je"*, *"I"*, *"io"*, and *"yo"* by turns, but it was never *"you"* or *"Du."* It was *her Amerika Reise* to hear her Caruso, and Father was, for some reason, *her Goldpfoterdl,* her little golden paw. For me it was the golden paw of a miniature lapdog and for Father it was the red cloth to the bull. She said *"Weh, Weh"* (ouch, ouch) before, during, and after all ordeals, as having her nails filed or her hair washed. Having her in the house, doing her daily opera act and using his car irritated her *Goldpfoterdl* beyond endurance. She spent her time in bed, at the opera, and in the car, and in what—I now realize—was the systematic wrecking of Mother's household.

All well-brought-up ladies in Austria were taught to cook so that they could guide or control either their cooks or the house-keepers who controlled their cooks and doled out the proper rations. It was fashionable for the lady of the house to have her specialties. Grandmamma's Vanilla Horns were her thing, and when she was safely at home in Austria, Father would think nostalgically about her *Apfel Kuchen* with the combined sentiments of "the pies that Mother used to bake" and the "greener pasture." Before she left she always let herself be persuaded to bake HER **Huzarengeback** and her "keks" for her little Golden Paw . . . so that he could eat, for once, in the manner he had been born to. So once during each winter visit Grandmamma and Mother and Fräulein and I trooped downstairs to the kitchen to participate in Grandmamma's big bakeoff. "Keks" was Grandmamma's word for cakes just as her "plait" was wrapped around her knees by her maid when she sat sedately in Carlsbad's Stadtpark to hear the Sunday concert. Her "plait" was a small cashmere rug in Scotch plaid design with which every self-respecting Austrian warded off the unspeakable illness (now known as "the trots") which resulted from sitting with a draft across the knees. I remember that Father teased her unmercifully about taking seriously a *Konzert* at which the conductor faced the plaided audience with his back to the orchestra. Grandmamma maintained that his position was justified since it enabled him to bow to the more exalted guests. Since he always bowed deeply to her, she didn't really care whether the second violin got his cue or not.

When we arrived in the kitchen, set out according to Grandmamma's taste, Scotti (my misnamed smooth fox terrier) and I always sat under the table. We were tented and shrouded by yards of white damask. Grandmamma couldn't have cooked on an undraped table—*unmöglich.* I was given a small piece of dough so that I too could make My Strudel, My Horns, and My "Keks." For reasons I never could explain, my piece of dough became darker and darker and the grubby little pancake which Scotti and I finally produced never saw the inside of the oven.

I have always delighted in the reminiscences of my friends who insisted that they produced their first matchless Country Pot Roast or their unrivaled Roast Stuffed Turkey when they were six, and knew how to spin sugar before they were ten. Whatever I produced before I was in my twenties was either My Fudge, My Scrambled Eggs, or a great failure.

Although I knew nothing about cooking, even a backward child would have seen that Marie creamed the butter, Marie beat the batter, Marie kneaded the dough, Marie scalded and ground the almonds, and Marie shaped, cut, baked, sugared, and finally produced Grandmamma's specialties. The only thing Grandmamma did was to hover and finally carry them upstairs and present them to her Golden Paw as the work of her own loving hands. Mother stood by shuddering lest Marie lose patience and depart. Each time Grandmamma left New York, Father and Mother packed their bags and went off for a rest cure.

As I grew older and parental anecdotes became more interesting, I was (and still am) delighted when I heard that Mother once inadvertently locked Grandmamma in the ladies' room in the Naples Museum where she had to spend the day before an Italian locksmith could be located. This was an even more fortuitous happening (and I like to think it was carefully planned), since Grandmamma was in Naples only because Father and Mother were on their honeymoon and Grandmamma interpreted Father's need for his mother's blessing as having to be administered anew each day. Grandmamma was the reason for my parents' move to America. When my school friends told of descent from ancestors who had come to America for socially acceptable reasons, such as religious persecution, I could only produce parents who came because Father's mother was what they would have designated as a "pain in the neck." Having opposed my parents' marriage for seven years, Grandmamma succeeded in wearing Mother down into accepting an invitation to visit friends in America. No sooner had Grandmamma breathed a sigh of relief than Father—unmoved by tears or prayers—sailed for America and married Mother the instant he set foot in the New World (neglecting in his charmingly *schlampig* Austrian way to notify his regiment that he had made other arrangements).

Nine years later, in 1914, when he was the father of two small children, this omission plunged him into prison in Lofer near Salzburg (where he was motoring, disregarding the war) under sentence of death as a spy and a traitor.

When Grandmamma was faced with the American marriage of her Golden Paw she set sail from Hamburg with blessings drawn and just happened to book passage back on the same Italian liner on which Father and Mother were taking their honeymoon voyage. The ladies' room episode in the Naples Museum becomes even clearer when we consider that because of the greater comforts of the double cabin, Grandmamma arranged to share with Mother while her Golden Paw enjoyed the discomforts of the single cabin. A very handsome Italian fellow passenger was so moved by Mother's plight that gifts and photographs (of himself in ever more and more braided and bemedaled splendor—he ended an Admiral) followed us for years.

During the period in my life when all children like to dramatize themselves, I was told—in whispers—that my little playmates either were foundlings, adopted children, orphans, or were born-out-of-wedlock, natural! Being by nature a very modest child, I settled on (and was saddened by) the tale that I had been one of twins and my smaller sister, or brother, had died at birth. This turned out to be far too unsensational and I was casting about for a more exciting circumstance when I came across a large glossy photograph, mounted on a thick beveled cardboard, of the sinister Italian in full uniform, rich in epaulets, decorations, sash, and saber. The fact that the picture was secreted under a stack of bath towels in Mother's linen closet made it doubly romantic and mysterious.

Since he had a nose as long as mine, hair as dark as mine, and a rapacious expression, which I tried out in front of the mirror, I decided that here was the true love of my mother's life—and that he must be my father. He became an entirely satisfactory imaginary father: He explained my out-of-the-family looks, my love for Italy, spaghetti, and sunshine, and his medals supported my tales of heroism. My friends might *think* they were the daughters of Woodrow Wilson or John Drew, but I had a picture that could be shown (provided Mother was out). Whoever he was, this fellow passenger of my parents helped me enormously at moments when the man who thought he was my father was being particularly Austrian and strict, and he added tremendously to my prestige at school.

Father and Mother, having had a short taste of America and *Freiheit*—freedom—came back for several reconnoitering visits, during two of which both Edward and I were born, two years apart, in New York. My first trip to Europe was made at six months, the occasion when I was dramatically lost in London, and shortly afterward my parents decided to make New York their permanent home. They promised their widowed mothers that they would visit them twice a year and fulfilled the adage, "What the son takes pains to forget—the grandson and/or granddaughter tries to remember." They loved America up to but not always including its cookery. And the fact that they had New York to themselves, unburdened by relatives, added to their happiness. Edward and I, on the other hand, adored Austria.

Food was the only struggle. Father would have defended America (after he was finally canceled out of the Austrian Army), but he would not put up with its fried clams, canned fruits and vegetables, and griddle cakes—*warum* griddle cakes when there were perfectly good *Palatschinken* and **Crêpes Copenhagen** in the world? Poor Father—Carlsbad-born, educated in Austria, France, and England, he was at home in several gastronomies and utterly out of place in America's. He swam, with great splutterings and puffings, against the stream. He fought a losing battle but comforted himself at the best tables of Paris and Vienna, at Walterspiel's and Pforte's, during his four yearly European visits. He also took comfort in the various floating Ritz Restaurants during the eight or more weeks he spent on shipboard each year leading his Austro/American life.

The difference between the food he was served when he went to the homes of his friends and what he set before his guests was extreme. He would give shuddering accounts of dinners he had eaten (which sounded like seventh heaven to us), and I have no doubt that the children of his guests heard equally shuddering reports of dinners they had to sit through (until midnight or later) at Father's table. He described dinners at which he was given steaming hot bread on an empty stomach, ice cream on a full stomach, and ice water throughout the meal. Added to these impositions on his interior, the main course had been fried and the vegetables had been of the variety which was known to produce gas.

To Father, eating was a matter of constant stratification. If he described a dinner party it was not so much a report on the menu as a cross section of what had been placed on what in his stomach. He would not say there was a *Pêche Andalouse*, he would say, "There was a peach *on top* of cucumber salad." Nothing he ate was ever out of context. We couldn't put this under that and he wouldn't pour a good wine into a stomach full of—God forbid—creamed onions. Little layers of bread had to be interjected under the wine and over the food. When bread was eaten it was only a fastidious piece of the crust and the lovely foamy, pulpy, wonderful center part was discarded. In the case of "Papa" Fred Muschenheim, owner of the Hotel Astor and a little white beard, it went to make cannon fodder. He rolled little pellets and fired them surreptitiously and with absolute accuracy into the deep clefts (proudly displayed in those days) in the center of his guests' décolletages. Dinners were punctuated by the little jumps of the ladies who were hit.

When, on the other hand, Father was served with something that had been breaded (in spite of *Wiener Schnitzel*, which never happened to him at home) he opened the bread shell, ate the contents and left the golden crust on his plate (clean plates were only for children). He approved of crisp homemade Melba Toast, rusks, Carlsbad Zwieback, and parched bread, but he considered a sandwich and plain white bread a vulgarity.

We always wondered why Father's friends put up with him.

Children notoriously do not appreciate their parents' charm and we knew nothing of the attractions that an amusing guest held for his hostess. Father took his duties as a guest just as seriously as his duties when he was the host. He might arrive an hour late and deplore his hostesses' menus, but he kissed their hands, amused their guests, was gallant and sophisticated, and Austrian. When they, in turn, were his guests, they might complain of the late dinner hour, the unaccustomed delicacies, the four or five wines, and the fact that the table was never "lifted" until Father felt the proper time had come (even though that time was a good two hours after his guests might have wanted to stretch their legs), but they never refused his invitations.

Entertaining was not limited to home. Father made a fine art of traveling and exploring, as his mother and grandparents had done before him, and no stone was left unturned to add another good restaurant to his itinerary. He cultivated a little group of food appreciators in all the cities where he had favorite restaurants and he rendezvoused with American friends. All the annual European musical and dramatic events had to be further embellished with good food— he could not live on music alone—and friends had to be imported to share his discoveries. During the Munich *Festspiele* he stayed at the Vierjahreszeiten—Four Seasons—and planning little meals with Herr Walterspiel was half the fun.

I experienced Alfred Walterspiel's idea of a little luncheon some years later and came to understand why he was so gently rounded. He ordered *Huîtres Bernadotte* (Oysters in Sauce Verte), *Consommé Froid à la Russe*, a little tiny **Sole Francine** and a *Tournedos Caruso* garnished with Neapolitan Macaroni and a tomato, and after a refreshing green salad there was his lovely Raspberries Walterspiel. Since it was only a very little luncheon, there were only two wines.

Long before travel became tourism, there might be Thomas Cook who provided couriers, but there was Father who planned his friends' trips down to the last detail. He told them not only where they should eat but what they should eat *and* drink when they were there. In later years he moved through Europe as a sort of gourmet pied piper with a queue of friends behind him.

There was Bayreuth and La Scala and Milan's great cookery in winter, and the Salzburg Festival with **Salzburger Schneenockerl** at the Goldene Hirsch and **Montblanc** at the Oesterreichischer Hof.

Father enjoyed the *Wiener Oper Saison* all the more for living across the street at the Bristol where he ate his suppers and for Demel's where he ate a sort of high tea before the opera. "High" at Demel's was an extravaganza of unbelievable pleasures. Father enjoyed Covent Garden and the London theater as much for the dinners that preceded the performances as for the suppers that followed them. And then there was Paris, the Opera, the Comédie Française, and an entire firmament of restaurants that he ate his way through.

In later years, after Mme. Blé was gone, I think that of all their musico/gastro explorations I looked forward to Bayreuth the most, since it was the only one I was allowed to miss. Father and Mother were so involved with Wagner, friends, and food that they neglected my *Kultur* and left me anywhere that I wanted to be. There was one utterly happy Bayreuth season when they left me in Elbogen (a medieval town on the elbow of the Eger River) while they concerned themselves with Siegfried (the son), Siegfried (the tenor) the doings of Frau Cosima and all the Bayreuth scandals and schisms. While they were eating with and being photographed with Wotan (Friedrich Schorr), Siegfried (Johannes Sembach), Gurnemanz (Carl Braun), the Walter Bakers and all the various gods and goddesses of Valhalla, I sat quietly on a terrace above the Eger and ate floating Bohemian Povesen and such lowly goodies as *Dampf Nudeln*.

Father and Mother came back with note-by-note descriptions of the *Ring*, newly published biographies or newly found Wagner correspondence and everything connected with the Wagnerian syndrome. I was always expected to read Father's Wagner library and came away with a strong sense of money being needed, money being demanded, and money being borrowed—there was little or nothing about money ever being returned. Between Wagner's velvet tam o'shanter, the Abbé Liszt's clerical collar, Mr. Belasco's priestly habit, and Cosima always the completely weeded widow, I was confused.

One year I was taken to Bavaria to see the Oberammergau Passion Play. We had rooms without bath, negligible food and nothing but bearded Bavarians who let their hair grow for their Biblical parts, starting about three years before each performance. Now they have an inconspicuous hippie look, but then they stood out with their haloed heads and short lederhosen, their beer steins and their beatific expressions. Father refused to stay for the crucifixion and solaced himself with a dinner of **Münchner Schweinebraten** (Munich Roast Pork) and a Bavaroise Religieuse at the Alpenhof in Garmisch-Partenkirchen.

As rather ponderous European travel became more and more chic, Father became his friends' guide and leader. Weeks were spent over pleasurable little dinner parties, planning trips, recommending restaurants, and giving introductions. Father pointed the way to a very comfortable and highly civilized era of European travel, isolated bits of which still exist. We now follow Father's routes, nostalgically, and often find improvements when I had expected deterioration. Just recently I ate a superb *Spargel Salat* (Asparagus Salad) at what was once the great Pforte's restaurant in the Hotel Atlantic in Hamburg, and the Hotel Eisenhut in Rothenburg ob der Tauber gave us a **Saddle of Hare** with juniper berries that Father would have emphatically approved.

7

Maiden Voyage of the Vaterland

THE SUMMER OF 1914 is the first I can remember without assistance and my first clear recollection is of the bridal suite on the S.S. *Vaterland* and food. Someone had sent me a replica of a small red tin trunk filled with cookies and Father had the steward, Oscar Schwarzer, take them away.

Father never missed maiden voyages and the *Vaterland*, then the largest ship in the world, later the *Leviathan*, rated a round trip. He was always having to sail abroad at the drop of a letter from Grandmamma or for business reasons, and usually his trips managed mysteriously to coincide with glamorous European events. The opening of a new opera invariably concurred with a crisis in Carlsbad. It just so happened that he came back to New York on the maiden voyage of the *Vaterland* and returned to England with us on her return demimaiden voyage.

The Steinways were in the other bridal suite and all of them ate at Commodore Ruser's table. At the right hand of the commodore was the most desirable spot on the ship. I only remember great celebrating, music, deck games, people in evening clothes, dinners in the suite, Squabs in Sauerkraut, Apple and Apricot Fritters, and **Kirschenkuchen** (Cherry Cake). And Oscar. He had been Father's steward on many crossings, and when the *Vaterland* was interned in Hoboken he came to us as butler and stayed until he went off to open his own restaurant after the war. (Years afterward I sat down in a Madison Avenue restaurant and suddenly had a large napkin knotted around my neck from the back in child fashion. It was Oscar, by then a successful restaurateur).

While he was with us I rode about the house on his shoulders or head—a sport that Father never indulged us in—and always looked away when he galloped me up the stairs to the top floor, where he had pictures of his children in the traditional German pose, naked on a white fur rug.

In London I remember that Edward was given a grown-up bed while I was still put into a brass crib. Toward the end of June (on the 28th) there was great sorrow and consternation over the assassination in Sarajevo, but Father felt it would only be days before it was all settled and we crossed into France. There we met the car, Edward Lawrence (Mother gave a vacation to Lawrence's wife, who was part maid and part second governess), and Fräulein Chaudière.

The next thing I remember was Venice and the Lido and a **Langouste Fra Diavolo.** Father didn't let the distant roll of drums deter him from his planned summer trip and our introduction to certain fruits of the sea. One of them was apparently past its prime and within days of getting to Venice I complicated Father's plans with a high temperature and a face swollen into a ball. As far as I know, the plan had been a tour of the Dolomites and a swing to Meran for a little wine tasting and that is exactly what he did. When we arrived at San Martino di Castrozza Father was badly frightened and entered the hotel saying, "Is there a doctor in the house—we have a sick child."

As it turned out, there was a young American doctor right in the lobby, awaiting a bus that was going to take him, his mother and his fiancée, and the other waiting guests to Genoa and a passage home. He stayed to take care of me and was separated for weeks from his ladies and a passage home. (In 1924 we visited him—Dr. Camp Stanley—in Washington, and in 1944 we met a Mrs. Benz in Maryland whose son had just married his daughter.) The only thing I can remember besides Dr. Stanley was a promise. Scotti had long since been given away and Father said that if I would take my medicines and get well I could have another dog.

I think Lawrence was having a hard time getting benzine or perhaps the pressure pump broke, but after a time the Stevens Duryea could no longer go uphill. We were on the wrong side of the Dolomites and I remember that Lawrence backed the car around the dizzying hairpin curves of the Falzarego and Pordoi passes and the Stilf-

serjoch—the Passo Stelvio. As soon as an incline lay ahead, not to say
a mountain, that ponderous car had to be turned and backed up it.
Then it was turned again and we came down the other side going
forward. Father, it seems, was feeling the urge to join his regiment;
this meant that the family would be in Carlsbad for the duration.

Europe, in 1914, was not of a single mind as far as driving was
concerned, and as we went from country to country and hill to hill,
the car not only had to be put in reverse from time to time; it had to
be driven alternately on the right and left sides of the road. We apparently passed from the Tyrol into Salzburg without Lawrence (or
Father the map reader) realizing it, and on one of the curves along
the Saalach between Lofer and Salzburg we ran head-on into a small
Wanderer car driven by a handsome Austrian officer who was speed-
ing to join his regiment. The officer subsided into a ditch, and Mother
sat with us unde a wayside crucifix, which is still there, to await assistance. When it came it was in the form of a group of belligerent
peasants who saw their injured officer as the victim of a plot. They
brandished pitchforks, hitched oxen to the cars, and drove us before
them to the magistrate in Lofer.

Father was traveling with a French triptyque, or permit, and
since the car had been unloaded at Le Havre the local authorities had
simply given Father a Le Havre residence. No one traveled with pass-
ports or identification and when Father said, "But I am an officer in
the Emperor's Regiment," they laughed and pointed out that the regiment was in Serbia and if that were true, he was a deserter; and if it
were untrue, he was a French spy from Le Havre and the penalty for
either was bullets at sunrise. They put Father into the local prison,
locked Mother and Lawrence into their rooms at the Hotel Post and
put Edward and me into another room with two local gendarmes at
the door. They stood with drawn bayonets and sabers at their sides.

They searched the car and luggage and were able to prove con-
clusively that Father was a French spy sent to poison Austrian wells
because they found a bottle of iodine and an eyedropper. They were
doubly enraged because it was obvious to them that he was using
innocent children—someone else's—to camouflage his activities.

Mother apparently pounded on her locked door and insisted on
seeing the local magistrate, who was celebrating the imminent
outbreak of war in the local Gasthaus. When he agreed to see her—
in the middle of the night—she threw on a robe over her nightgown,

and with streaming hair (as Father later told it), threw herself at the befuddled magistrate's feet.

Father always drew an operatic or dramatic parallel, and in time he accused Mother of having done a sort of combination Lady Godiva and Monna Vanna to save his life. (Monna Vanna is the heroine of Février's opera, in which Mary Garden went naked under a robe—actually in pink tights—to offer herself to the conqueror in exchange for the freedom of her people.) What Mother really did was to throw not herself but a few related names about and this frightened the magistrate into agreeing to a stay of execution until word could be gotten to Vienna. Edward and I were unaware of much of this and were enjoying our house arrest. (I remember that the room had tall Gothic beds that looked like two wooden cathedrals and when we stopped in Lofer a few years ago I asked whether I could see Zimmer Zwei, and there it was, with its two Gothic beds and the same pictures on the walls.)

I heard afterward that Father's uncle, who was president of the *Advokaten Kammer* (Chamber of Advocates) and in constant touch with the Emperor, drove down from Vienna during the night, walked into the prison, threw some papers at the magistrate, said *"Dumm-kopf,"* and drove back to Vienna. Ours was always a dramatic family. Father was released under guard and the long months of waiting began: proof of identity, papers from America, had to come; the two cars needed repairs at the local blacksmith's; and we needed to know that the injured officer would recover.

The Post belonged to the Poschackers, and while we were blissfully being neglected by Father, who still had a gendarme at his heels, we helped in the hotel. I'm sure I never brushed my teeth and we left the light on as long as we liked. Our guards were called off and we watched the romance between one of the local girls and the officer, whose broken rib had mended, but his convalescence dragged out interminably. As far as I know, he was still there when we were finally able to leave.

Edward helped with the sausage making, which I abandoned, after a day of making *Kalbsleberwurst,* when they started on their *Blutwurst.* Instead I watched the daily baking of the **Haustorte** which was the Hotel Post's much improved (and less dry) version of the Hotel Sacher's Torte. (It sounds like blasphemy, but at heart most people will agree.) When we were finally released we crept to Salzburg and Vienna, and Father stopped at all apothecary shops on the way, buying as much benzine as they would sell him, usually in four-ounce bottles. Filling the tank took hours. We left the car in Carlsbad, and were separated from Lawrence, who arrived in New York some months later, alone, as did his wife and Fräulein Chaudière.

We went to Berlin, and with a beautfully sealed and beribboned document signed by James W. Gerard, our ambassador in Berlin, which is still in our safe-deposit box and makes mention of the fair Lillian and the noble Edward, managed to get to Holland—the North Sea waves came right into our freezing rooms in Scheveningen—and we went on to London. In London it became instantly plain that two German-speaking children would not be well received, and Father produced a Miss Simpson who walked us all the way to Paddington Cemetery each day where we sat on the gravestones and crammed English. As a result, for some years the accents of Miss Simpson irritated our friends in New York. We crossed the North Atlantic on the S.S. *Baltic* and I can remember playing shuffleboard and hopscotch in an enormous life preserver with a girl from Duluth.

In New York I mulled over THE PROMISE and on Christmas Eve was disappointed to find the usual doll and a green book by John Galsworthy at my place. The book was called *Christmas* and turned out to be about Mr. Galsworthy's dog, Christmas, and when this dawned on me, Mother came in carrying a cocker spaniel, whom we immediately called Christmas. He piddled over Mother's Lucille gown and wouldn't walk on a leash for several days, but gradually he adapted himself, and until I went to study in Vienna, was my *Sorgenkind*—my worry child. If there was any trouble he could get into he did; he fought with other dogs, chased cars, barked, left hairs about and made little monuments here and there. But he endeared himself to us by greeting us with effusion and enthusiasm when we came home—he would leap into the air, run up several flights of stairs barking, run down again, and take about fifteen minutes to subside.

Edward went to school each day in New York with John Easton, and I was put into something called an ungraded class until my English improved. We both had riding instruction at Durlands, skating lessons and Wagner appreciation lessons, and I came home to cooking lessons once a week. When this got about among the mothers of all my little classmates, they joined me once a week. We labored over Chou Paste and watched Puff Paste being made. We made Nut Horns and *Tuiles* and left taffy pulling and fudge for the younger children.

When the *Vaterland* was interned in New York, Commodore Ruser had with him his wife, Marie, and son Hans, who was a forward-backward talker and called himself Snah Resur. They lived on the *Vaterland*, at the docks in Hoboken, and we often took the ferry over to play with Snah and his dachshund, Hexe. We prowled all over those vast ships, the *Vaterland* and *Imperator*, and the pride of Hamburg was our playground. I was Naillil and Edward was Drawde and Snah came up to Norfolk, Connecticut, to stay with us the following summer. At that time there was a flutter among the New York German families, and a *Deutsche Bazaar* was arranged at Madison Square Garden. (The United States was not yet in the war, of course.)

I remember being taken there and buying lots of chances on a white goat and cart and meeting the three Muschenheim children. Our young connections all dispersed over strange playgrounds. Snah had the *Vaterland* and the Muschenheim children had the Hotel Astor at their disposal, and our playing extended over endless corridors and hide-and-seek meant never being found. I was notified that I had won something at the German Bazaar and I looked with rapture for the goat and cart. Instead I received a very large Isolde *Puppe*, a doll that someone at the Metropolitan had fashioned to look like the singer Melanie Kurt. She had hair like the diva's wig, the same kind of costume, and was about as large as I was (who exchanged the chances I do not know—someone who didn't want me to have a goat and cart in the house, I suppose).

I was bitterly disappointed and loathed the doll, which had to stay and be admired whenever Frau Kurt came to dinner. Years later I felt for a woman at a dog show who went around screaming, "Nothing but a damned blanket," when she had been notified that the door prize had won her "a beautiful afghan"—she had expected an Afghan hound. It was altogether a period of great disillusionment. A friend of Mother's said, "I'll give you a ring." And I waited expectantly for Mother's new ring and all she got was a telephone call. A friend of Father's promised Edward and John a hunting trip "if nothing unforeseen occurs," and for ten years something unforeseen always happened. If we said anything in German, Father said "Use your heads," and Edward Lawrence went to work in a factory.

Our friendships had always been interrupted by our constant traveling, and with the exception of John Easton, many of them could not survive Father's curfews, the shut-off telephones, and the Fräuleins. Other children played with the children of their parents' friends, but our parents had strange friendships based on vocal chords and musicality.

The only thing that anyone needed to endear himself to Father was a voice. If he had one he could do no wrong. We grew up surrounded by people with voices or musical talents, and when they had children we were expected to play with them. Fortunately people who are constantly occupied with the condition of their own voices do not seem to be overly prolific. Most opera singers had none or at most one voiceless child. I remember that we were expected to "Oh" and "Ah" over the pictures of Wotan-Karl Braun's children and the anecdotes about Felicitas and Paul Bender's babies. We played with pretty (younger than we) Florence Steinway, who was most acceptable because most singers were accompanied by the Steinway piano, and because at four, she told five-year-old Carl Artur Bodanzky that he was no gentleman when, blindfolded, he pinned the tail on the donkey. We didn't play with Eva Goritz (who turned out to be too old) nor with a frail and pretty little girl with heavy eyes. She was—unbelievably—the daughter of overpowering, mighty, double-chinned Brangäne-Isolde (yes, both), Venus and Erda, Margarethe Matzenauer. Her name was Adrienne, pronounced as though the *a* were an *ah*, and if we were told the truth, her father's name was Edoardo Ferrari-Fontana.

We were wintering at the Château de la Galère, at Théoule near Cannes, eighteen years later in 1932, and Mother joined us in early spring. When she disembarked she asked us to wait and drive Madame Matzenauer and her daughter, who had been on the crossing, to their hotel. A grown-up and very beautiful Adrienne came down the gangplank with her mother, a double vision of fuchsia and lavender, magenta and purple, lilac and amethyst. Matzenauer was enormous, Adrienne was a miniature; they each had one purple and one magenta shoe, one purple and one magenta glove, one purple and one magenta stocking. If they had been nearer each other's size, they could have split a pair between them but they were sizes apart, and each must have had two pairs of everything to achieve their fascinating fuchsia effect. It was the last time I saw either of them.

I met and liked a girl at school some years later, and we became friends without benefit of our parents. Her name was Wally de Luca and it took me months to realize she was Giuseppe de Luca's daughter, the Metropolitan's reliable Italian baritone whom we loved especially in *Gianni Schicchi* and *Così Fan Tutte.* My only friendship that grew out of a we-want-you-to-like-our-friends'-children beginning was the daughter of Edward and Suzanne Ziegler, young Suzanne, now Mrs. Charles Gleaves. There was a slight difference in our ages and we met just at a time when that difference left me with my hair down my back in low heels, while beautiful Suzanne, with her hair pinned up into a bun, had graduated into pumps with baby French heels— the green envy of everyone who hadn't yet grown into them. Suzanne also was an experienced opera-goer and generally unreachable, since she had a soft mole coat, while I was dressed in those days according to the unfertile imagination of Burberry of London. But by the time I too was in baby French heels, the differences were outgrown, and our friendship, which was originally handicapped by our parents wanting us to like each other, is now more valuable because we share each other's memories of Neddie Ziegler, Big Suzanne (so called only while Suzie was little Suzanne), Rudi, and Ida (always pronounced Eeda).

Table Manners

WE SPENT FOUR YEARS in America, 1915 through 1918, spending two summers in Norfolk, Connecticut, one in Katonah, and one at Lake Placid and Canada. While we were in New York we went to school and spent the whole week dreading Sunday, which was spent with Father. He devoted the day to gastronomical researches in what he called *les environs de* New York and never found what he wanted. He had visions of discovering *haute cuisine* on the Hudson, and the Pyramide on Long Island Sound.

I can remember that we went to recommended duck farms on Lond Island, where he expected *Caneton à la Savoisienne* and got a simple roast duckling. We went to mushroom farms in Pennsylvania where he expected *Cèpes à la Russe* and got broiled mushrooms on toast, and we went to seashore restaurants where he expected the delicacies of Genoa and Naples and got a shore dinner that ended with pie. We did find a few places that Edward and I loved: The Port of Missing Men, Longue Vue, and the Claremont, with its French Waffles with Strawberries. We had our first Baked Alaska (Father was appalled) at the Gramatan in Bronxville and Corn Pudding at Gedney Farms in White Plains. I remember that Father expected so much of a place called Beau Séjour that he engaged rooms for the weekend and returned to New York on Sunday morning in a silence.

The evenings fell into three categories: when they were invited out, when they had guests at home, and when they were home alone with us. When Mother and Father were out it was heaven; when they had guests we hung over the banister and had a sort of hair-part and décolletage-view of their friends. New York was full of what we called "private houses" where guests trooped up two flights of stairs before they were greeted by their host and hostess. We watched them come up and saw them go down to the dining room after a lengthy stint in the library, where Father gave his guests concoctions that apparently brought instant relaxation. Long before the cocktail hour was established, he was giving them something that tasted like equal parts of Pinaud's Hair Tonic and benzine. I had this straight from a girl whose parents had once been Father's guests. We watched trays of hot profiteroles filled with icy caviar, barquettes filled with mousse of pâté de foie gras, **Warsaw Tartlets, Cucumber Slices Filled with Crab Meat,** eggs filled with smoked salmon, mushrooms filled with chicken livers, and artichoke bottoms filled with eggs suédoise.

Everything was filled with something else. A dinner menu in those days was a long list of fillings and housings into which to put them. Mother's **Squabs with Scrapple** were as good as her **Trout in Aspic** and her **Filet of Beef with Duxelles.**

When Mother and Father were at home during the winter without guests—a rare and dreaded occasion—we all ate as though we were patients recovering from surgery. A little strong beef stock laced with beef juice, a sliver of white meat, veal or chicken, and a stewed fruit, home-stewed and hygienic. There was none of the elaborate fare that they set before their guests, no sauces, no *friandises.* They yawned, Father preached about his eating rules (in theory only, since there was practically nothing on our plates), and off they went to bed. When Father was asleep it was almost worse than when he was awake —total silence had to be observed. I remember that a baffled principal called Mother to report that I was the only child in school who always tiptoed and whispered. Father had a device installed—against the law—which silenced the telephone and all bells after he retired. While he slept we were completely cut off from the outside world, which was a great irritation in later years when I hoped for calls from young men. They were called beaus in those days and we lived for their calls.

On the evenings when we were alone Father administered his unshakable set of eating rules and table manners; they sounded like a codicil to the ten commandments. *"Du sollst nicht bei Tisch kochen"* (You shall not cook at the table) was a flexible commandment which covered everything that went on our plates. All pleasant pushing around of food was forbidden. Swooshing the asparagus and West-phalian ham through the Sauce Maltaise, stirring the Cauliflower into the Polonaise, edging the rice over into the curry (via the chutney), or creating little Japanese gardens with the mashed potatoes and broccoli, were all classed as "cooking at the table." If I tried to manipulate the *Poussin Bismarck* into the Green Grape Sauce I was stopped, but when Father dunked toast triangles in his Sauce Crécy or swirled croutons and cream through his **Potage St. Hubert** that was fine. He frequently dropped a little piece of bread crust into the sauce left on his plate, impaled it with his fork and went through an exercise that could only be compared to a garage attendant making a thorough job of cleaning the windshield. Such pleasures were not for us.

"You shall not speak when your mouth is full," went without saying, since it was covered by the second commandment, "You shall not speak at the table." This also covered "You shall not make sounds at the table," which included grunts, *schlürfen* (slurping—a sound produced when eating soup), sighs, hiccoughs, and something the Austrians called *schmatzen*—a sort of smacking, chomping sound comparable to a ravenous pig's noises at the trough. A small burp would have probably put us out for adoption but Father allowed himself the pleasure of some very fine sound effects in that direction.

Posture, while eating, was important; we sat up straight and placed the fingers of the left hand up to the second joint on the edge of the table. Elbows were about as improper on the table as feet. "You shall not let your food get cold," came next. Blister the roof of your mouth, scorch your tongue, scald your throat, but don't let the food on your sizzling hot plate fall below the boiling point. If we blew on a spoon of simmering soup we were excused from the table.

Most baffling of all the rules was, "You shall not spoil your appetite." (*Du sollst deinen Appetit nicht verderben.*) An appetite in America was something our friends worked up several times a day and satisfied with anything that took their fancy—like a hot dog. An appetite in Austria was a precious God-given gift that must be cherished and preserved. If you were a child the only acceptable way of fulfilling this recurrent blessing was with three sensible meals served punctually at the same time each day, and two of the meals started with soup. If you were an adult in Vienna you spoiled your appetite to your heart's content about seven times a day. There was tea in bed —or coffee—with a crescent roll and a touch of Green Gage Confiture.

A second breakfast, before which you couldn't go out of doors because of the fresh air. A bite just before lunch, lunch, tea (*Jause*), and an *Imbiss*—a snack here and there—dinner and supper and something called (in Germany) a *Betthüpfer*, a little sweet to generate enough energy to hop into bed.

The soup for which we children were not allowed to spoil our appetite was not a delightful **Cold Senegalese Soup** but a footbath of hot beef stock with a large dumpling floating in it. (A *Knödel*—a term also applied to tenors who produced a certain adenoidal sound in the backs of their throats which suggested that it was coming from behind a dumpling.)

After the hot soup the proper appetite-appeasing meal for growing children was a sober meat, marinated, braised, or sautéed with wine, two healthy vegetables, and a pudding. Here again it was not a divine **Fig Pudding** with a runny Vanilla Ice Cream Sauce, or an Almond Pudding with Brandied Peach Sauce, but something made of farina or, worst of all, tapioca or stale bread or elderly apples.

Needless to say, Father's last commandment was, "You shall leave nothing on your plates," and that meant every crumb unless there was a meat bone. Besides eating everything on our plates we had to eat everything that was set before us—there were no preferences expressed, no curling of the lip, no tantrums at the table. We learned to eat everything, although I once came close to putting my foot down on some old and woodeny plain boiled carrots and I still do not go far out of my way to eat tripe.

While Father was seeing to the inner children and the manner in which we should eat, Mother started on a program for showing us the great. She always said, "I would rather have you remember Pavlova when you are old than play in the sandbox now," so Edward and I were dragged (with short white gloves and cartwheel hats, secured to the backs of our heads with elastic bands that ran under our chins; we learned to make a hideous grimace by opening our mouths very wide and rolling our jaws in order to keep the elastics from slipping) to see Pavlova dance at least three farewells. In 1916 we were taken to see the entire Russian Ballet on its first American tour with Nijinsky and Lopokova, and ravishing costumes by Léon Bakst. In later years we were taken to hear Duse, Yvette Guilbert, Caruso, and finally Sir Harry Lauder. My chilblains itched and my legs fell asleep and Duse, especially in Ibsen in Italian, dragged badly. I have since heard that my parents' friends were sorry for us and the parents of our young friends—the ones who were presumably playing in their sandboxes—thought our case should be reported to the Child Protection League, but now I can remember Yvette Guilbert singing *"C'est le Mai, C'est Le Mai, C'est le joli mois de Mai,"* and it still brings me pleasure.

Norfolk Picnics

$\mathcal{W}$HEN I WAS A CHILD it was customary to change the body twice a year—the body of the car, I mean. This meant that our New York limousine went into the workshop each spring and emerged, after several weeks, with a very dashing open "touring" body for summer use. Apparently they stripped the car right down to the chassis, since the "touring" body was a sporting dark green, while the limousine was of course a sober citified black.

The touring body meant not only a new season and new activities but a totally new outlook on life. We all had to lay in a touring wardrobe consisting of dusters and goggles. I had a dust-colored object that looked like an enormous nightcap to cover my hair, ribbon, and most of my face. Mother had a long dust veil, a scarf as long as the one that killed Isadora Duncan.

For us the change of body went deeper, it brought a change from detested long white stockings and high-laced shoes to short socks and —joy of joys—low brown oxfords. We also changed our diets. Hot-milk rice was replaced by cold **Malteseritter Reis** and while for the children nothing was to be served ice-cold, we were given cooling drinks and lovely cold foods and we started on a series of marvelous picnics.

The American picnic and the Austrian *Ausflug* had very little in common except that food was eaten in the country, preferably in the fresh air. An *Ausflug* did not necessarily imply sitting on the ground with the traditional ants, but it always included a walk, a tramp, or a hike. The Austrians could make an *Ausflug* an excursion into the woods and along streams, and they could always depend on finding a strategically located *Gasthaus,* or inn, wherever they happened to feel hungry and wherever there was a pleasant aspect or beautiful view. In Austria if one carried food from home it could be anything from a simple *Schinken Brot,* carried in the rucksack, to delicacies for the most elaborate *fête champêtre* with several courses, *Bowle,* and an impractical torte. There was always, naturally, a well-guarded jar of whipped cream, *Schlagobers,* which was placed in the shade or put into a cool stream before anything else was unpacked. When we went on *Ausflug* in Austria, we were always sent off to pick wild strawberries so that the *Weinbowle* could become an *Erdbeer Bowle.*

When Father organized an American picnic, there was always a good half hour before luncheon while the fire was being built by Lawrence Cluen which was devoted exclusively to us. It was spent in playing *Blinde Kuh* (blind cow, or blindman's buff), and considerable time had to be devoted to find a suitable picnic spot which also provided the necessary number of trees, the proper distance apart. Father was invariably the blind cow, and the ladies squealed so pleasurably when he caught them that we were never certain whether the half hour was really for our benefit or for theirs.

I have a faded snapshot, which anyone would take to be a visit to Peking but is in fact a picnic in Norfolk, Connecticut, in 1915. Reading from left to right are Dr. George Steel, our deliverer and godfather, *Tante* Emma Easton, Father, Lydia Steel (our godmother), Roswell Easton, and Mother. John Easton, Edward, and I are in the foreground. The trees are in full leaf and I would judge the day to be hot and in August. John and Edward and I are dressed in cool summer clothes, with Chinese pagodas on our heads, but the adults are all in elaborate mandarin coats, dwarfed under high headdresses with long black pigtails attached to the back. It was apparently a formal costume picnic for six and they must have felt pretty silly putting on mandarin coats on a hot summer's day in Connecticut to go out into the woods to eat a cold collation. The snapshot was probably taken by the Steels' chauffeur, since Fräulein and Lawrence Cluen can be seen in the left background building the fire.

Father's picnic menus were incredibly involved. There were ponderous wicker picnic cases full of porcelain, crystal, and silver, thermos containers for ice and fruit, and, of course, silver champagne buckets, and I remember that there was an old-fashioned ice-cream freezer, complete with a piece of carpeting, so that a refreshing

lemon sherbet could accompany the cold game birds. A proper
American picnic always started with a lobster salad, and ended,
several courses later, with a Macédoine of Fruit absolutely drenched
in some—despised by me—liqueur. Usually the fire was built only to
boil the coffee, but in Norfolk there were always freshly caught (at
the trout hatchery) trout which were grilled on the fire. There were
no hot dogs, no corn on the cob, no marshmallows or sandwiches, but
there were always stuffed eggs and there had to be a potato salad.
The only acceptable beverage was champagne, with Rhine wine for
Father and for us there was one depressing bottle of milk. Even on
picnics we had to prepare for growing big and strong.

Next on the list of annual pleasures, after the changing of the
car body, was the advent of the house painters. Father arranged to be
in Europe during these visits after he selected the same colors, and
Mother and Fräulein were so busy protecting everything in the house,
except the vertical wall surfaces, from the painters that they could
not be too concerned with Edward and me and we were free. We
watched their meticulous color mixing, the picking out of the moldings
and the highlighting. I prayed for new colors but it always ended
with a painstaking match to the old ones. (I never dreamt then that
I would one day be a mural painter and a member of the Scene Painters and Painters and Paperhangers unions and would be fined
five dollars for not wearing white overalls and a peaked white cap.
Furthermore, I never took part in parades, which was also a finable
offense.)

It was believed at that time that the smell of paint was injurious
to the digestion and we did not eat at home. There were reciprocal
invitations; we had the Poors for meals when they had the painters
and they had us when we had the painters. Having the painters was
like having the measles in the house. When we were not at friends',
we ate at Constantine because of their Créoles and *Tuiles* or at Mail-
lard, and later on at Longchamps, which was the accepted painter-in-
the-house or servants'-night-out restaurant in New York. Once we ate
in a Chinese restaurant, which we adored, but Father never knew.

The final pleasure was closing the house for the summer. We
usually missed the excitement when we went abroad, but we spent two
summers in Norfolk, Connecticut, and one summer in Katonah during
the war and we stayed in New York until the upheaval was over.
Everything had a fitted and labeled slipcover of its own, made out

of a self-striped beige ticking and bound and tied down the back with beige tapes. They were called dust covers, as much for their purpose as for their uniform dust color. When every last picture and footstool had been covered with its own cover, woolen dresses and furs were sent to cold storage, the carpets were rolled up and sent to be shampooed, the silver and plate went to the bank vault, and the plants went to the florist. Books were wrapped, accessories and bric-a-brac were packed away, and chandeliers and sconces were tied into muslin bags. Edward and I tunneled under cases and hid under shrouded tables, and our world diminished as heavy shutters were bolted to the windows and each room was finished and locked. When we were finally isolated in the foyer with neither space, nor light, nor air, we took up our dog Scotti and our canary, and Mother handed the house over to a uniformed patrolman who plugged it into the Holmes Protective Agency.

There is a rhyme in Wilhelm Busch's "Max and Moritz" about some chickens which, in extremis, each lay one more egg before they depart this life. *"Und jedes legt noch schnell ein Ei, und dann kommt der Tod herbei."* Accompanied by a suitably moving illustration, it was one of those never-to-be-forgotten things in every child's life. I always thought of it whenever some last ritual was performed. And so we posed for a picture each year, with covered canary birdcage in hand, with Scotti on his leash—he was a smooth fox terrier, named for Antonio Scotti, the famous Scarpia of the Met, and not a Scottish terrier at all—with Fräulein, Marie Michel, Maggy Mulligan, Anna Gorsky (a fabulous Hungarian cook who preceded Marie), Lawrence Cluen, Mother, Edward, and I. Once the Holmes man joined in and once Mike, Father's mad Italian furnace-man, disposed himself among us in front of the closed door of the house. As every better English home has pictures of the staff lined up in front of the Manor to greet them on their return, so we had utterly useless pictures of our departures. In one of them Anna Gorsky is clutching the last bottle of milk and Maggy has a bunch of flowers.

Then off we went on the then eight-hour (now three) drive to Norfolk, singing all the way. There Father had just happened to rent the Crocker Cottage next to the Julian Streets. Edward played with Pete and I played with Rosemary while the older generation pursued their interests and pleasures in wine and food. I had my first cup of cambric tea and all sorts of good things suitable for young children from Mrs. Street while Rosemary's Mademoiselle and my Fräulein made the best of their private war. Sometime during the summer Mother fell into Doolittle Lake while paddling about with Dr. Peasley, and Father never let her hear the end of his amusement.

When war prevented Father's shuttling across the Atlantic, he chose to come to Norfolk apparently because it had a music festival. There was a short tryout (without Father) of the Lake Placid Country Club, where we played happily with the Scranton children and were crammed with golf, tennis, swimming, and riding lessons. If it couldn't be culture, it had to be sports. When Father joined us he caught a cold in the head and spents his first two Lake Placid days in bed. On the third day he rose, ate two meals and on the fourth day he departed saying "*Schauerlich*" (It is to shudder). We had been perfectly happy and I had embroidered a balsam pillow for him, which he rejected as he rejected **Lake Placid Corn Chowder** and Adirondack Pumpkin Pie. We thought it was superb food.

Norfolk was *Ein Kultur Zentrum* (a cultural center) compared with Lake Placid, and Father was as happy as he could reasonably be expected to be in a region that did not provide famous vineyards or cellars where he could taste wines and speak his "wine evaluating" language. Various stranded Central European opera singers, including conductor Artur Bodanzky and mezzo soprano Melanie Kurt, came to Norfolk and spread about an extremely Wagnerian atmosphere, which was somewhat incongruous, considering we were at war with Germany by then. I remember that Gertrude O'Brien, with whom we rode each day, brought her tallest horse, High Tower, to play Grane to Frau Kurt's Brünnhilde for a series of pictures. She first brought a small white mare (Wagner was not Miss O'Brien's forte) called Mimi, but Mimi looked as though Siegfried had played polo instead of galloping through the skies, and Miss O'Brien went back for High Tower—Frau Kurt's makeup running the while.

The photographer of musicians (but not of horses) Carl Struss came from New York, and we watched while poor High Tower—who subsequently threw John Easton onto an asphalt road and calmly ambled away—took an equine dim view of having to get out onto the Connecticut hill above the Housatonic River that most nearly resembled the home of the Nibelungen on the Danube.

Frau Kurt had on her full armor, with a great shining helmet surmounted by two white eagle wings (probably goose feathers). She carried a spear and a shield large enough to cover her, and she was afraid of horses. Competitor Johanna Gadski had been photographed most successfully with a horse, both looking as though they were standing in a steam bath (the mists of Valhalla) and something along those lines was wanted. Frau Gadski's horse was innocent of all harness, while High Tower had to wear his halter. When it was removed he immediately departed and had to be recaptured with a measure of oats. High Tower also had saddle scars as a result of his riding-school profession and a properly trimmed mane. After a morning of trying to pose Frau Kurt in such a way that her body hid the saddle scars and her arm hid the missing mane, Mr. Struss finally backed High Tower into some bushes, from which only his head emerged. The resultant picture showed Frau Kurt peering into infinity in front of some pyramidal maples with a horse's head looming over her right shoulder, looking more like a stuffed trophy than Brünnhilde's steed, who, though courageous, never rated a motif in Wagner's score. Mr. Struss stayed to lunch and I find his name among Mother's ever-reliable notes about who was fed what under **Smaragd Suppe** (Emerald Soup) and cold filet of beef with **Green Bean Salad Mimosa**. Dessert finds him listed under partakers of Melon in White Wine.

Our life no longer revolved about annual wine buying, but Edward and I grew up to know a great deal about opera singers and their strange ways.

Opera Singers

*J*UDGING BY THE sounds I have heard from opera singers in the early morning—and they need not come from the next room: when the wind was right in Norfolk, we could hear Melanie Kurt waking up across the entire valley—there is apparently a moment of doubt for all of them. Has the voice gone in the night? Will they ever sing another note? Light-opera singers can wake up and trill out a carefree breakfast order or sing a rousing "Good morning," but for them it is not a matter of life and death as it is for the Isolde or the Kundry who has just opened her eyes.

First there is a tentative clearing of the throat and then a squeaky little note. All this, for some unknown reason, has to be done with a hand mirror in the hand and an agonized peering down the throat. Then comes the plunge: not the "Liebestod"—that cannot be sung lying in bed—but the long, drawn out P–a–r–s–i–f–a–l (with enchantment) or the Rhinemaiden's motif in half-voice.

Melanie Kurt sang the *Walkure's* "Ho-jo-to-ho" and then let everyone in Norfolk—music lovers, townspeople, and summer guests—know what condition her voice was in. *"Ho-jo-to-ho, ich bin verschleimt"* (I am full of phlegm) or *"Ho-jo-to-ho, ich bin bei guter Stimme"* (I am in good voice). Norfolk could breathe again.

After establishing that the voice was still there, there came another long scrutiny down the throat and then BREAKFAST. And when nature distributes her gifts they never come alone; where there is a voice there is always an appetite.

Performance days started with a raw egg. Non-performance days began with a deep sigh and *Oeufs Brouillés Don Juan,* **Jenny Lind,** or **Offenbach.** If it wasn't just the right day for Don Juan, if the humor was more sentimental, then the proper thing was **Oeufs Héloise.** The theory at that time was that for true resonance the vocal cords had to be embedded in a layer of fat. More than vocal cords were embedded. Sometimes the entire singer was embedded. When I was a small child I once saw Emma Calvé against the light, and the memory did not have to be kept alive for me by Mother or Fräulein. Whoever devised Apples Calvé must have heard but not seen her. Schumann-Heink, in silhouette, could be remembered too, especially when she was wrapped in an American flag to sing "The Star-Spangled Banner." They named a suitable dessert for her: *Bombe Schumann-Heink.*

I have never felt that voices were more beautiful in my day or that opera singers were greater, but they certainly were larger. When chubby Siegfried-Hans Sembach leaped back after removing Brünn-hilde's armor plate, and exposing her to himself and the audience he sings, *"Das ist ja kein Mann"* (This is no man), there was always an audible murmur from the Met audience. Brünnhilde's, that is to say Margarethe Metzenauer's, *belle poitrine* was showing in no uncertain terms.

But all opera singers were diet prone. There were cures and diets, and after the diets there were deluges of calories and carbo-hydrates, and then came another and a newer diet. Some little self-indulgences were needed to offset the endless performance days of starvation and nervous indigestion. Swimming and singing are never done on a full stomach, and part of the suffering before a performance was from hunger. There was a story about a pale Tristan, having just died and been died over, leaving the stage after a dignified curtain call—he was heard to say loudly, *"Und jetzt Sauerbraten."*

Opera singers always made "days." They made milk days, apple days, water days, raw-egg days, herring-salad-roast-goose-with-baked-apples-stuffed-with-goose-liver-and-Mozart-torte days, then back to milk days, apple days, water days. And every autumn Madame Musa-eus let out the costumes. It is no wonder that so many operatic cos-tumes were designed with lacings and thongs and straps and let-out-able features.

On practice days the stomach was left moderately empty and the food was of a soothing nature. The throat was pampered. During hours of going up and down the scale with a flourish at the top, there was a little *Imbiss* at intervals. An *Imbiss* means something that is bitten into (and incidentally also swallowed). Tiny packages of smoked salmon stuffed with minced chives and capers mixed with riced egg yolk went down very well and were known as **Lachs Imbiss.**

After a few hours of *Imbiss*-punctuated practicing came the *Leckere Stunde*, the Delicious Hour, the hour for rewarding the throat and the ego and for fattening up the dogs—Don Carlos, Mario, Fidelio, or Mimi, as the case might be, was released from the kitchen and came flying directly onto its master's or mistress's lap. There was great licking and cooing and making much of each other. Singers and dogs shared the pastries, and in time a strong resemblance developed between them. And every autumn, while the opera costumes were being let out to suit the new dimensions, the dog's collars and coats were let out proportionately.

The Delicious Hour meant tea and pastries—Victorias, Madeleines, *Poupelins,* and **Linzer Augen.** And sometimes, on very special occasions, it meant chocolate-covered meringues filled with throat-soothing-vocal-cord-embedding whipped cream. They were called *Indianer Krapfen.* The *Indianer* reminds me of a series of cooking classes I attended in 1956 in New York's Greenwich Village. Toward the end of the course we were each asked to select one recipe that we wanted to prepare under expert supervision. I chose *Indianer Krapfen* and tried them with a marked lack of success—they came out flat and wide instead of round and high. After three guided attempts, the instructor said *he* would make them. I looked modest when his turned out to be even flatter and wider than mine. It was spring and the end of the series and I left—straight for Vienna and the school for hotel and restaurant cookery on the Juden Platz. When asked what I wanted to learn, I asked for special instruction in *Indianer Krapfen*—just another madwoman of New York. The appointment was made and I sat in the amphitheater with a few strays who wanted to see *Indianer Krapfen* made.

The pastry chef began by placing an old wine bottle on the table. He uncorked it, sniffed at it (they always sniff at everything before they add it to a recipe in Europe—only Americans have full faith in every egg and every shrimp), and emptied it into the beater. I raised my hand, which meant a question: "Week-old egg whites," was the answer, "with as little air on the surface as possible," hence a tightly corked narrow wine bottle with only about half an inch of air surface at the top. Every small child, I was later told, but not every American cooking teacher, knows that you cannot make meringue-like pastries stand in a perfect globe unless the egg whites are several days old and have been exposed to practically no air.

And so we learn and while we learn about egg whites we wonder why the little student chefs, in their wooden shoes, always step out of the kitchen into the garden or courtyard to beat their egg whites. And why they beat them on a wide flat porcelain platter with a fork or French wire whisk. I remember sitting in the enclosed terrace restaurant at the Hotel Post in Partenkirchen and suddenly hearing the ping of the beater. Why did the boy go outside, why the flat platter? Because you expose egg whites to the minimum amount of air while you store them and the maximum amount of air while you beat them. This is particularly important when you make *Salzburger Schneenockerl*.

The *Nockerln* at the Post are very good, though Bavarianized. Every Central European town has a Post Hotel, where the post chaise used to stop. The Post in Partenkirchen is hidden on the lovely Ludwig's Strasse—mad Ludwig's Street—above Garmisch and caters more to Germans than to tourists. But even the Post has a busload now and then during the skiing season. It is pleasant, unpretentious, and furnished in part with some very good antiques. The porter is also an antique but the concierge is a pretty girl. There is the Barbarossa Bar and three restaurants and they take less of your money than others do. At Claussing's Post Hotel in Garmisch, where the post chaise still stops and the postilion still blows his horn, and the cows come clanking down the main street from the alp each afternoon—and drop cow plops—and the Bavarians yodel at the Bavarian evening, and all is not entirely free from *Korn*—but it is all very sweet—they make absolutely divine *Salzburger Nockerln* with a strong apricot flavor and as large as sofa pillows.

We stayed there one winter—in the turret room—and fumed through our dinners because a Dutch family of copycats ate everything we ate at every meal. With generations of menu-choosing forebears behind me, I came up with some divine combinations, only to have them imitated across the aisle. They didn't even try to disguise their method of choosing, they simply pointed at our selections and said, *"Auch"*—also. I was tempted to order a gastronomic atrocity, but appetite was stronger than dislike—until I thought of *Salzburger*

Nockerl. With the accumulated knowledge of my forebears, I ordered one portion for the four of us. There were six Hollanders, and when each one said, *"Auch,"* Herr Claussing wrote down six portions. They were served with twelve enormous sofa pillows (almost bed pillows) of apricot-flavored, floating egg whites, and I had my revenge.

A year later Herr Claussing had been discovered by all the world and we became true to the Post in Partenkirchen, which has a better parking lot and no cows.

For *Waldmeister* (woodruff) the herb that cures all ills, go to the old pharmacy next to Claussing's Post Hotel. It is housed in one of Europe's finest S'Graffiti, buildings, and then make a *Waldmeister Bowle* on a warm spring evening.

To return to the singers. After their Delicious Hour came the pause (a little *Bowse* or nap) and then some really serious eating—dinner. Opera singers' dinners were notoriously lengthy, since the waistline was not as important as the voice, but a new generation of opera singers came along who had both waistline and voice. Singers began to permit smoking in their presence, and some actually smoked themselves. Some singers managed to sing without the feverish voice-preservation precautions, and although many of them lacked all sense of humor about themselves, there were exceptions. Jeritza never went to any lengths to guard her voice, and Lauritz Melchior and Friedrich Schorr were both well voiced and undeprived.

Melchior was able to laugh about himself, had a wonderful repertoire of jokes which he collected to tell the king of Denmark, and took only reasonable care of his voice. On our way to a dinner in Philadelphia, in the late forties, we were caught in an incredible press at Pennsylvania Station. A hurricane was raging and the tunnels were flooded. Standing head and shoulders over the crowd was Lauritz Melchior and standing head and shoulders under the crowd was *Kleinchen* (little one), his wife. Melchior was doing a sign-language act—he pointed to his throat and his hermetically sealed mouth. He dimpled and rolled his bright blue eyes, but not a sound. Kleinchen told us he was going to sing in Newark. We waited an agonizing two hours, and by the time we made a train Lauritz was completely relaxed and opening his mouth to every draught of air. According to his watch, the concert had begun and he would arrive just in time to make an apology and bow. We found seats in the bar car, and great quantities of drinks and unsuitable foods—hot dogs, potato chips, pea-nuts—were consumed by an unmuffled Melchior.

At the top of his voice, Melchior regaled us with stories of every singer who ever missed a concert. He was amused to think he was missing the concert but would get there in time for a jolly good Dan-ish fellow dinner. He talked every inch of the way; the car became smokier and smokier as we were held up under the river. The crowd was noisy and Lauritz had to shout to be heard. They detrained in a deserted Newark and we went on to Philadelphia.

We found the remains of a dispirited party and at midnight our host turned on the radio for news of the hurricane. A cheerful an-nouncer came on to say that a bedraggled Lauritz Melchior had ar-rived at the concert hall in Newark after incredible hardships, but his loyal audience had waited for the concert and he took great pleasure in introducing Lauritz Melchior—ovation, ovation. We listened to the concert. Without benefit of muffling up, keeping the mouth closed, starvation, cold sobriety, silence, sprays, and raw eggs, Melchior sang superbly. We knew what lay in his supposedly empty stomach and about the thick smoky air he had been breathing and the shouting he had done. When we saw him again he said, "You know what—I sang on all those frankfurters—very good too." So all the precautions are not necessarily necessary. We heard the Danish dinner included **Norsk Fiskfärs.** Our Philadelphia dinner was dull, but there were wonderful filet steaks, which were the beginning and the end of our host's reper-toire—*Filets de Boeuf Gastronome* with a garnish of glazed chestnuts.

Thieves and Joseph Urban

*I*N THE MIDDLE OF the first Norfolk summer, Mother and I drove to
New York to fetch something Father needed from the house—
probably a spice to add some infinitesimal nuance, an exotic breath,
to his ever-changing salad dressing. The Holmes man detached our
connections with the main office, unlocked the door, and departed.
Mother and I felt our way up the dark front stairs with an unlighted
candle stub in what must have, even in its initial stages, looked like a
Mack Sennett comedy—and ran smack into the arms of three burglars,
who were just as frightened as we were. We finally extricated ourselves, and they flew up the stairs to escape down the back leader
while we left hastily down the stairs. Outside the front door, Mother
threw herself into the arms of a huge black-eyebrowed policeman,
pleading, "Come into the house with me, come into the house with
me!" It did not move him at all. Any small child, except me, would
have seen that he had on a long double-breasted coat and an old-
fashioned high gray helmet and that he was not a real policeman—as
it turned out, he was an actor taking part in a movie being filmed at
the corner.

Everything thereafter was confusion and pure slapstick. The on-
lookers enjoying the movie making thought Mother was part of the act,
and in the meantime our own burglars took themselves over the back
fence and were gone. They had apparently removed several suitcases
of our possessions before we arrived but had abandoned whatever else
was packed for the next load. Their point of entry had been the coal
chute, from the pavement to the cellar, which was the only vulnerable

entry to the house, but Holmes had failed to wire it. This too was un-derstandable, since any thief would have to send a very tiny thief down the chute and he in turn would have to cut wires before he could open the cellar door and the back gate for the bigger thieves.

When a real policeman was finally found, his only contribution was a flashlight. As it turned out, only Edward and I had been robbed. Our savings banks, our War Savings Stamps, our Christmas $20 gold pieces, and our stamp albums and penny banks were gone. Everything we had been good, obedient, truthful, and unselfish for, and for which we had washed our hands and had our hair washed for years, was gone. The only silver that had been left in the house were our starter sets of silver spoons (a very popular gift in those days from aunts and godmothers), and they were gone. (Afterward we both continued to receive coffee spoons for Christmas and birthdays, and we were always bitterly disappointed. Eventually the spoons ac-cumulated and now I could give a black-coffee party—if I had that many cups and that many friends—for more than seventy people. But for the burglars I'd now have more than eighty spoons for people to stir a Coffee Mélangé or a *Café mit Schlagobers,* or an *Eis Café* simul-taneously in Lunz-am-See.

In any case, we the victims were never recompensed and I was secretly afraid of burglars as long as we stayed in the house. Our three burglars had come in through the coal chute; the next ones, I felt cer-tain, would come over the roof and directly into my bedroom, two flights below.

After Fräulein came Mme. Blé, and when she left and Edward went to boarding school, I had the fourth floor of the house to myself and my fears. I took certain simple precautions, always slept with a loaded water pistol under my pillow and arranged my bed across the locked bedroom door. I reached the room by going through the front living room and dressing room, where I arranged undependable (as it turned out later) booby traps at strategic points. The only other ac-cess was through the back hall into the bathroom and through the bathroom door into my room. This approach was guarded by Christ-mas, who slept soundly in his basket before the radiator and would have greeted any visitor with delight and joyful barks, which at least would have awakened me and so the fear of surprise was mitigated.

I was awakened one night by a great fat man, endowed with the great-grandfather of all double chins, sitting down on the side of my bed. Christmas was sound asleep; I had no time to think about the failure of the safety devices and ineffectual traps I had contrived—my instant concern was to cover myself to my chin. He turned on the dressing-room light and I could see enough to know that he was human and he was laughing. While I have been hinting at certain quiet virtues and a good character, the fact remains that somewhere deep down within me there was a worm that had turned the moment my last governess left. I had been the infant who had never cried, I was the child that was roused at dawn for Father Kneipp's Cold-Water Cure. I was the meek child who had never opened her mouth in the presence of her elders. I was the child who wore braces on her legs so that her Indian-type feet would turn outward in the approved officer's march step of the Austrian Army. But now I was the child who, the moment Mme. Blé closed the door, changed her entire mode of life to conform with her ideas of practicality and comfort. After taking a bath every evening, I brushed my teeth and combed my hair, and then dressed fully for the next day—even putting on gloves—and got virtuously into bed (I taught myself to sleep without moving). I got out of bed the next morning five minutes before I was driven to school. I put on a hat, fetched the breakfast tray set in front of my barricaded bedroom door, and flushed the breakfast down the john. I slept two luxurious hours longer each day than anyone ever suspected.

So now I pulled the covers up over my neat Bromley dress, the uniform of every young girl in the 1920's, with gloved hands and I tried to act as though I didn't have my shoes on in bed. My visitor was in tails and all he said was *"Das Kind ist begabt"* (The child is talented), and went off into great vibrating chuckles. He had wandered into Mother's room (my parents might be strict, but they had devotedly framed and hung my first attempts at art work) and asked if he might see me. This apparition turned out to be Joseph Urban, Viennese architect and stage designer who came to the Metropolitan from Boston in 1917 and later turned into my inspiration, my mentor, and finally my employer. He was my first precious piece of Vienna, *Mein Stück von Wien.*

I cannot remember what I had wanted to be or do before I met him—but after that night I wanted to be, like him, a stage designer, an artist, an interior architect. I wanted to study art where Urban had studied art—in Vienna; I wanted to paint and design and chuckle. A door had opened for me—opened by a fat man who shook with laughter because he had found a nine-year-old-girl in bed against a barricaded door with all her clothes on. He was my release from what had looked like an empty future of Coming Out, Finding a Husband, and Having Children. No one at school looked an inch beyond that project, and everyone but me seemed satisfied with it.

Nobody knew that I had made up my mind, and nothing is as formidable as a child's determination. I still wore my clothes to bed and had my secret sleep, but I had an object in life and the quickest way to achieve it was to get school over with. Obviously the only way to get out of school was to graduate and the only way to graduate was to apply myself, so I set myself not to learn but to memorize. And four years later I went to Vienna to study art.

12

Artur Bodanzky

*T*HERE WAS NO ROOM in our upbringing for wasteful pastimes or idle diversions. When we played games they were supposed to broaden our minds, and rainy days in Norfolk were spent sitting around a table (with two adults) playing "Shakespeare," "Paintings," or Riddles.

"Shakespeare" was something halfway between drama and bridge. Cards of Shakespearean quotations were dealt, and I think that a sort of primitive form of bidding followed, which showed us who was strong in *King Lear* and where there was no *Taming of the Shrew*. At the start one of us led with, say, "When sorrows come . . . ," reading it aloud as it was put down on the table. If anyone recognized whose sorrows they were, he or she could cover them with, "I could a tale unfold . . . ," reading or reciting it with feeling. If we had no *Hamlet* we could try to slip in a little something Caliban said, and if we didn't recognize the quotation at all, we discarded a singleton. There was opportunity for a great deal of bluffing. The trick was taken by anyone who had "To be or not to be . . ." (the ace *Hamlet* quotation), and we then knew that three *Hamlets* and one *Tempest* were out. We piled up our tricks and he who had the most marched on to victory. I always discarded *The Merry Wives of Windsor* and *The Winter's Tale* from dislike, regardless of trumps, and I am now able to recognize—and, if necessary, recite—four telling quotations from each of Shakespeare's twenty major plays. About bridge I learned absolutely nothing and my card playing is limited to patience at which I win enormous sums of money from myself. Our friends were limited to people who were willing to give up an evening of bridge for eating and conversation and—if they dared—the playing of one of our puerile educational games.

The one called "Paintings" has stood me in better stead than "Shakespeare." I can hold forth at museums and can recognize four Andrea del Sarto Madonnas as opposed to four Raphael Madonnas. I can distinguish Titian's voluptuous ladies from Palma Vecchio's fleshy blondes, and no one can fool me where Tintoretto and Veronese are concerned. Just recently we came through Winterthur where I saw a ghastly Böcklin in a private collection that I had frequently fought over on rainy days in Norfolk.

Another favorite game was Riddles, which, in Father's rather cultured version, had to be a famous quotation at the same time. We were supposed to guess the riddle and know who asked it, all in the language of its origin. You can see why we played our games with knowledgeable adults—our little friends were still deep in Slap Jack and Old Maid when we were being grounded in the classics. Riddles was rather limited and many of the quotations were unanswerable. We knew perfectly well it was Lowell who said, "and what is so rare as a day in June?" in *The Vision of Sir Launfal*, but we never did guess what was rarer. So it was with special interest that we greeted new riddles. I remember playing with Mother and Melanie Kurt (they never kept their minds on the game) when Mother asked, "Who said and what is, *Noir comme le diable, chaud comme l'enfer, pur comme un ange, doux comme l'amour?*" * It was my turn to guess, but Frau Kurt spoiled the whole thing by singing out "Der Artur Bodanzky" and broke up the game laughing.

Derarturbodanzky became a disliked rhythm in my mind long before we heard that he was coming to stay. Preparations for his visit were hectic—Derarturbodanzky would not like this and he would like that. The only light spot was that we were not going to practice piano or violin while he was there. The piano had to be tuned; we vacated the guest bathroom (not completely, as it turned out); and an even deeper silence than usual was to be observed. Derarturbodanzky wanted no children underfoot, and as for Christmas, he was not to bark, jump up, come into the dining room, or pant. Derarturbodanzky, had we been allowed to express our feelings, was going to be *ein Schmerz im Hals*—a pain in the neck.

* Talleyrand gave this as a description of the best coffee.

When he arrived it turned out that he really was exactly like a cup of burning-hot strong, black coffee. I sit now over a biographical dictionary and try to think of the very old men I knew in the light of how young they really were at the time. Artur, it turns out, was thirty-eight when he came from warring Europe to stay with us before he started conducting at the Metropolitan. The things I remember about him are the least important in his life, but to me they were profoundly impressive. I had never seen anyone eat twelve *Zwetsch- genknödel* (Plum Dumplings) in a row. He swallowed the pit of the first one because Mother didn't believe in substituting a lump of sugar for it (on the grounds that it would make the juice run out or jet across the table with the first puncture of the fork), but he slung down eleven more without reservations. He ate as enormously as only a wire-thin man can eat, and when, after three or four courses with double helpings, he fell on the fifth one, he turned to Mother and said, *"Sehen Sie,* Das *esse ich"* (You see *this* is something I eat)—it was his standing joke as was his sudden interruption of all conversations by commanding *"Die Kinder sollen nicht so viel reden"* (The children shouldn't talk so much). This always delighted everyone, as Edward and I hadn't opened our mouths since we were alone together several hours—or even days—before. We were entirely speechless for such long periods that when we tried to say something we usually started with croaking sounds.

Bodanzky deserves better than my six-year-old biographical recollections of him, but I very much doubt whether he ran his extraordinary bony hand down over the faces of the Metropolitan's artists or box holders and said, *"Du bist eine Canaille,"* which is what he always did when he saw me and I doubt whether he was admired for the same talents by anybody else but me. I was absolutely carried away by the way he blew his nose, which is more than you can say for his greatest musical admirers. The entire performance took several minutes and was an awesome spectacle. It involved throwing an enormous handkerchief over his face while he trumpeted loudly and almost broke his thin rudder-like nose, which he pushed savagely from side to side. There was a shake of the head and a final, never-to-be- forgotten dig with the handkerchief covering his two forefingers and then it was furled into his pocket and he smiled sweetly, as though he had just regained consciousness after a serious operation.

He was full of the sort of delightful, earthy remarks we had never heard before. He said, *"Ich wünsche ich könnte jetzt in den seinen Magen essen"* (I wish I could now eat into that one's stomach), after he had just eaten a long and hearty meal into his own. His anecdotes of stage disasters were endless: the trapdoors that opened by mistake, the tenors who stood on the soprano's trains, the substituted props and the effect of the footlights on the digestive tracts of various animals. There were many stories about Lohengrin's swan, but I particularly loved the tenor-laden swan that got stuck behind the tall grasses and the stagehand who crawled out on his belly to get him started again; pleased with his success, the stagehand stood up in the full glory of the footlights. Artur always got up at this point to portray the stagehand's departure from the stage, doing a slow and dignified breaststroke into the wings while Lohengrin sang *"Fahre wohl, mein lieber Schwan."*

About a week after his arrival, Artur came down to breakfast and asked sternly, "Who in this house has red hair?" He had arrived hairbrushless and was using the one in the guest bathroom in which he found a red hair. From Christmas 1914, for more than ten years, I had spent my life protecting, defending, and shielding Christmas from Father. Anything he did—a thoughtless bark, a spot in the hall (where he had a favorite place created by, in Father's eyes, the irreproachable Hans Sachs, a dachshund belonging to a Wagnerite), or just leaving about some of his red hairs—always meant "That dog has to *go.*" Everyone shook his head at Artur's question until he came to me. I admitted leaving the dog brush in his bathroom, though I knew that Father would now really dispose of my Christmas, but Artur thought it uproariously funny and Christmas was allowed to stay.

It was Artur who said, "Give that poor child some sugar," when he saw I couldn't swallow the **Chou-Fleur Ignatieff,** and taught me to love it. It was Artur who cried *"Genug"* (enough) when we were playing Forfeits, and my musical Fräulein, thinking the forfeit hanging over her head belonged to Melanie Kurt, asked for a song. It turned out to be mine and I got out an agonized opening bar of "Hark, Hark the Lark" when Artur's *"Genug!"* rang out so loud that it could have stopped the Metropolitan orchestra and chorus. He was with us over the Fourth of July and my birthday and instituted the custom that the birthday child could order all the meals. I thoughtfully ordered his favorite Plum Dumplings, which are my favorite too, a Walnut Birthday Torte, with Capon Drouant, Chestnut Purée,

Rice Pudding, and Biscuit Tortoni. It was not really a well-composed menu and I remember that Father sulked. I also wished for a croquet set and sneakers. I always wished unsuccessfully for sneakers until I was old enough and independent enough to buy them for myself, and then—tragically—I didn't want them anymore.

I was born early in the morning on July 5, when Mother, knowing nothing about Independence Day, was badly frightened by a firecracker, and for some years I thought the celebration on the eve of my birthday was for me. I remember that we all drove to Winsted, ostensibly to buy firecrackers, with Father in the front seat, Mother and Artur in the back, and Edward and I on the jump seats. They left me sitting alone in the open car and presently a large wooden, gratifyingly croquet-set-shaped, oblong box of firecrackers was brought out, and Artur gave elaborate instructions for placing it carefully with the firecrackers standing up. He fussed over it all the way home and we all acted as though we didn't know that he was going to give me my wished-for croquet set—though not my sneakers.

Dinner was a great sucess and the Plum Dumplings were divine as always. Since reaching my growth I have eaten fourteen at a single sitting and without other courses, but I have heard that the world championship is for eating over a hundred. I later met architect Adolf Loos, when I was a student in Vienna; I went to see him participate in the *Marillenknödelwettrennenessen* (the Apricot-Dumpling-Eating Race), and cheered for him all the way. I don't think Artur would have qualified for that event because we only counted twenty-odd pits on his plate, but then he had eaten capon and chestnut purée and had to leave room for birthday cake.

After dinner there were fireworks. Father was not one to simply light a match and send off a few 'crackers for his children; he approached the whole subject, which he called *Lustfeuerwerkkunst*—pleasure-firework-as-art. What Father concocted and Lawrence Cluen carried out (with the assistance of an old gardener and his gangly boy) would have put the Ruggieris into the shade, and it is a wonder that I did not grow up with a Versailles complex, since they insisted it was all for me. It was only when I went to school for the first time that winter that I gradually learned about our Independence Day and the insignificance of my birthday.

We sat in a row of ponderous wicker porch chairs arranged across the top of the lawn and watched (and heard) Father's artistically arranged Roman candles, Bengal lights, stars, Chinese fire, fountains, and shells cut across the Norfolk sky. There was an extravagant display of stars and bursts, and the whole thing worked up to a final *Pyrotechnische Entfaltung* of colored Catherine wheels and a triumphant portrait of Woodrow Wilson all done in red, white, and blue explosions.

Artur was as endlessly tall as a long shadow on the wall, cadaverously thin, saturnine, dark, and so completely unrelaxed that I always thought there would be a wiry twang if I were to touch him. He was capable of the most unexpected, tumultuous, and infectious laughter that stopped as suddenly as it began. His incredibly expressive Gothic hands were heavily knuckled, thin to the bone, with rounded nails and fingertips. He seemed completely unselfconscious and he was capable of the most unexpected, tumultuous, and infectious laugh- could be fierce. His children, Lisa and Carl Artur, who came to New York the following winter with their mother, Ada, were as frightened of him as we were of Father—Ada was apparently frightened too. Being afraid of fathers and loving non-fathers, who were always called *Onkel*, was the European custom—adoring Dad or even knowing one's father well enough to call him Dad was unknown. Dick and I are uncle and aunt only to the four Thrane children, the youngest of whom improves on this old-fashioned and charming custom by calling us Uncle Liesl and Aunt Dick. Artur was not an uncle type, so we called him Artur, which was unprecedented in those days. Artur looked exactly as though someone had pulled Gustav Mahler into twice his length and half his width and called him Bodanzky.

After a time Artur moved down the valley to stay with Melanie Kurt, but they continued to come for dinner every evening, Mina Hackelberg being more a Prussian factotum than a creative cook. My recollections of both of them consist of the things a child would notice, added to obscure things that were said in our presence (and sometimes understood years later). At the time I certainly didn't understand how Norfolk, Connecticut, could possibly object to Artur moving down to Frau Kurt's house; I could see that *he* would mind, because of Mina, but not Norfolk. We were so silent that adults invariably forgot we were there and said curious things. We heard that Artur had to work with Tante Melanie because she was going to be Brünnhilde in his first *Götterdämmerung* and I heard Mother say that there was friction.

During that summer the Stoeckls had a charity bazaar, and Rosemary Street, dressed as a Harlequinette, got to sell some beguiling little kittens while I, dressed as an orphaned *Dirndl*, sold picture postal cards of Melanie Kurt as Isolde. I can think of nothing the New Englanders wanted less than a postal card of a German singer in a German opera, and one old lady came up to me and said, "Think of the poor Belgians." When I asked what she meant, Frau Kurt was furious.

Frau Kurt was the Metropolitan's leading Wagnerian soprano, but to her maid, Mina Hackelberg, she was *Frauchen*—little woman— a misnomer if ever there was one. Frau Kurt was tall and large and loved to eat, and wherever a bone should have protruded she had a dimple instead. She dwarfed her tenors—Hans Sembach, in particular—and was hysterically fond of animals and reptiles. When the car passed a Connecticut turtle on the road, brakes had to be applied and Turti was brought home to live her life in a New York apartment, listening to scales, arias, lieder, and *Wutanfälle* (tantrums). Amazingly Turti finally listened to her own voice and laid a single brown egg in Mina's bathtub.

We were invited down especially to see the oval brown turtle egg, since it was one of the few things that occurred in Frau Kurt's apartment which could be considered of juvenile interest. Somewhere in Frau Kurt's past in Berlin (she was the wife of Doktor Max Deri, art expert and author of *Die Neue Malerei*) there had been Flink, a fox terrier who stood at Doktor Deri's ankle at every curb until he was told to cross the street. Stories about Flink were the sum total of Mina's and Frau Kurt's conversational material for the young. In Norfolk they all went off in the car and came back with a melancholy chocolate-colored cocker spaniel whom Frau Kurt called Bluntschli after the hero of Shaw's *Arms and the Man*, which later became the opera *The Chocolate Soldier*. In a matter of days he became less chocolate-colored and more flesh-toned as his hair fell out with the mange. Bluntschli went back to the Bloodgood Farm's kennels to be exchanged for a black-and-white dog of the same breed whom she called Loge—God of Fire. Loge was always called Lucky because of his great good luck in being chosen as the best friend of a Wagnerian soprano who loved to eat. Actually I always thought the Prima Donna and Dog relationship a little overdone and we secretly called him

Unlucky. We loved Christmas, but a dog (if I may be forgiven for saying so) is a dog, and watching Lucky sit on the sofa next to Frau Kurt while she divided her meals with him shocked us. It was not as though she gave him every other *friandise,* or sweet—she always bit into candies, petits fours, and pastries, and gave him the other half. The Lucky Dog became so fat eating half of Melanie Kurt's meals that he finally died—as Father had gloomily predicted—of fatty degeneration of the liver.

The next summer the Bodanzkys rented the Flynn house in Margaretville and Frau Kurt rented a cottage nearby. For some reason I was asked to spend a week with her before the others arrived. My only recollection of that stay is that the elderly spinster who owned her cottage came to call each morning because (as I heard her explain to Mina) she was used to going to that particular loo. To compensate for this use she always brought a pie. Her **Apricot Raisin Pie** and her pineapple-apple pies were a melting delight and Frau Kurt put off discouraging her visits. During that week Unlucky dragged her mistress into a ditch where she turned her ankle. Mina and I helped her back to the house and arranged her on the sofa. We spread a cover over her and called the doctor. He was most concerned about the swelling; he bandaged it and prescribed treatments. He asked her to try and stand on it, and when her uninjured other leg came out from under the covers—an exact mate to the first—he left.

The Bodanskys arrived with an entourage of musicians and admirers and I met a quiet little man called Otto Baumgarten, owner of Voisins, the Crillon, and the Esplanade, where I later always ate my absolutely favorite Artichoke Hearts Stuffed with Chestnut Purée. He also served *Dobos Torten* and *Indianer Krapfen,* and as we grew up we were allowed to lunch our friends there. About this time everyone became very serious over Gatti's cancellation of German operas and the ultimate departure of Melanie Kurt, Unlucky, Mina Hackelberg, and Turti.

The Bodanzkys stayed on and moved into Alma Gluck's house, and we sometimes played with Lisa and Little Artur in the park. They had a Fräulein Meyer who was so stern that she served as the prototype of punishment-giver in our family—it wasn't the goblins that would get us, but Miss Meyer, if we didn't watch out. She sometimes sat in the park, with our comparatively benign Fräulein, making what looked like consecutive cat's cradles and produced yards of tatting, which always struck me as an unusually unattractive way of edging a handkerchief.

Edward and I were born New Yorkers, but geography had nothing to do with our upbringing, and for all the liberties we enjoyed we might just as well have been born in Austria. Bodanzky's children were born in Germany, probably Mannheim, where he conducted for many years, and where, according to the only thing I can remember hearing from young Lisa, the stork that brought her *zwickt* (pinched) Frau Bodanzky in the leg to wake her up and show her Lisa, and the pinch was so severe that Frau Bodanzky had to go to the hospital. Thus shielded from the German facts of life, we were all alarmed by the threat of the stork.

I remember a dinner at the Bodanzkys in New York—probably a birthday—and the Bodanzky birthday child had ordered **Vanilla Haselnuss Kipferl** and Plum Dumplings, and I marveled that Artur had ever learned to love the dumplings he got at home; they were thick with cinnamon, and a lump of sugar was substituted for each pit. I was slightly disillusioned when he ate them with his usual speed and gusto. The vanilla *Kipferl* were small, hard, and dark (unblanched almonds I later learned), and for the first and only time in my life I fell into the deplorable phrase of the food experts: These are not as good as ours.

13

Son et Lumière

ATHER'S ENTIRE LIFE was divided into opposing halves. On one side were the rigid rules by which everyone else was expected to live, and on the other side was the complete absence of all rules, which was the way he lived. In some people this might have created a complex, but not in Father. He spoke of himself in Goethe's words for Faust, *"Zwei Seelen wohnen, ach! in meiner Brust"* (Two souls, alas, live in my breast), by which he meant his serious love for art and music and his hedonistic inclination to put the arts aside while he devoted himself to the pleasures of the table and the cellar. Whenever he spoke of himself in this way, I deplored Herr Goethe's *"Ach!"* with the exclamation point. There was no alas in Father; he loved both his souls.

To him music meant the infinite pleasure of both listening and relaxing (like many music lovers, Father was able to sleep soundly through much of it) as well as the never-ending delight of entertaining musicians and artists. It was then that his two souls met— food and drink in an aura of music. Most of our musician friends were a special race unto themselves and Father understood their foibles and graces. I have come to the conclusion that he was, in fact, a great musician who just happened to have been born without an ear, a voice, or a talent. But he did truly love and appreciate music. He also loved to be a sponsor, but though he gave to various music and art institutions and helped to keep some of them alive, he never let his name appear.

I think Father was unaware of the vagaries of his procedure;

everyone else had to be absolutely correct in all things—he pronounced the word with German emphasis, on the *r*—while he allowed himself the most illogical liberties. Nothing that applied to his fellow-men applied to him. Even the recognition of time was for the masses. He was not actually unpunctual; it was only that he did not feel himself bound by anything so commonplace. He continued to drum into us the maxim that punctuality was the politeness of kings and then left us to wait—regally—at the appointed time and place while he was having a perfectly happy time somewhere else. There were never any apologies or explanations, and as a result, he was a dreadful guest and a really appalling house guest. I never knew why anyone invited him, but off my parents would sail on their weekend invitations, hours late, and loaded down with gifts that I always thought were in the worst possible taste.

Mother must have felt the same way because, years later, when she went to weekend with her little group of widows—Mrs. Griswold at Hillhome in Stockbridge, Mrs. Steinway in Tuxedo or Watch Hill, Mrs. F. A. O. Schwarz in Greenwich—she always took the same gift, caviar from Maison Glass. The ladies sat together with their happy memories and their courage and guzzled (I quote) caviar. Mother was at heart a caviar purist—warm toast, cold butter, and nothing else—but I think she enjoyed her friends' gastronomic innovations. Mrs. Griswold always had it served with cocktails throughout the weekend, Mrs. Steinway believed in the classic first-course service but other friends served Mother *Caviar aux Blinis*, **Fonds d'Artichauts au Caviar,** and Mrs. Baker's lovely **Caviar aux Tomates.** (Our imaginative friends the Lamonds have served us *Huîtres au Caviar*, and once we were given *Caviar à l'Andalouse*, which is nothing more nor less than caviar in a steamed onion—but *Ach*, how different. But I, too, believe in the classic treatment, although I have served thick slices of cold rare roast beef covered with an equally thick layer of caviar as a main course at a special sort of dinner party. In Iran we could give these fine tastes full scope. I must also admit, however, that I also love what Pforte used to do with caviar in Hamburg, *Palmenherzen mit Kaviar* (Hearts of Palm with Caviar) and **Caviar aux Crêpes de Pommes de Terre.**

But back to Mother, who was always a very popular guest. She also brought her friends' servants, *kleine Aufmerksamkeiten* (small attentions), and tipped generously and tactfully. Mother and Father, more than anyone I have ever known, had a talent for endearing themselves to restaurant and hotel staffs and their own and their friends' servants. With Mother's Napoleonic memory for names she sent her friends' servants properly addressed and thoughtfully selected Christmas presents—she was never one to consider her duty done by sending three pairs of stockings or a box of candies or a necktie addressed to Mrs. Steinway's Henry. Nor did either of my parents ever descend to thinking that they would be less respected if, by some dreadful chance, they were to overtip.

Now that we have moved to Austria, I have come to understand that Father was burdened by the Austrian approach to the bearing of gifts. Here no one comes empty-handed—even to dinner—and they do it casually, not with great gift wrappings and boxes. It can be a single flower or a bouquet, a bottle of wine, or a slab of *Bauern-Speck,* delicious home-cured bacon. There is no limit to what people bring; it can be a box of chocolates, or bulbs or corms for our garden. We have received all these things since we have moved here, in addition to an antique washstand, two antlered monarchs of the glen—masterpieces of taxidermy—an enchanting sphere of dried flowers, a table, and a wooden bowl carved by the giver. Father's weekend gifts had to be transported in the trunk of the car and sometimes even in ice chests or thermos containers. They ranged from Lenox service plates and braces of pheasant and wheels of cheese to ginger jars.

There were two things about Father's gifts which added to my embarrassment. They were invariably selected to fill deficiencies or weaknesses in his host's home, and they were obviously planned for instant consumption—by his host and hostess and by himself. Mother's gifts of caviar might be for mutual enjoyment too, but it always seemed to me that Father's iced wines, his *Terrine de Pâté Maison,* his hothouse grapes, his Hazelnut Torte and goose livers, and jars of turtle soup and bottles of brandy pointed up certain shortcomings in the cuisine or in his host's cellar. Certainly they had to go to their kitchens and do an immediate about-face with their planned menus. Father once brought Mrs. Thomas Beck a complete china service— hers was unbelievably chipped—and thereby severed a perfectly pleasant friendship. If his host served brandy out of liqueur glasses, or burgundy out of white-wine glasses, Father thought himself thoughtful when he brought brandy snifters or the proper goblets for red wine. He had to be taken as he was, and most of his friends did just that.

The worst feature of Father's weekendings was the equipment he carried for his own comfort. He considered himself a first-rate, almost a professional insomniac, although he laughed at his mother who always maintained, if anyone made the mistake of asking if she had slept well, that she hadn't closed an eye all night. Father did not lie awake all night only because he went to the most incredible lengths to ensure his eight hours of sound sleep. If Mother woke up in the night she was not allowed to turn over in bed, let alone turn on a light. If Father woke in the night he turned on the light, read, sighed, woke her, and insisted that she stay awake as long as he did.

Light and sound, *son et lumière*, were his problem. While it was an era when everyone traveled about carrying the most outlandish personal possessions and equipment, Father's paraphernalia must have been the worst.

I remember that Mrs. Polk and May Baker had Schaffer's Market send snow-white eggs to the steamers when they sailed or to the hotels where they stayed. Others carried silk sheets, cashmere throws, and lace pillows. A certain set carried silver framed pictures of the Queen Mother or their own mothers, provided they were recognizably distinguished. Byron traveled with his Michaelmas geese, and Ronald Firbank never stirred without his palm tree, but Father had, to my utter shame, a whole special Vuitton trunk for his anti-insomnia blackout equipment.

Anyone else but Father would have localized his horror of light and sound with a chic black velvet mask, not necessarily with eyelashes embroidered on it, and earplugs. (Harry Bull of *Town and Country* later came to absolutely silent New Milford with earplugs and referred to them mistakenly as his Meds instead of his Flents. He also brought a mirror tray that he adjusted around his neck when he sat in the sun to reflect its rays beneficially and turn what might have been just a weekend pink into a summer tan. When he fell asleep on our terrace he looked like the severed head of a latter-day Jokanaan on Salomé's platter. Harry also took up a large rug from the floor and put it on his bed when he was cold in the night. We adored him.)

Father would not consider eye patches or earplugs or anything that had to be attached to himself. He believed in an untrammeled sleep, but he didn't hesitate to shut out light by rigging up strong wires over the windows and draping the entire room in heavy black. If he could have put a gigantic black tea cozy over the entire house, he would have been completely happy. The weight of the double black curtains was so great that the wires that carried them had to be secured to deeply embedded screw eyes or even togglebolts. If the plaster wall was too resistant, the whole thing went into the wood-work. A really restful and relaxed weekend for Father might mean a plasterer and painter called in by his hostess on Monday.

The dark curtains shut out all light and helped to muffle some sound, but there was nothing Father could do about disturbances in the night and early morning, except that he could refuse the next invitation from friends whose homes were noisy. Sea gulls, small children, and dogs were his *bêtes noires,* so he avoided the coast and children and always inquired solicitously about where the dog slept. If the pet slept at the foot of his mistress's bed, or better still *on* it, Father was content; such well-situated dogs rarely got up early to bark.

Father had grown up in hermetically sealed Austria, where the first faint break of day was not seen until the maid drew back the curtains, inch by inch, at some quite advanced hour of the morning. My memories are vague but I cannot help thinking of Countess Attems in Vienna, who always boasted of her extraordinary sixth sense which told her (*before* the maid knocked) whether it was raining out. I never disillusioned her about the millions of Americans who wake in rooms with windows and daylight and so are perfectly aware of the weather. The Austrians I knew never exposed themselves to any of the elements until they got into their baths.

Generally we didn't accompany our parents on their weekends, but I do remember being included in an invitation to visit Yolanda Merö and her husband Herman (Dudie) Irion in New City. I think she must have been as outrageous as Father was and decided that two could play at his game. She apparently salted away all his gifts and determinedly served us her planned menu and wines. She also gave me my first memorable gustatory shock—tripe (all Francophilic gastronomes notwithstanding). It was Hungarian tripe and it was awful. Father kept a stiff upper lip and enjoyed **Spätzle** and a sort of tart which was called **Kossuth Blitztorte,** made in a few minutes. For me the weekend was great fun, as I played with their graceful white Russian wolfhound (male), called Polly, or possibly Poli, who loped about the green lawn and filled Father with dreadful forebodings about barks in the night. The dog was far too large to sleep at the foot of anyone's bed, but all must have gone well because the friendship continued. I was always taken to Yolanda Merö's rare and beautiful recitals, and once I heard her distinctive Hungarian voice across half the Metropolitan telling Mother what she thought about various performances, including Jeritza's last *Fledermaus*, during Jeritza's last *Fledermaus*. Johann Strauss was all delightfulness and charm, even in his own personal life; there was unending youth (aided by black hair-and-mustache dye), but he didn't compose for aging singers, and Yolanda said so at the top of her voice.

The only other weekends on which we were sometimes included were at the Heubleins' Tower near Hartford. Of all the homes that have passed I think I am saddest about the Tower. When we now drive toward Hartford from Farmington and pass the inconspicuous entrance, I remember the excitement of turning in, passing Montevideo, and driving along the wooded mountain ridge to the Tower. It stood near a great flat rock on which a bent iron rod marked the spot where an open observation tower once stood; it was here that Mrs. Heublein had accepted Mr. Heublein's marriage proposal. Few husbands commemorate such events with a monumental tower and I was enthralled. I think the Heubleins invited us because they knew they lived in the fulfillment of a child's dream—originally young Gilbert Heublein's dream. The Tower combined the fascination of a medieval castle on the Rhine looking out across Connecticut's tobacco fields and the enchantment of a German fairy tale. They were all there, Rapunzel with her golden hair and her prince, Sleeping Beauty with her roses and *her* prince, and just a touch of Lorelei and Gambrinus.

It was a tribute to the Tower's perfection and to Mr. Heublein's wine cellar, which was probably as good or better than Father's, that Father confined himself to weekend gifts in the best of taste. I remember that Mr. Heublein years later showed me some Chinese porcelain and Georgian silver that Father had brought them. Since all windows were heavily curtained, Father could leave his blackout trunk at home, and as each guest room was by itself on a separate story in the Tower, Father was undisturbed by sounds.

There was no room for improvement in the kitchen, and Father ate **Codfish Balls** (the only time I ever saw him eat a deep-fat-fried food) for breakfast—a time of the day when usually he never made any demands on his "system." They were as large as tennis balls and as light as Badminton shuttlecocks, and I have tried for years to duplicate them. The Heubleins were German in some ways yet loyally New England, and the food at their table was one of the happiest combinations I have ever tasted. I remember a tender **Faisan Titania** and traditional Celery Root Salad being followed by the most melting **Latticed Apple Cake.**

Apple pie anywhere else would have evoked Father's worst manners. He would have gently raised the upper crust and removed it to the side of his plate. He would then have eaten the apples with obvious distaste and he would have regarded the bared lower crust as though he had just turned over a moist stone. He would have then inspected all the other plates with alarm, and if he found everyone else had eaten the lower crust he would have looked sad and prepared for the very worst. At the Tower he ate everything. Mr. Heublein was the first man we ever saw cook on an outdoor grill and his corn roasted in the husks was the first and best I ever tasted.

All this enjoyment of life, and many philanthropies, were built on A-1 Sauce and (later) bottled cocktails (which Father refused to think about) especially during prohibition, when alcoholic content was reduced. Mr. Heublein, on the other hand, was a source of endless prohibition jokes and his children's children have prolonged their grandfather's wisdom with Smirnoff vodka, a division of Heublein. Fräulein von Beckmann, Mrs. Heublein's companion, spoke French to me and Mr. Heublein's chauffeur took Edward on a secret motorcycle ride—and now we have a Queen Anne chair here in our Austrian home which was their constantly enjoyed wedding present.

In 1928 Mother and I crossed from Cherbourg with the Heubleins, Harry Bull (not yet *Town and Country's* editor), Maria Jeritza, Baron Popper, Mr. Burton Holmes, Mrs. Holmes, and his photographer Lamarre on the *Majestic*, and I spent the sort of week between the sun deck and the Ritz Restaurant (which provided a staircase for sweeping up and down) that air travelers, belted to their seats, cannot visualize. In those days we boarded steamers, looked at the passenger list, found friends, wrote invitations and gave little dinner parties in the liner's Ritz Restaurant. It meant a different gown for every evening and hours of conferences about menu and wines.

We had all been showing Vienna to the Burton Holmeses for one of his famous travelogues and had taken part in a fortunately never-publicized travelogue of Mr. Holmes doing a travelogue of Vienna. There were scenes of us picking our footsore way across cobblestones which would have gone far to discourage his devoted audience. There was a sort of Holmes-thing in our lives—Burton was distinguished, goateed, and the man I always wanted my father to look like. My daughter Toni, on the other hand, always wished that her parents looked and acted like the Frank Graham Holmeses, nice, sedate, settled, unsensational, and utterly dull. I remember seeing the travelogue of the travelogue at the Holmeses' one evening and suddenly saying, "That dreadful young woman has my dress on." It was I. After that I looked for the scrawniest, most hungry-nestling-like creature on the films and learned to recognize myself as others saw me.

During the last years of the First World War, when Father could not go to Europe and had to stay in America where window shades were flimsy and white and where everyone knew when it was morning, he decided on a change to a more Continental atmosphere.

Father had lived in France and loved it, and now having become disenchanted with the Lake Placid Club, he decided on more sympathetic fields and better food in French Canada. Accordingly he took his better-sleeping trunk and we started on what was to be the nightmare voyage of his career. The inspiration for these sudden whims could never be traced to any one person, so there was no one whom Father could kill (slowly) after we came back from the upper reaches of the Saguenay River in Quebec.

We drove from Lake Placid to Montreal, where Father had friends and all was still civilized, then to Trois Rivières, where we had a French **Tarte au Sucre** (I found the recipe among Mother's notes) and on to Quebec. Father insisted that he had found a bedbug at the Château Frontenac, but if he had actually seen one, there would have been a crisis comparable to our evacuation from the Hotel Regina in Vienna. (After our peaceful house arrest in Lofer we reached Vienna in the turmoil of 1914 and Father had to descend to and at the Hotel Regina—opposite the Votiv Kirche—in a city where there wasn't another bed to be had. I remember that we were torn from those precious beds in the middle of the night, stood in pails of cold water while more water was poured down over us and porters were carrying out our luggage. We were rushed into our clothes and departed the Regina to drive round and round the Ringstrasse behind a sleepy Lawrence until the sun came up—all because Father had met a bedbug.) Since we were not roused or doused with water in Quebec, it was probably a false alarm. In the morning we left the security of the car and Gostike and sailed down the St. Lawrence River to Tadoussac, the oldest European trading post in Canada. There we made a sharp left turn into what Father considered the uncharted wilderness.

Father had always enjoyed his little trips on the Rhine and the Danube and it was undoubtedly in the hope of recapturing some of their glamour that he had planned the Saguenay voyage. On the Rhine he could point out Rheinstein and Slotzenfels with a glass of Rheinwein in his hand, and the Danube trips were made dazzling by a distant cousin who was president of the Donaudampfschiffahrtsgesselschaft, the Danube Steamship Line, and provided special food and drink for us. Father said afterward that he had not expected great vintages on the Canadian steamer but he *had* expected good French wines and he had looked forward with pleasure to little huddles with the chef over his wishes for dinner.

I do not know whether there was a chef on board. What was set before us could certainly have been achieved by any person with a sharp can opener, and as for the wines, there weren't any. Father always recalled for the benefit of his friends that there was nothing to drink except something that tasted like boiled Saguenay water. There were no villages or inns; there was no shoreline; the trees grew down to the water and into their black reflections without definition. There were no rocks or shale, no wild or human life—only a dark river over six hundred feet deep, with a black and bottomless look; it was like sailing down a nightmare.

Mother and Edward and I could have enjoyed ourselves anywhere, we didn't know what boredom meant, but being confined with Father on that small steamer was like being marooned with an angry bear. As it was, we could hardly keep serious over the names. We passed Capes Trinity and Eternity, and the halfway point, after which things became even worse, was called Ha Ha Bay. At the end was Chicoutimi, supposedly Indian for the End of the Earth, and it was. The Saguenay River drains from Lake St. John by two channels called the Big and the Little Discharge. We never told Father.

His greatest fears were realized within an hour of sailing. He was bored, the food was appalling, there was nothing to drink, and the noise of the engines was deafening—so he retired to his hole of a cabin to shut out all light and drape himself in black. It was then that he discovered the screw eyes for his curtains had been forgotten at the Château Frontenac. Father had always pulled out all the stops for something as simple as eating breakfast, his life had been one long crying of "Wolf, wolf," so he had nothing left with which to express his feelings. He took every pointed instrument he could find to nail up his draperies and was finally reduced to using his beloved chamois-lined manicure case. I remember that I came to the cabin just as he drove his favorite Sollingen Zwillingswerk German steel file into the wall and bent it double. He literally howled, the attendant came running, and when he saw the black curtains he went for the captain. The captain thought Father was preparing for a corpse—or possibly a black mass—and fled.

The area is all probably a beautiful resort now, with hydrofoils skimming across Ha Ha Bay, but from Father's standpoint it was an experience that should have made him eligible for membership in the Explorers' Club.

We returned to New York, and Father checked himself immediately into Lenox Hill Hospital for observation. He had, after all, exposed himself to malnutrition and the complications which can arise from an empty stomach. Actually he probably wanted to mull over the indignities he had suffered at the hands of these unfortunate descendants of his beloved French and the frustration of having no one but himself to blame.

The only American trips he made after that were to follow the opera to Atlanta, and from his tales about eating terrapin and Pompano with Limes, the artists must have performed with very full stomachs. He went, of course, occasionally to East Liverpool, Ohio, where he had established an office to reach the American pottery industry who were his customers, his friends, and his hosts, but where there was *überhaupt nichts zu essen*—nothing at all to eat—at the local hotel, and in 1928 he showed me Chicago. Atlanta and Chicago were the farthest points south and west he ever reached, and the Saguenay River was his only venture completely beyond civilization à la Ritz.

14

Der Rosenkavalier Chez Nous

*T*ODAY YOU HAVE made an old woman out of me"— *Heute haben Sie ein altes Weib aus mir gemacht*—sang Father (off key in a quaking baritone) with more truth than musicality as he peered at himself in his shaving mirror. He was dressed in the wig and costume of the third-act Marschallin from the Metropolitan, and he was trying to decide whether or not he should shave off his mustache.

We were giving a *Rosenkavalier* party, and everyone had gone—unbeknownst to everyone else—to Madame Musaeus at the Opera's wardrobe department to borrow a costume. It was the era of theme parties, and everyone threw themselves wholeheartedly into the trouble and expense of appearing as someone else, even at small dinner parties. Every possible occasion was celebrated with a party—birthdays, anniversaries, farewells, welcomes, Saints' days, openings, and holidays. The *Rosenkavalier* dinner was for either Bodanzky's birthday or Richard Strauss's, and weeks had gone into its preparation.

They say that choice of costume reveals the inner nature of the chooser (we used to say of art director Willis Conner, "He is the sort of man who goes to costume parties as Casanova—look out for him"), and there was Father looking like Maria Theresa with a mustache, while ever-modest Mother was in her dressing room putting on the little blackamoor's turban and silver-belled yellow costume and effacing herself behind a layer of black paint. As far as I remember, the only things the little blackamoor does are to bring the rose to Octavian and the Marschallin her chocolate—he backs out of her presence dancing—and he closes the opera by returning to fetch Sophie's handkerchief before the curtain comes down.

We pleaded with Father to spare his mustache, which added considerably to his interpretation of the role, and fled upstairs—to take up our banister positions—when the first guests arrived. Mme. Musaeus must have wondered what was going on when twenty people in one week asked to borrow *Rosenkavalier* costumes, but she apparently kept her counsel and all the guests greeted each other with screams of surprise. Bodanzky came as himself, the *Meister*, in tails with a wide red ribbon across his chest and a spangling of decorations over his heart. Frau Johannes Sembach was Annina, and pretty Ada Bodanzky came as Sophie.

Mother and Father had a shadowy pianist who strummed *"Ohne Dich"* and disappeared from the piano before anyone was aware that the theme party had started off with a theme song. Melanie Kurt came in a shimmering Octavian costume with her silver rose, and Clarence Whitehill, the handsome new American baritone, came as Sophie's (Ada Bodanzky's) father, the wealthy parvenu Herr von Faninal. Edward and I had our eye out for Carl Braun, who would undoubtedly be Baron Ochs von Lerchenau, but when Carl Braun came no one recognized him. It turned out he was the very splendid and, in the opera, never-glimpsed Feldmarschall Prince von Werdenberg, the deceived husband. Handsome Mrs. Braun came as Marianne, Sophie's duenna.

After Carl Braun arrived, even Edward and I, suspended from the banister above, felt the tension rising: Who would be big and fat enough to fill the Baron Ochs costume? Various guests came as footmen and the majordomos, and George Meader came as Hypolyte the hairdresser, who in the opera is responsible for turning the Marschallin (Father) into an old woman. I remember being thrilled that a guest, probably Mrs. Meader, came dressed as a shabby, dusty man and maintained she was the *souffleur*—the prompter—and when Julia Steinway came as the third-act Octavian dressed as Mariandel ("the girl who drinks no wine") everyone was delighted. Frederick Steinway was the police officer and the Alfred Deliagres were the Italian intriguer Valzacchi and the milliner.

And still no Baron Ochs—all the big men had arrived—and Fred Muschenheim was a surprisingly goateed Hugo von Hoffmannsthal. Johannes Sembach came as the singer, and Elsa Muschenheim and

Mrs. Whitehall were two of the three orphans. Everyone was having a hilarious time with their lines, Father's deadly cocktails, and Mother's Hot Stuffed Mushrooms and **Cold Stuffed Mushrooms** when Baron Ochs von Lerchenau arrived. Edward and I hung way out over the stairs to see the biggest, fattest Ochs of all time, a waddling Ochs, his costume filled to the brim with small inflated red balloons. As soon as Ochs opened his mouth we all knew it was Yolanda Merö, the great Hungarian pianist with the high Hungarian voice. Her benevolent husband, Dudie Irion, was, of all things, a very convincing Richard Strauss.

They went down to the dining room where small explosions could be heard for the rest of the evening as each guest was moved to stick a fork into Yolanda. Mother told me that before dinner was over she was so deflated that she had to remove Ochs's costume and finish the evening in the dress she had on underneath. Madame Musaeus must have been alarmed to find prong marks all over Baron Ochs's satin coat and breeches.

Mother's menu records indicate that a certain Viennese atmosphere permeated the dinner. The theme usually influenced the food—within reason—and the flowers were of the period. We usually went down the backstairs to hang over the backstairs banister, where we could at least hear whether the party was a success. When we heard Artur's great barks of laughter and roars and rolls of mirth, we stopped listening and went up to do our homework. We always wanted these parties to be a great success, and they always were, although it took a certain indoctrination period before some guests adapted. I remember having a visit one evening from a pretty young American woman who was so overcome with the lateness of the dinner hour and the length of dinner that she rested on my sofa, belching, while she gathered her strength to go back down. Now that I think about her, she was probably more overcome by the wines than the hour.

On that evening there was Turtle Consommé, which was more like drinking a cup of hot sherry after the cocktails than a soup; Crayfish on a Plank (the lowly plank was made to set into a silver platter), of which I adored the **Dilled Potato Ring,** mysteriously supported with cream cheese; **Suprêmes of Pheasant,** and as in Vienna they were dressed against a hill of Glazed Apple Slices which were arranged over a heart of sauerkraut cooked in wine and bound with brown sauce—a better sauerkraut than they prepare now. With pheasant there always had to be Celery Root Salad, and the dessert was a Bavarian Ring filled with strawberries, embellished with spun sugar and accompanied by **Nusshörnchen.** Coffee was always served at the table—Father didn't approve of the separation of the sexes—and only after coffee did the ladies leave the table with Mother.

Just before the *Rosenkavalier* party there had been a terrible upheaval in the house: a new cook in the kitchen. It was like a new king on the throne; nothing was ever going to be quite the same again.

In 1914 Anna Gorsky decided to retire to Hungary (she just made it before the war broke out) and a replacement had to be found. No one ever wanted it said of them that they couldn't keep a cook, and a good cook, like a Rolls Royce, was expected to last a lifetime. Grandmamma had her Resi for a good fifty years, but Anna had saved herself an ample dowry and she wanted to go home to see what it would fetch her. For a few years—no time at all for a cook—we had a tall dark Marie who made the loveliest little *Heidesand* and *Linzer Kräpfchen* and fried a beautiful **Grinzing Backhendl.** But Father was not one for frying, and one day when I came home from school I found an unidentified older woman in Mother's room with a beautiful young woman, Marie Henneberger, who turned out to be her niece, fresh from an Austrian Chefs Training School, asking for the position. Marie came to us, a trained chef and a dedicated cook. I never knew where she came from or why she came to us instead of to the hotel position she had trained for, but she stayed more than twenty years and I do not think there was an instant's dissatisfaction on either side.

Marie was *ein Talent* and undismayed by the largest parties. Being Austrian, she had a feeling for birthdays and anniversaries and didn't care how many events were celebrated. Her only fault was an absolute block about sandwiches. By this time I had become a master of the art of flushing food down the toilet, but there was none on my way to school after I picked up the sandwich packages she placed on the foyer table each morning. Since I walked to the school door with my governess, the tempting rubbish cans on the way did me no good. Each pupil brought her lunch and ate it under the eyes of the others. Mine were usually the leftovers from Lucullan dinners. Marie cut bread as thick as a finger, never removed crusts, and would fill the sandwiches with a cold Wiener Schnitzel, a slab of Filet Wellington, or a piece of pâté as thick as the bread—they would have fed a day laborer, and they were wrapped in anything she came across. Irma Fulton, across the aisle from me, Janet Lee (who later mothered Mrs. Onassis), and the Cobb sisters all came to school with their delicate sandwiches, innocent of crusts, filled with girlish lettuce leaves or blameless cream cheese and wrapped in immaculate white sandwich paper. I used to put my head inside my desk to bite into the forerunner of a hero sandwich.

When I grew older Marie made such irresistible *Plätzchen* (cookies) and tea cakes for me that she added enormously to my popularity with young men who came to tea. Whatever she had to say, it always started with "Alle While": "Alle while she eats not enough" (me) or "Alle while he stays too long" (Julian Hawthorne) or "Alle while dey tink they make *Kugelhupf* und alle while dey make plain cake." Her letters were classics, and she either had a perfect memory or kept careful records because she always knew what we had served on any given day. If Mother suggested shad roe for Grete Stückgold's birthday, Marie remembered that she had been given just that on another occasion. The only guests for whom she repeated —and that was always by request—were Maria Jeritza and Baron Popper; when they accepted an invitation they always said, "And please could we have . . ."

The day was bound to come, although Mother didn't face it, when Marie would want to retire. Marie was devout and thought of retirement to some Catholic order where she could devote herself to good works, quiet retreats, and prayer. She put off this project while visiting all the Catholic hospitals, orphanages, homes, and convents near New York but apparently didn't find the place where she felt her intentions would fit. Finally she wrote Mother in Europe that her search had led her to the perfect place in New Jersey. It was a monastery, a place secluded from temporal concerns, a haven for religious retirement. She would be a handmaiden, a simple servant to the elderly head of the order. Mother with foreboding said *"Das wird schlecht ausgehen"* (This will end badly), and so it did.

As soon as we came home Mother went in search of a cook, and finding no single person who could do what Marie did, she engaged an English couple, George and Caroline Latham, and after Marie's final departure we were plunged suddenly into English food at its best. Joints, tarts, lovely tea biscuits and scones. We had **Trifle** and Fig Pudding, Steamed Mocha Pudding and Yorkshire Hot Pot, Apple

Amber, and something called Cocktail Roquefort Ice Cream. They stayed with us until we gave the house away and made our headquarters in New Milford.

Marie wrote long letters. It didn't take the ascetic monks long to discover their humble handmaiden's talents; some of their contemplations of the spirit turned to contemplations of the table, and in no time at all Marie's cloistered retirement was a full-time cook's job—quantity cookery—and her good works were directed toward the non-monastic inner man. But Marie had her revenge: Her letters changed in tone and her cookery became a cross betwen nostalgic memories of life with us and a sort of you-asked-for-it attitude toward the monks.

One December she wrote, "Last night, December 16th, on Mr. Bodanzky's birthday I gave the monks his 1928 birthday party dinner. We had **Cocktail Turnovers,** Consommé with Marrow, Pompano with Anchovy Butter, Parslied Potato Balls, **Poulets en Chaud-Froid Talleyrand** with Spiced Crab Apples and **Endive Salad Valencia.** For dessert I repeated the *Apfel Strudel* that Mr. Bodanzky loved. On January 8th I am repeating Frau Kurt's 1917 *Fidelio* birthday dinner with **Sénègalaise au Kari,** the **Partridge in Casserole Madeira** and on January 27th they will be given *Gnädige* Frau's birthday dinner that we had in 1930. On February 12 I always give them your wedding anniversary dinners and the following day I give them Mrs. Bodanzky's dinner, as her birthday fell on your anniversary. On the 14th of February we will have Mr. Lincoln's birthday dinner and on the 15th we will celebrate the name day of Saint Faustian. During Lent they will get nothing to eat and on June 11th we always repeat the *Rosenkavalier* menu to celebrate Mr. Strauss's birthday."

The food budget of the monastery must have been colossal and the monks' robes must have hidden some vastly expanded waistlines, but Marie made her contribution. Father only worried whether the monastery cellar was up to the demands Marie's dinners put upon it.

15

Father's World War I Effort

*A*FTER WE RETURNED to New York, the war left Father mercifully untouched, since the kindly Americans looked upon the
Austrians as a race apart (which they are) and did not identify or
confuse them with the Germans. I remember that they were always
referred to as "the poor Austrians."

Just before the end of the war, Father apparently decided that
he had to make himself independent of all employees and that he
would learn to do it himself. For a man who had never raised a hand
to take care of himself, this must have been a major decision and it
was one he pruned down considerably after the first glow had worn
off. I suppose he did his own nails and trimmed his mustache for a
few weeks, and I remember some newfangled electrical appliances
that were to substitute for his masseur. One of these stood for many
years in its red velvet-lined case on the top shelf of Father's bathroom
closet and was one of the objects we children stared at whenever
our parents went out. It looked exactly like a small vicious vacuum
cleaner and made a frightening *plop-plop* sound when he ran it over
his face. The suction was so strong that he could hardly tear himself
away from it.

What it all boiled down to in the end was that Father learned
to drive a car. Up to this point he had taken an unusually active
interest (compared with my friends' fathers) in the administration of
his own daily comforts, but all of it had been verbal—he simply gave
orders or asked questions. When out in the car he availed himself of
the speaking tube to make the car stop, turn, back up, or start.

When Father came home in the afternoon his first two questions settled the evening. "Where are we going tonight?" and, if the answer was that he wasn't going anywhere, "What are we having for dinner?" Of all his questions this was the most devastating, since he always had his answer ready: "But that's what I had for lunch." How the various clubs where he lunched and the old Manhattan Club, which was nearest his office and where he acquired his worst indigestions, ever managed Squabs Stuffed with Scrapple or Asparagus with Westphalian Ham Sauce or **Veal Gaston** with a brillant green Mousse of Green Peas, I will never know, but Father's remark was always the same, and his long reproachful looks across the table at Mother implied that the dish as served at lunchtime had been the better of the two.

His third favorite question was, "Where is the car?" even though he might have dismissed Gostike and sent him to eat his big Greek dinner only ten minutes earlier. This question continued after he drove his own car and simply left it wherever he saw a space. Taking it to the garage would have meant having to back it up. I remember that Mother sometimes wandered through many neighboring streets looking for it. Father's questions were designed to alert his family to what he wanted done and what he was dissatisfied with. Many of them were unanswerable, especially when they were in the third person. He would ask, while he looked sternly at me, "Why is she pale?" The other questions which brought him into close contact with the minutiae of his daily life were, "Who starched this collar?" or "Who stood up this bottle of wine?" or ominously, "Who barked?" He would turn to Mother on the morning after a rich and wine-full dinner and say, "What disagreed with me?" And finally he always asked "*Wo ist mein Hut, mein Stock?*" (Where is my hat and my cane?) all in the spirit of Johann Strauss. Where, what, and why—*wo, was,* and *warum*.

Our dear friend John Easton spent so many vacations and outings and holidays with us that he said, "*Warum*" the moment he saw us. When he was little he thought it meant where and not why and invariably said, "*Warum ist Liesl?*" and I often wondered too. Later I had a dog called Warum.

I remember that when we were in Europe just after the war, we had to take a train and share a compartment. John was with us and the sixth seat was occupied by a dignified elderly gentleman. After a time Father turned to him and said loud and clear, "*Leiden Sie von*

Fuss Schweiss?" I refuse to translate. Father always waited until there were guests before he asked us, "Did you wash behind your ears today?"

There was no danger whatever in the autumn of 1918 that Greece or the United States would draft Gostike Kotti and send him *Over There,* but the fact became more evident every day that Gostike was getting too fat and too old and too nearsighted to drive a car, although he never ceased to be giggly and benevolent. So Father made his decision and pensioned Gostike. I was too young to know who taught Father to drive or how he went about it, but having been a *Kavallerist* he knew the principle of a relaxed seat, of applying pressure with the feet, and guidance with the hands. A photograph, which I still have, reveals Father sitting (tense and unrelaxed) at the wheel of the first car he drove himself.

Obviously he couldn't drive a great hulking Delaunay Belleville or an enormously high old Rolls limousine around the countryside, let alone in New York. He had lived his whole life on softly upholstered back seats or a chic green, soft leather-lined tonneau, from where he had controlled the driving without realizing that the chauffeur's seat was straight-backed, hard, upholstered in unrelenting black leather, and exposed to the elements. So, judging by the picture, he bought himself a rather dashing sedan in which to start his non-dependent life.

The first thing he did after he had a driver's license was to get himself suitably dressed for what he always called his "chauffeuring," after which he made a rendezvous with a professional photographer at some picturesque point between New York and Yonkers, probably Riverdale, where the rocks and snow-clad trees would make a handsome background with which to impress his mother regarding his wartime economies and sacrifices. (He had somehow heard, with considerable resentment, that she had turned in all her gold jewelry to the government. After the war her jewelry box contained only one item, an Iron Cross engraved on the back *Eisen für Gold.* This was the Kaiser's total compensation for her sacrifice, and a lot of good that did.)

As I look at and finally dispose of, by immolation, great boxes of photographs, I marvel at the support we gave to what must have been a flourishing profession. Everything we did was commemorated with a picture; there must have been men with cameras and tripods and large black cloths around them at all times. They were a background adjunct and I was never conscious of who arranged for them to be there. I have pictures of Mother and Father on almost all their occasions—with May and Walter Baker at Bayreuth, in full evening clothes in full daylight, with Wotan and Siegfried or Parsifal or Hans Sachs.

And this tradition went on long after I grew up. The most frightening one of all is of me taken in 1933 clinging to Rudolf Laubenthal's little tunic while he turned a Grecian profile as Aegisthus. He had on golden laced elevator sandals, a curly black wig, and a golden wreath. I have on a black dress and hat, and I don't wonder that Father used to ask, "Why is she pale?" There is a second picture of me crushed under Klytemnestra's train while Maria Olszewska, who sang the role, is assuming an imperious pose with her back to me. I had just done the costumes for *Elektra,* and the pictures were taken after a rehearsal to illustrate some human-interest story. What was so remarkable was the effort expended in summoning the photographer, posing, and finally distributing the pictures.

My picture of Father in his new sedan in a snow-covered landscape is almost my favorite. He wore, for what he evidently considered "sporting" reasons, a very dashing fedora hat at a devil-may-care angle. It appears to be gray with a black band and pearly binding around the brim; below it he wore a black winter coat with otter collar—I remember it had a beaver lining—and a bit of Charvet neckwear at the throat. He had on gray gloves with black stitching, which were always ordered by the dozen from Paris, and he is caught leaning well back with arms outstretched and gloved hands clutching the top of the steering wheel. It is a lovely imperial sort of picture and I can't imagine anybody passing him on the road. As I recall his driving, he speeded up or drew over to the left to prevent such infringements.

I remember later agonizing drives when Edward and I had to report from the back seat whether there was a car behind him, even if it was just a dot on the horizon. He drove fast, which I suppose was to be expected, took a very superior attitude with other motorists and, to my certain knowledge, never learned to back up. Just as soon as he felt confident he exchanged the dark-blue sedan—I think it was a Nash; just a modest unassuming little car to learn chauffeuring on—for a long green Pierce Arrow sedan with lights out on the fenders. He kept it so long that I grew old enough to drive it and to be photographed—at the Schniewinds'—looking slinky and leaning against one of the headlights. Like Father, I too was rather unsuitably dressed in a floppy garden-party hat.

In the meantime, Mother too had learned to drive—after all, someone had to fetch the car from the garage so that Father could drive it, and she drove extremely well, which Father did not know since he never drove with amateurs. Soon he found himself an extremely nice chauffeur named George and did his chauffeuring himself only on rare occasions, presumably to prove something to someone or himself.

Father's do-it-yourself program began and ended with learning to drive the car. For what were called merciful reasons, which was presumably his poor mother in Carlsbad, and by pulling every possible political string, he was one of the first to go back to Europe in 1918. Thereafter he took up his travels with gusto and vigor. On one of these postwar trips he drove out to a garage near Carlsbad to look at the 1912 Stevens Duryea (which we had abandoned in 1914 when the benzine we could buy in little bottles in drugstores ran out). It had great brass lanterns and leather straps that ran from its touring top down to the front fenders. We still have this car. It has been ripening behind the Iron Curtain for years and I was recently offered a staggering sum for it. Though legally mine, I feel that the local authorities might well produce obstacles that would equal its value.

Edward and I didn't go abroad until 1920, when Father and Mother left us in an odd pension on the Boulevard Victor Hugo in Neuilly to brush up on our neglected French while they made a round of the various opera houses that had reopened. It was the first of a series of surprising freedoms they allowed. Having brought us up strictly, they now had confidence in us, and Mother always maintained that independence and true self-confidence were more easily acquired by unspoiled children, whom no one took special interest in, than by overindulged ones, such as the typical debutante. In any case there were two of us and we acquired an unexpected guardian angel.

My first recollection is of a green-aproned houseman with a yellow-and-black vest whose name was Gaston. He was the typical Parisian servant, with a black curly forelock, a swirling mustache, and a certain bounciness. There were housemaids who stepped right out of the engravings in my pink-bound Bibliothèque Rose books and the atmosphere was pure Mlle. Zénaide Fleuriot, the swooning heroine of *Plus Tard*. As we arrived, there was a rainstorm and all the long

French windows were closed. It stopped a few minutes later when the maid was in my room and she opened the windows and threw up her hands in delight: "*Voyez, Mademoiselle, un arc en ciel—ça porte bonheur*"—there was the arch in the sky, a brilliant rainbow that would bring good luck, and it did. It was a lovely rainbow summer.

There must have been owners, but I do not remember seeing them. There was a young Dutchman and a fantastic old Southern lady (who was then probably in her late fifties but seemed ancient to us) under a brilliant red wig. Her name was Mrs. Carter Payne, and her daughter was Mary Carter Payne. Mary was older than Edward, but Mrs. Payne dressed her as a little girl. We both still wore our hair hanging down our backs; I had been allowed to give up a great silk hair ribbon tied in a bow on top of my head two years earlier, but Mary still had a lopsided bow, and we both had barrettes, which I loathed. Mary seems to have felt the first stirrings of romance, since she adored Edward and they wrote to each other for months after we left. She had deep-raspberry crested paper and she sealed her envelopes with a blob of wine-red sealing wax into which she diligently pressed her crested seal. I cannot now described how profoundly this impressed me.

Mrs. Payne—after her dead-white powdered skin, her green eyes, her kohl, her red wig, and her Toulouse Lautrec attire had been overcome—turned out to be delightful. She had a deep husky voice, great bursts of hearty laughter, and an enigmatic way of implying she had a past. I remember being called into her room and finding her sitting at a dressing table covered with great flagons of perfume in silver bottles which were engraved with flowers and cut out here and there to show glass and perfume. There was also an atomizer. I who had only seen Mother's *Secret de Bonne Femme* was deeply shocked. The writing desk was just as lavish, with quill pens, silver mountings, and heavy pink writing paper.

Mary was tall and always dressed in some shade of raspberry, including the floppy hair ribbon. She wore braces, which we admired, and a wide gold hoop bracelet on her upper arm outside her crushed *framboise* sweater. She and her bizarre mother sat at a corner table in the dining room next to one of the long windows. Hugo, the Hollander, sat in the opposite corner and we sat at the center table between them. Gaston changed into his butler's disguise to serve dinner, and the *femmes de chambre* turned into proper Daudet waitresses with little crumb scrapers and trays, and we were all given numbered napkin rings. We conversed across the dining room in English (the summer did our French conversation no good whatever), and Edward and I felt our first intimations of personality—we even discovered we could talk. I remember that I pinned up my long hair once or twice, because it was so hot.

Most notable was the food. There was a long hard roll next to our rolled-up napkins when we came to the table; it was the first time I had seen bread without a butter plate, a butter knife, a butter ball, and a little bud of parsley. We were at an age when we could take it or leave it, and I planned to leave everything I didn't like and to take lots of desserts and French pastries, which I had never had a chance to do. It was a good French bourgeoise cuisine, but the service was startling. The first dinner began with soup, as all subsequent meals did, and everyone ate it out of deep wide plates with enormous spoons which they brought around in such a way that they headed straight into the mouth, point forward. The handle of the spoon was then raised and the soup tilted into the mouth with a smack. For the second course they gave us large hot plates and then brought in a huge round platter piled high with a mound of green beans glossy with butter and delicious. The mound was at least nine inches high and fourteen inches in diameter, so we ate green beans until we were satiated—thinking it was probably an obscure French fast day. Then came another round of large hot plates and **Veal with Cold Sauce Espagnole** without one single blessed thing with it. Alone, ungarnished, and unaccompanied.

I was and still am, in spite of all my disapproving American friends, a Continental eater. I never gave up the knife in my right hand or the fork in my left, and if I have nothing to impale under, spread over, or balance with the meat on my fork, I am bereft. Meat without vegetables, potatoes, without anything was worse than no meat at all. I have never wanted the beautifully thought-out taste combinations to meet after the fact of eating them; I want them to unite as I eat them and I want to be the one to know that the **Côtes de Mouton Cyrano** were perfect with the *Fond d'Artichaut* filled with Mushroom Purée by tasting them together and not by eating them consecutively. It was a summer of beautifully roasted chickens without a single *Petit Pois à l'Ancienne,* Poached Sole without Steamed Potatoes, and **Langue de Boeuf Mentchikof** *sans* Chestnut

Croquettes. Nothing with anything. I think it was all done so that each meal could consist of seven impressive courses.

Sometimes the second course was not just a mountain of carrots or beans; certain less constructible vegetables were contained in rings of other vegetables or starches. Creamed Mushrooms were served in a Chicken Liver, and Rice border, and cucumbers were controlled by a ring of **Pommes de Terre Duchesse** (only butter was used), while *Epinards à la Crême* was hemmed in by a wall of **Pommes de Terre Ménagère,** and the *Petits Pois Bonne Femme* (full of onions) were surrounded by *Chou-Fleur Ignatieff*—Father would have said, "Gas, gas, gas." I was, after all, without suspecting it, my parents' daughter, since I can remember every detail of those meals, which *ein anderes Kind*, another child, would not have noticed. (Father once told me that his mother always compared him so unfavorably to *ein anderes Kind* that he thought he had an older brother.)

At the pension they always put a menu card on the table written in purple ink and giving not only the menu but a name for each course. It started with the heading *Déjeuner* or *Dîner*, which was followed by *Potage* and some pretty name like *Crème Dubarry*. After that came *Légumes,* followed by **Choux de Bruxelles aux Marrons,** and then came *Entrées* or *Rôtis* or *Viandes*—something impressive like *Suprême de Volaille Grand Siècle*, which was still an isolated, unaccompanied piece of chicken. The fourth course was something unexpected, a salad or what they called *débris* or a pâté. The fifth course was no problem—*Fromages*—and then came *Fruits Variés* or just *Corbeille de Fruits*, which consisted of a basket of assorted fruits that had reached room temperature several days before. The ending was called *Frivolités* which usually meant nuts, dates, figs, and raisins. Of *entremets*, or desserts, there wasn't a whisper. After the fruit there were *bols rince-doigts* containing warmish water, and a slice of lemon. After the meal, Edward used to tear down to the Porte Maillot for an ice or chocolates.

I never left that lovely walled garden all summer or those long French windows that opened to the floor with classic metal grilles coming up to a point well below our knees—I fell out of one of them on the ground floor, the only one that opened on an areaway, and everyone, especially Mrs. Payne, nursed me in my recovery from bruises so that Mother and Father need not be told. Mrs. Payne's medicine cupboard turned out to be as formidable as her dressing table. Her negligées were very like her street clothes, only drapier and there were bits of batik all about. She never spoke of herself and took an amused interest in everything we did.

In the midst of all this bliss we were called to Carlsbad. Mary qcame to see us off with red roses and kissed Edward good-bye, which so stunned him that he sat in his compartment without saying a word until we arrived in Carlsbad. A few days later there was a long letter from Mary to explain. Mrs. Carter Payne was the famous actress Leslie Carter, and Mary was the child of her second marriage to an Englishman called W. L. Payne. Many years later I had two invitations to first nights: Mary and Mrs. Payne and I embraced tearfully behind the scenes of *The Circle*, whose cast included John Drew and elderly greats, and again when I saw her as Madam God Damn in the *Shanghai Gesture*. She was the glamour girl of her day, and had played in *La Tosca, Zaza*, and *The Second Mrs. Tanqueray*, all great tearjerkers of the period.

In Paris, the lady of the long bead necklaces, flowing velvet robes, great droopy felt cloche hats, scarves, and bangles had taken an interest in all our activities and been kind to two children who, up to that point, had never opened their mouths. She was our mystery lady and the first adult friend we made without our parents' help.

16

Where Would You Like to Go This Year?

$\mathcal{E}$VERY SPRING, LONG BEFORE the New York Board of Education thought that the school year should end, and long before we had learned as much as its final examinations required, Father said, "*Also, Kinder,* where would you like to go this year?" From my present experienced age, I think he was trying to ship us off to Europe and Grandmamma's house before he followed in solitary splendor. While I don't want to be unfair, I think the ships he took were a shade larger and faster than ours and he was able to indulge himself without family encumbrances. Nothing hampered a gallant shipboard style as much as two gangling half-grown children, no longer kept absolutely silent by a governess, a wife, a chauffeur, and odd members of the New York staff.

It was at that time my heart's ambition to be listed on a passenger list with "and maid" after my name. Marie usually crossed with us, but "and cook" would not have been suitable, especially since Marie enjoyed her role as the mysterious woman in black, the shipboard enigma. She never spoke to anyone, least of all to us, and she emerged from her cabin only to go down to dinner, late, in one of Mother's discarded little black dresses from Drécoll or Poiret. Marie was still a pale blonde, and looked like a pale Memling Madonna with a slight limp. I was always tempted to run about and say, "That's Marie Henneberger, Mother's cook!" She apparently ordered dishes that would enhance her repertoire when she returned to New York but she never learned to make the Hamburg-Amerika Line's divine **Hering**

in Senf (Herring in Mustard Sauce) or the *Hamburg Hummer Ragout* (Lobster Stew), which they served the first evening out.

The goal of our spring trips was always Carlsbad and Grandmamma's Haus Garfield. (I asked Miss Eleanor Garfield, the President's granddaughter, whether she knew why Grandmamma had a minor *Schwärmerei* for her grandfather and named her home after him, but she pooh-poohed the idea of any connection.) Father never changed our ultimate and dutiful destination but he allowed us to select the places via which we got there. He believed that travel, if it was systematically administered, would teach us as much as we could learn in school, and he always hoped we would choose to go via Kamchatka or Sevastopol or Rio, but we were stodgy children and I always said, "Please may we go via Vienna." So to Vienna we went via a different and less direct route each year. We chose Greece twice, Madeira and Corfu once, and another time (one of the winters when the school year ended in December) we went to Cairo on our way. One spring it was North Africa and several times it was Portugal and Spain, but most often it was Italy. Our springs in Italy were a slow winding and traversing from Naples to the Brenner Pass.

One year Mother needed what she described as an informal tiara, and it was her illusion that she would find it in Naples. Mother was one of those meek wives whose husbands went alone to see all the Paris collections and ordered their clothes for them. The numbers that Father selected were then executed on Mother's *buste*, which stood labeled and ready at Drécoll and Poiret, and when the boxes arrived in New York, Mother had her first inkling of what she was going to look like that season. If she had the temerity to buy herself a dress, Father always compared her appearance to a Christmas tree or an epergne until she took it off. If he discovered a new house in Paris that did not yet have Mother's *buste* in the storeroom, he selected the mannequin who most nearly approximated Mother's size and had the selected models made on her. (This thoughtfulness entailed taking the mannequin out to luncheon and the races, to judge her measurement in relation to a public space, of course.)

Mother's Parisian clothes, by proxy, were sometimes very attractive, but the hats were frightful. Father went to Reboux and bought any hat that had a drooping brim. "A hat is not a toque, it is a cloche," was his principle. "It does not sit *on* the head, it is a lid that comes down over it." She sometimes went to Herman Patrick Tappé in New

York, under Father's strict supervision, but the result was always a top-heavy *Mushroom Sous Cloche.* The same buying processes were applied to accessories and jewelry, and whatever made Mother think she was going to buy herself an informal tiara in Naples was a dizzying departure—almost worth a divorce.

We stayed at the Hotel Excelsior, and every morning I went around the corner to the first jewelry shop on the right (which is still there) on the Via Santa Lucia and mooned over a tiara of gold leaves with little lapis-lazuli berries. It looked as though Diana had worn it and I urged Mother to buy it, with an eye to later borrowing.

When she wrote to Father to describe her find, he cabled, "Tiara on way is child eating decently." The tiara arrived a few days later from Cartier in Paris and discouraged any further thoughts of independent action. It consisted of an intertwining of pearls set in platinum with a distinctly Nouveau Art flow of lines and it was exactly the very tiara I would never want to borrow. Father's inquiry about my decent eating meant: Was I being properly introduced to squid, cuttlefish, octopus, sea turtles, and assorted Tyrrhenian bivalves and the specialties of Naples? Father's cable address was Kudolerta New York and I composed, but did not send, a clear and inexpensive answer to his question—No.

I did learn to love *Brodetto di Pesce* and Broccoli Sauce and Eggplant Sauce for pasta. In those days the pizza, which did originate in Naples, was practically unknown and unobtainable there. We were finally sent to a pizzeria and ate some pre-Americanization pizzas. The bread bases were shaped with much higher sides than they have today, to create a deep olerium in which olives and anchovies floated in oil over a bed of tomatoes. I have heard the making of a pizza compared to the playing of a piano; nothing is hidden—you see the hands, the keyboard, and the music—everything is, so to speak, aboveboard. At the pizzeria you see the bread dough, the filling, the oven, the tomato sauce, the hands—there are no secrets. Watch carefully and you too can play the piano or make a pizza, but just try tossing a piece of bread dough over your hands sometime. After that, we had silver dollar-sized pizzas with cocktails whenever Father was away.

Mother was always told to take the children to the San Carlo Opera and La Scala, but she also took us to movies such as *Il Piccolo Lord Fauntleroy,* with Mary Pickford, and a movie which I shall never forget called *Senza Musica.* She took us to tea each day, a meal that

Father considered a mere appetite spoiler, and we learned our pastries, from *figaros* to *fedoras*. On the whole we acted like the mice when the cat is away. Father was somehow a constant presence even on the trips he wasn't on and the organization required to remind us of him was formidable. We never sailed into a harbor without seeing a little man on the pier with a large bunch of flowers. We never came into our hotel rooms without more flowers and cables and long letters of instruction telling us what and where to see and eat and drink. People were constantly showing up with presents and attentions.

Most beautiful of all, as I now look back, was Mother's Letter of Credit; worst of all were the letters we had to write Father. What we said never seemed to come through, but how we said it and our calligraphy and spelling came in for criticism by return mail. Father even took exception to Mother's handwriting, which, as the years went by, became indistinguishable from his own.

Our gastronomical upbringing suffered on the trips with Mother. I can remember abandoned desserts of Naples' Biscuit Tortoni, Rome's *Pandorato,* and Orvieto's devastating Boiled Chestnuts. We ate pasta to our heart's content, carried home bars of Torrone in Perugia and actually *ate between meals.* We read in bed such daring authors as Vernon Lee and Elinor Glyn, E. Phillips Oppenheim and Edgar Wallace, and we spoke at table without first being spoken to.

After Edward went to boarding school with John Easton, Mother and I took the spring trip alone, and on two occasions with Tante Emma Easton, who was a giggler. Both Mother and Tante Emma turned serious when they wrote their husbands each day, but for the rest they were extremely frivolous. Frivolity had its limit with Mother, who drew the line at speaking to strangers and considered one of Tante Emma's activities as just plain *picking up men.* I remember that Mother was quite undone when she found that we had several male escorts, thanks to Tante Emma, when we once emerged from a moonlight visit to the Coliseum.

In Florence we ate **Gelatina all' Arancia** at Doney et Neveux or opposite at Giacosa in the Via Tornabuoni each afternoon. In Bologna we had **Caffè Granita,** and in Verona at the Hotel Due Torri we ate *anasso.* In Venice we had *Scampi di Venezia* and lovely *Risotto con Aragosta* at the Hôtel Royal Danieli, and when we got to Vienna's Bristol, Tante Emma said, "That child needs a good dose." In defense of Mother, I will say she argued against the Méthode Easton, but

Tante Emma won and went out to buy oranges and castor oil. She told me how obediently John always downed his dose and shamed me into a bottoms-up performance. By evening they had to call a doctor, and after several days in bed I was able to have a light broth, although it took years and a spring in Spain before I could drink orange juice again.

Except for Father's ever-present "Interior," we were a healthy family, and Mother only took to her bed on rare occasions when she had Her Cold. She had it one evening that autumn and couldn't go to the theater with Father. After trying all available single ladies, who were all unavailable, he had to make do with me, and off we went—silent as always—to the play. During the intermission he must have realized that we were alone together, and casting about for something to say, he made the mistake of asking, "What would you like to do?" He meant, of course, did I want to stay in my seat or walk in the lounge, but I was so startled at being addressed at all that I took it to be Life we were talking about and I had my long-pent-up answer ready, "I want to go to Vienna and study art." We were both stunned into silence until the curtain went up. In the next intermission we finished our first conversation with two more sentences. He said, either from shock or sudden understanding, "You may go to Vienna as soon as you are through with school," and I said, "Thank you." Ordinarily that would have meant six more years, but I had left Miss Veltin's Conventional Classes on 74th Street, where I had taken the brunt of speaking English with a German accent in a school that flew the Tricolor, and changed over to the Blessed Sacrament Convent School on 79th Street. At the convent Sister Dionysia, our Mother Superior, allowed us to advance as we learned, and with my Joseph Urban resolution before me, I decided to be through with school when I was thirteen. Enough of all that waste of time.

The convent was perfect: we ate jelly sandwiches at eleven on Fridays and during Lent, and peanut-butter sandwiches on all other days. We fasted with zeal and had mad crushes on Father John. By December 1921 I passed all my exams except algebra (in which I had zero), and Sister Dionysia said I could come back and learn algebra before I went to college, but I never did either.

Father lived up to his promise, and Mother and I sailed on New Year's Day in 1922 after spending New Year's Eve with the Urbans in Yonkers, and I went to Vienna to art school. (Urban still said *"Du* bist *begabt"*—and when I returned in 1924 I went to work for him.) In Vienna Mother and I lived at the Bristol and I started at the Kunstgewerbe Schule (applied art school)—where Urban wanted me to go—as a pupil of Josef Hoffmann and as a Ferdinand Schmutzer pupil at the Academy—where Father wanted me to go. In the meantime Mother looked about for someone with whom I could live.

There were vast housing shortages in Austria then and everyone who had a large apartment was forced to share. Mrs. von Inten and Mrs. Steinway wrote that the Gerickes were looking for a paying guest and they could be found spending the summer with a friend in Munich. Wilhelm Gericke had founded the Boston Symphony Orchestra and been the Vienna Opera's conductor before Schalk. Father decided this musical atmosphere was a good one and off we went to Munich to see the Gerickes. Their friend turned out to be the majestic (and undisfigured) Milka Ternina. I moved into the Gerickes' apartment at Beatrixgasse 30 that autumn, and serious schoolwork began—also some really serious eating, at least six times a day. Urban sent two more Americans, Jo Mielziner and Edward Beegle, to Vienna to study at the Kunstgewerbe Schule, and we had our growing-used-to-life-in-Vienna pains together.

Vienna, Vienna, I Love You More Than Ever

*L*IFE IN VIENNA TURNED out to be even more food- and music-oriented than in New York. For one thing everyone had live music in the home, once a week or once a month, in the form of *Kammermusik* (chamber music). The Gerickes had a quartet that couldn't be sneezed at, although there were hostesses who had quintets and even sextets. But the Gerickes' first violin was a Philharmoniker, the second violin was from the Oper, the viola was Volksoper, and the violoncello was Musikverein. In some homes the host or a member of his family participated in the music making, but at the Gerickes' the string quartet was entirely professional and very chic.

Having a trio, quartet, or quintet in the house meant a good deal of food, as everything in Vienna did. The Gerickes had their quartet once a month during the season, with elaborate refreshments for the listeners and a dinner afterward for the four musicians and their wives. A second minor gathering—tea or possibly an informal supper—took place each month to discuss the next program so that the refreshments and dinner menu could be suitably planned. No one wanted to eat a *Soupe de Concombres* after Brahms or a *Wiener Gulash Suppe* on top of Debussy's Quartet in G minor. Mozart called for *Salzburger Nockerln* and Ernst von Dohnányi (who always came to dinner with Father and Mother in New York and on whom I had a modest crush) called for Paprika Chicken.

There was considerable rivalry among hostesses and much snaring away of first violins or cellos, as the case might be, but everything was done with food, audience, prestige, and friendship to cement a good relationship. Frau Direktor Gericke's unassailed position in top music circles ensured her against such losses; after all, her musicians could drop her name very pleasantly when they were chatting with their second violin at the Philharmonie, the Oper, the Volksoper, or the Musikverein.

Vienna was all for *Kultur*, and the Gerickes' daughter Katharine, who had grown up in Boston, went to lectures with me at the Urania, the Albertina, and the Museum. We went to concerts and the opera, but the pivotal point of every month was Mrs. Gericke's *jour*—her day. "Quartets" and *jours* were always accompanied by the first person possessive, and when I first arrived in the Gericke household, Mrs. Gericke was in the turmoil of setting the day for her quartet and her *jour* so that it would not interfere with other similar events she wanted to attend, or with the programs of the Philharmonie and Oper which had first call on her musicians.

When the days were settled, after telephone calls to and from all of Vienna's major hostesses, Mrs. Gericke's card was printed with FIRST WEDNESDAY in the lower corner. It was then hand-delivered by one of the old *Dienstmänner* (servicemen), who were still in existence, to the homes of the elite, and all of Vienna knew that on the first Wednesday of every month the *haute volée* and the music world would be at the Gerickes', eating superb food and making brilliant conversation.

I remember that at the first *jour* I sat down, all unknowingly, on a settee (only for a few minutes), and it was pointed out to me that only the hostess and her oldest and most distinguished guest ever sat on that settee. As the most distinguished guest departed, the hostess patted the seat of the settee and invited the next in line to sit with her —and so on. There were a good fifty years and considerable achievement still standing between me and a seat on the sofa. I was reminded of all this lately when we dined at Schloss Stiebar, where our hostess's mother gave a quick look at the other ladies and led me to the settee, where she (I could hardly believe it) patted the seat and asked me to sit next to her. My life has come full circle and I now frown when I have to sit on a hard chair while the new youth sprawls on the sofa.

The Gerickes were wonderful. I loved them and shocked them and Katharine is still a friend. Professor Gericke was a beloved figure in Vienna's music world, and Bruno Walter came to lunch once a week to hear him reminisce and to bring news of Munich music. Another close friend who came each week was the portrait painter Herr von Mayhofer, who was a famous raconteur and looked exactly like an elongated Emperor Franz Joseph. There was a great deal of calling before and after invitations, and since everyone pursued the same social pattern, the Gerickes were constantly attending other chamber-music evenings, other *jours*, and all the *Empfänge* (receptions) of the season. I was a sort of curiosity, the Gerickes' P.G., and was included in everything.

My own day started with coffee, two Turkish crescent rolls, and a Meindl preserve in bed. A brisk walk, past the Johann Strauss and Pfarrer Kneipp statues in the Stadt Park, to the Kunstgewerbe Schule and Professor Oberbaurat Josef Hoffmann's classes. Hoffmann had been a student with Urban and had gone out to found and run the Wiener Werkstätte, which Urban brought to New York, unfortunately long before it was appreciated. (A recent exhibition of Wiener Werkstätte treasures and Art Nouveau in London was a sensational success.) Hoffmann was stern, supposedly from shyness, and an inspired teacher. He flew through the class with monitor—later professor—Haerdtl and frightened us all to death. At the first criticism session he came into the hall, and giving me one look—as I labored over my little design—said, *"Die betonung der horizontale ist gelungen"*—The emphasis of the horizontal is a success. For a moment I was quite encouraged, but then I realized it wasn't my design that had caught his eye, but my Tutankhamen-inspired sweater. When he looked at my design he said, "Cut everything in wood," and left. For months I cut everything—costume designs, stage settings—into blocks of hardest pear wood and into my knees, and learned to eliminate every unnecessary line. When he saw I had done that, long before I did, he said, "Paint everything on the walls." So paper was mounted for me and I splashed all over the class walls, and incidentally I learned to eliminate all finicky details. Carving a line into pear wood or teetering on a rickety ladder, twenty feet up, left no time or strength to go into detail. Whatever he prescribed for me was a great physical effort and I learned to do it all with one line. All the other pupils were given similar unexpected media, and most of us ended in quite different careers from those we had originally planned. I had wanted design and ended with mural painting and interior architecture, with stage and costume design thrown in.

At eleven each morning there was a midmorning *Schinkenbrot* and a *Bäckerei* (not the bakery shop but the piece of pastry), and at noon I walked back to the Gerickes' for a heavy dinner almost always including a *Hauptgang* (main course) of Boiled Beef with Dill Sauce, Horseradish Sauce, Tomato Sauce, Mushroom Sauce, Potato Sauce, Pepper Sauce, Bean Sauce, Green Sauce, Spanish Sauce, Mustard Sauce, Watercress Sauce, revolving on a two-week cycle. I spent every thirteen days looking forward to the return of my favorite, Mushroom Sauce. As a result of all the boiling of beef, there was always a strong soup with something floating in it. A piece of marrow, dumplings, *einlauf*—an egg run in—noodles, *Nocken* and *Frittaten* (a pancake cut into strips). Dessert was always a lovely *Mehlspeise*, flour dish, *Wiener Pfannkuchen* (pancake), or **Metternich Pudding.** Friends came in for dessert and coffee, and I walked to the Academy for my afternoon classes. These too were interrupted with a little *Backwerk* (bakery work) or *Konfekt*, and we ate *Pischinger Torten, Nuss Kuglen*, and *Mandeln im Schlafrock* (coated almonds) to keep up our strength.

Die Jause—tea or coffee—was the pleasantest meal in Vienna. I always returned from the Academy in time for the less formal *Kugelhupf, Bishof's Brot*, or *Kuchen* and the Salty Tea Sticks. *Jause* was set at the dining-room table; many friends stopped in; and it finally broke up when Sophie or, later, Monika came in to clear and reset the table for supper. Supper was something lovely made from vegetables or a little meat dish. Spinach Pudding, **Gebackener Karfiole,** or Mushroom Soufflé with a light dessert. When there were no guests we all did *Handarbeit* (hand work) at the table, after supper was cleared, and ate a small pastry before we went to bed.

Father's lawyer and close friend Albert Washburn was then American ambassador in Vienna and I went to the Krügergasse Embassy for such functions as my age permitted. Lincoln Washburn was even younger than I, but we met when I was included at informal dinners at their summer house outside Vienna. Jo Mielziner, Edward Beegle, Father's cousins, and a few passing New Yorkers made up my life outside of the Gericke home, and I was just beginning to overcome my shyness when Artur Bodanzky came through Vienna with Gatti-Casazza, general manager of the Metropolitan Opera.

My dinner with Gatti-Casazza was, if not the most memorable meal of my life, certainly the quietest I have ever eaten. Not a single word was spoken. He made only a few of those perfectly natural sounds which people make when they are eating and the final rasp of the napkin across his handsomely bearded chin—otherwise nothing, literally nothing. Why they asked me to dinner I will never know, unless it was so that I could hear the silence he was capable of producing. They say there wouldn't be any sound in the world if there were no ears for it to fall on and apparently the same can be said for silence. There wouldn't be any if there were not someone to hear it . . . me.

The whole thing was probably Bodanzky's mad way of killing two birds with one stone: he could feed Gatti and check on a friend's daughter, all on a clear, cool, summer evening. We drove up to Schloss Cobenzl above Grinzing, with Bodanzky talking in Italian about Viennese auditions all the way. Gatti contributed some grunts and a sigh and I sat shivering on the jump seat.

Bodanzky ordered while Gatti stared straight ahead, and my attempt to introduce my new acquaintance Bruno Walter as a subject of conversation fell completely flat. I remember that we started with a **Ungarische Fischsuppe** accompanied by friendly slurps from both of them, which established the musical atmosphere. They both ate soup from the front of their spoons and tilted their plates, and Bodanzky shouted *"Falsch"* (wrong) at the small orchestra. Although a complete lack of conversation had begun, it was not really oppressive while the musical accompaniment lasted. We ate **Polpettini** (every Viennese menu has an Italian specialty), but when we came to the *Zwetchken Kuchen* it settled in for good. I cast about for another subject but when I began to say something about Mahler, Artur turned away.

Gatti, when he spoke at all, spoke only French or Italian, which some of his German artists (the less kind ones) suspected was all part of a very clever ruse. They accused him of being an absolute linguist, speaking English, German, and even Russian perfectly whenever he wanted to. They said the reason he handled all his temperamental prima donnas and star tenors so masterfully was that he understood all their muttered discussions with their agents and interpreters, while he spoke to them only monosyllabically through his business manager and his interpreters. Nothing clips the wings of a demanding Parsifal or Flying Dutchman as quickly as having to relay his wishes through a bilingual mouthpiece—the bluster wears thin in translation.

When an infuriated Brünnhilde told her interpreter to tell the *alte Esel's* (old donkey's) interpreter that she wanted a guarantee of twelve performances but would settle for ten, Gatti stared into space with a look of profound un-understanding. When his interpreter gave him an abridged version of the acceptable terms, Gatti said, "Six," a very long sentence for him—in Italian—and via his or her interpreters, settled for eight. Whether or not he understood any language save French or Italian, and he certainly stood by while his cleverer staff (like Bodanzky) learned Italian, he was always at an advantage because of his monumental silence. If black is the absorption of all color, then Gatti was the absorption of all frivolous sound. There was always a hush when he appeared and all sounds subsided, especially as he appeared most often (at least to me) in the form of a huge soundproof silhouette at the Metropolitan Opera House.

Gatti was brilliant and taciturn and always looked his part, always aristocratic and grand. If he had been short and voluble, articulate and fat and cuddly, the Metropolitan would never have reached the heights it did during his regime. I remember being enormously impressed when I heard a Wagnerian mezzo tell Mother in an awed, not to say jealous, sotto-soprano that Gatti had sent a huge box of roses to the prima ballerina Rosina Galli, who became in 1930 the second Mme. Gatti-Casazza. (His marriage to Frances Alda lasted from 1910 to 1929.) The entire Metropolitan had it that a card had accompanied the roses with three whole words on it, *"Con grande ammirazione."* He must have used at least two more words when he proposed marriage to her and two more to express the conventional consent at the wedding ceremony.

I later designed costumes for the Metropolitan and sat in on rehearsals, where I constantly seemed to get under Gatti's feet, and lost some of my fear—he even spoke in my general direction on several occasions. But for a young and awkward art student that night in Vienna, there was not a single word—not even a friendly belch. The lights of the city came up from below the Cobenzl balustrade and my appetite disappeared completely . . . even the most ardent student *Schwärmerei* fades after two hours of total silence.

Well below Gatti-Casazza, but still on the Metropolitan Opera staff was a long-faced man called Otto Weil, whose actual claim to distinction, in my young opinion, was that his wife was called Ottilie —Otto and Ottie. He must have been a sort of early day talent scout. When they came through Vienna each year he boasted far and wide that he had found, discovered, invented, nurtured, trained, fed, encouraged, and finally engaged the Baroness Leopold Popper—Maria Jeritza—for the Metropolitan. He never claimed to have fathered her, but everything else to do with her was his doing, according to him. She was going to make her debut in New York in Erich Korngold's *Die Tote Stadt* and her long blond hair was her very own.

In those days all opera singers got under enormous capes of wavy hair. Wigs were mantles rather than head coverings, and every singer traveled with her wig trunk. For some operas there had to be a wig for every act. Geraldine Farrar's wig for the first act of *Carmen* was glossy black and piled high, complete with flowers, comb, and curls. For the mountains in the third act she wore a sort of sports cut, and in the last act the elaborate wig showed the touch of success and money. (I remember being impressed when I heard Mme. Kurt give an interview in which she said with pride that she had *"begleitet"* [accompanied] the beautiful Geraldine Farrar when they were both Lilli Lehmann pupils in Germany. That was when I thought *begleiten* meant only "to escort," and I couldn't see why taking Farrar across Berlin streets was such a privilege.)

For Kundry the wigs went to great extremes. There was something rough and disheveled for the first act, something smooth and seductive for the second—a wig to wrap Parsifal in during that long kiss (I vaguely remember a resentful coloratura telling Mother that one of the tenors took advantage of the footlights and actually *kissed* and at the same time smudged the greasepaint of the helpless Isoldes and Kundrys who were at his mercy). Kundry then had to change wigs once more for something humble and contrite-looking and long enough so that she could dry Parisfal's feet with it. The wigs weighed a ton, and in an emergency they could be used as costumes à la Lady Godiva.

I went back to New York for a short visit in 1921 and happened to be there when Mr. Weil's glamorous protégée made her debut at the Metropolitan in *Die Tote Stadt*, the haunting opera by Korngold. The dead city was Bruges and Jeritza was wildly glamorous. I was just old enough to be spellbound and instantly enslaved—partly by Jeritza and her own pale golden hair, and partly by the Pierrot's Song. (We have just gone to infinite pains and expense to hoist Dick's Steinway up our Austrian mountainside so he can play it for me. His greatest interest runs to Bach, but when he wants to wrap a little knot around my heart he plays the Pierrot's Song, and I remember the whole world of beauty and enchantment which Jeritza brought to the Metropolitan.)

Up to then I had loved Geraldine Farrar and Frieda Hempel, who delighted my unmusical eye, and I never dared tell Father that Edward and I had numbered the five gestures which expressed all of Frau Kurt's (and several other singers') feelings. There was the extended arm, the balled fists above the head, the hand on the heart, the hand at the brow, and the hands joined in supplication. I remember that Edward and I were shhh-ed when we giggled while a Radames expressed his overflowing emotions in the *"Celeste Aida"* by extending his arms to left and right in the approved fashion for setting-up exercises. It was at the same performance that the chariot horses shied and a chariot wheel took one of the great columns along, and we thought that Amonasro had on long brown tights and brown gloves.

Backfisch *Year*

*T*HE AUSTRIANS HAVE a name for an awkward young girl, a *Back-fisch* (fried fish), and they define it as a schoolgirl, partially grown but still in short skirts. What they mean is the neither-fish-nor-fowl period when girls are rarely noticed.

I came back to New York for my *Backfisch* winter, going to Winold Reiss's Art School on Christopher Street in the mornings and Bridgeman's life classes at the Art Students League in the afternoons. When I had first started studying in Vienna I had been invited to join a small " 'akt' group," and accepted with pleasure. Just before the first session I asked Mother what an "akt" was and she made inquiries and discovered it was a naked man or woman. I immediately took to my bed and didn't recover until the group had filled my vacancy. Later on I went to evening life classes at the Kunstgewerbe Schule (the Vienna School of Applied Art) with Jo Mielziner and Edward Beegle and a determination to face life—in the form of an ancient man with a Gothic structure and a long white beard. By the time I went to Bridgeman's classes I was less shy, although the athletic supporters of the male models startled me and my drawings always had large blank patches.

My *Backfisch* evenings during that long winter in New York, when Father was out and the telephone was turned on, were spent next to it, waiting hopefully for a call from a divine young man, which rarely came. Every ring of the bell caused a flutter and every inquiry for Mother was a shattering disappointment. That was long before girls used their parents' telephones for hours of aimless conversation with other girls, singing, doing homework, and producing occasional long silences at so much per minute. There was no question of a girl calling a boy, so we were reduced to waiting, peering at our faces in our fathers' magnifying mirrors and waiting some more. No one who was well brought up used the telephone after nine, so at nine we went to bed in a cloud of despondency.

If there was a call from a man it meant an invitation; no one called just to talk, and an invitation meant—at least to me—hours of anticipatory indigestion and lots of little black pills called Bellans. The extent of the invitation depended on the young man's finances. It could be for as little as an ice cream sundae or lunch involving some refined white chicken dish such as **Chicken Hash,** Chicken Pie, or Chicken in Aspic and an equally white dessert, usually Meringue. The most sought-after invitation was to a *thé dansant*—we drank tea and moved like camels or jiggled like jelly on the dance floor, and conversation was quite unnecessary.

Most of my social life in New York was still with my parents and their friends, but the fact that I spoke German involved me in some agonizing events planned to entertain notables who had little or no English. Any hostess who needed a German-speaking girl didn't care whether she was an awkward *Backfisch* or not, just as long as she could understand what was being said. There was a bad period when various New York hostesses were entertaining Richard Strauss and his son Bubi while Strauss was conducting in New York, and I was one of those chosen to talk to the younger Strauss, who was hard to talk to anywhere. I had met them in Vienna, where Strauss and Franz Schalk directed the Staatsoper, and I knew that Bubi Strauss was a rival to Gatti-Casazza as a non-conversationalist.

A second torture was entertaining the officers of the *Graf Zeppelin* and the many young aristocrats who came to postwar New York to seek their fortunes or brides with fortunes.

Between our rare invitations from men, we went out with other *Backfisch* for tea and chatted with each other. When Doris Beck and I had tea together we went to Vantine's and drank pale China tea and ate quantities of cream cheese, guava jelly, and crackers. Doris always reported on the doings of her mad love, Scofield Thayer—whom she had loved for many years across the breadth of the old Brevoort dining room, and I reported on men who became young, rich, handsome, and single in the telling. Actually they were a gardener called Wilcox, a groom called Graham, and an American consul who had once given Father a photograph which I used discriminately. Not yet having any real loves, we made them up; the boys we had grown up with were away at boarding schools and were far too gawky and unromantic to speak about. They, in turn, were much more interested in older women at this point.

Doris Beck—daughter of Thomas Beck, then editor of *Collier's* magazine, and his beautiful Canadian wife, who had acted under the name Louie Roy—was a little older than I and extremely knowledge-able in the ways of the gourmet. They ate most of their New York meals at the Waldorf or the Brevoort and spent their summers in Morris Plains and later in Morristown.

Doris knew how to order lamb chops and hashbrowned pota-toes, cream of tomato soup and—of all wonderful things—a club sandwich. When I ate at their house there was steak and a baked potato, and Mrs. Beck always wore a hat at her own luncheon table. I remember that after a really good Sunday luncheon in Morristown, when I had eaten sparingly in order to go overboard with the dessert, Mrs. Beck suddenly "raised the table," and said "I simply couldn't think of a dessert." We laid in bottles of stuffed and ripe olives, cheese crackers, fudge, peanut butter, and all the things I had been so care-fully trained to avoid, and ate them in Doris's room after her parents went to bed. The Becks had individual dishes of salted almonds at each place on the table; they drank ice water; there were plain and chocolate-covered mints on the table; and when Mrs. Beck sat down in the drawing room she pulled her feet up under her. They were the most attractive parents I knew, and on top of everything else Mrs. Beck smoked and drove a car.

The endless *Backfisch* winter ended for me suddenly when I went to work at Joseph Urban's scenic studio in Yonkers, New York. The union day started at eight, so I started from town at six-thirty each morning. I couldn't very well fall back on my old school habit of dressing before I went to bed, as there was a sudden rush of popu-larity when I joined the workers and I was usually too tired to change from evening dress to street clothes when I came home. My first jobs were the mural decorations and curtains for a Palm Beach theater and odds and ends for the Hutton house and the Bath and Tennis Club there which Urban designed.

I went back to Vienna later that year for a stint of *gute Wiener*

Kuche and good *Demel Torten* and pastries and came back to Yonkers to start on the 60,000-foot mural for the Ziegfeld Theater, which was going to be on Sixth Avenue. Among the strange assortment of artists who worked at the studio was the Prague painter Maxim Kopf, who became one of Mother's and my closest friends and, during World War II, we succeeded in helping him come from Tahiti, via North Africa, to New York. Later he married Dorothy Thompson (who never shared his enthusiasm for us) and lived in their New York house and on the farm in Vermont. Dorothy at least shared the recipe of her cook's magnificent **Baba au Rhum** with Mother, however.

At the Yonkers studio we painted on the floor, so that color ran down in our brushes, as scenery is painted, and there was a lunch each day of *Gulyas* and coffee. The Munich painter Geitlinger and Maxim Kopf and I sat on the Ziegfeld mural together for more than a year, and Geitlinger dreamt of *Weiss Würste* in Munich, Kopf dreamt of *Böhmische Dalken,* and I dreamt of Demel's *Tee Gebäck* (tea cookies). We talked food eight hours a day.

As I grew older and threw off some of my *Backfisch* scales, I was doomed to attract the attention of older men with voices, since my parents exposed me only to singers and musicians, and the few young men I knew were in New York only during vacations from school and college. The Scene Painters Union, which I finally managed to join, had a forty-four-hour week and I went up to Yonkers even on Saturday mornings to put in my last four hours.

I remember that Walter Kirchhof invited me to go on a Sunday walk. In those days a Sunday walk in New York was still a refined occupation pursued in a silk hat and cutaway and with a walking stick. It ended in a smart little restaurant or at the Plaza with **Côtes D'Agneau Lavallière,** which gave one the opportunity of eating two ultra-favorite foods: artichokes and asparagus together. If it wasn't a refined little chop, it was invariably a *Crêpe de Volaille* or *Croquettes à l'Américaine.* The croquettes were nothing but codfish balls, a great favorite for a late Sunday breakfast, and no better for having a French name. If the walk was in the afternoon, it ended at a *thé dansant.*

Herr Kirchhof, who was a Metropolitan Opera tenor, picked me up early in the afternoon, a time that boded no good at all from the standpoint of nourishment. Before we left he wrapped soft white scarves around his lower face and throat and turned up his fur-coat collar. He pulled down the brim of his soft hat, put on warm fur-lined gloves, put his hands into his pockets, and off we went. He set a determined German-officer's-double-quick-time-semi-goose-step pace and I ran along two steps behind as best I could. After about twenty blocks we were held up by traffic at a cross street and I made a breathless attempt at conversation. He gestured emphatically toward his throat and made it quite clear that he would not open his mouth to the winter air. We were, it seemed, going to walk, silently breathing through our noses, down the length of Manhattan Island. And so we did, to Washington Square and back, ten long miles on a Sunday afternoon. We made it in three and a half mute hours—probably a record. He left me at the door and made eloquent gestures to show he had to take his voice back to his hotel to soothe it under a hot shower and relax it with a little hot **Blue Blazes.**

The next day a large box of flowers came with a card. Herr Kirchhof felt himself to be a second Caruso, master of the voice and the caricature. He didn't speak out of doors and he didn't use words on paper—all was said in caricature. The card showed a drawing of me—head forward, and pushing along on high heels while clutching my coat around me. A small balloon with an arrow pointed to the back of my ankle and contained the one word *"Loch"*—meaning that I had a hole in my stocking. That was my reward for running after him for ten miles!

Six years later he crossed to Germany with Mother and me on one of the North German Lloyd steamers. On this trip, which I had to make in a wheelchair, I was wheeled into the Ritz Restaurant to sit next to him every evening. Kirchhof, Mr. Campo Santo, as he liked to call himself, might not open his mouth in the fresh air but he was extremely articulate with a menu. He loved to order for others, and each dinner was the result of hours of confabulation (indoors) with the chief steward. I remember that the wheelchair evoked special solicitudes and he came up with some lovely dinners. There was **Potage à la Steward** and there was pheasant and partridge and all the game birds which German steamers always carried.

And one day there was *Hamburger Aalsuppe* (Hamburg Eel Soup), a specialty served with baked pears. It all sounds awful, but the soup happens to be one of my happiest memories.

When Herr Campo Santo came to dinner in New York, he was usually in high spirits and dominated the entire party. During dinner he produced an unexpected talent, sleight-of-hand—he made handbags and trinkets disappear and reappear and ended with a fabulous finale, in which he secreted masses of table silver in all the crevices of his tails and made them disappear completely. Mother's maid came up the next morning in tears to report the loss of lots of table silver.

I remember Mother speaking to Father about it and Father saying she couldn't very well ask. A week later he said he *thought* she might ask. Mother finally abandoned etiquette and wrote Herr Kirchhof to ask whether he would look in his tails for some inadvertently prestidigitated silver. Next day she too had dozens and dozens of red roses with a caricature of Mr. Kirchhof with the pockets of his tails turned out to show they were empty. As I recall, the silver turned up in a jardinière, and Mother never knew whether it was Mr. Kirchhof's joke or whether one of the other guests (there were three other Metropolitan tenors there that evening) was having a little extra laugh.

19

The Poppers

I DO NOT KNOW where Father and Mother met Otto and Ottilie Weil or when they met the Poppers, but by the time I came back to New York from Vienna for a second visit, they were friends. They had arrived at the sort of understanding and intimacy that allowed for small dinner parties and out of these Poldi and Maria had started to come alone—by special request—to more familial meals. They were due for lunch one Sunday. In those days I was expected to participate at meals silently, whether there were guests or not. I was certainly not an ornament but I was *die Tochter des Hauses*—the daughter of the house—and I was trained to appear when dinner was announced and to fade out before the coffee. When a story might become a little risqué or when there was a juicy scandal to discuss, I was sent to fetch cigarettes, although they were never passed until after dinner. This was a ridiculous formality, as cigarettes and cigars were already on their tray, and I simply went to the top of the stairs and waited for a burst of laughter before I came down again.

I saw Frau Jeritza for the first time offstage when she was curled up in a corner of the sofa in our library and while I was purposefully crushing any resemblance I might have had to Grandmamma for fear I, too, might go into a *Schwärmerei*. She was lovely, but my clearest recollection of that first meeting was of length. Jeritza could telescope down to cozy dimensions, but her hands were long, her legs were long, her hair was long, yet when she unfolded to an astonishing height— surely close to six feet—she still did not tower. She had a special gift of empathy and a talent for remaining, so to speak, at eye level. She

124

never dominated, and as I recall, she sang with Mario Chamlee and other middle-sized tenors without dwarfing them. On that day I took pleasure in her tall good looks and the fact that Baron Popper—Poldi —ate all the bones along with his **Squab Chickens in Casserole.** He expressed himself as always wanting just that whenever he came to dinner in future. All chickens of the sort that I have since encountered were braised in a casserole with bacon and mushrooms and cubed potatoes, but Mother's, straight from the Bristol in Paris, was steamed in a casserole with spinach leaves and finally doused with more yolks and cream than seemed possible

Dessert was Mother's **Almond Soufflé** with a thin hot **Raspberry Sauce,** but on other occasions it was her light Chocolate Roll or my favorite, Moor in a Shirt. First courses alternated between an Essence of Mushrooms or a **Consommé Sir James** and salads were *Moderne* or *Gauloise.*

There were changes in the rest of the menu, but the chicken was often repeated, and I can still hear Poldi crushing the bones with his strong even teeth. For years the Poppers wove through our lives in New York and Vienna and on ocean crossings. I cannot help thinking of Maria often, since part of my flat silver was her wedding present, and some years later, she became my daughter's godmother. She brought things into my life that didn't actually change it, but there was always some part of Jeritza. Before Jeritza there were shoes from Hanan and Saks and Perugia; after Jeritza there was a man called Hobersdorfer in Vienna who made our shoes—because Jeritza said he had to—for years. There were two men, father and son, called the Barrys—and naturally they became the Du Barrys—who came and did our nails as they did Maria's whenever she was in Vienna. Maria sent gifts—impulsive, wonderful, generous gifts—and flowers suitable for an ovation at the opera. I still have a seductive peach-colored taffeta Art Nouveau quilted chaise longue throw (I didn't even own a chaise) and a huge round pillow edged with great taffeta petals—the sort of thing that Erté inspired and was meant for a subtler creature than I was. When we dined with the Poppers in Vienna on the Stallburg-gasse I remember that the maids and footmen still wore white cotton gloves and there were little crystal dumbbells to rest the silver on.

The Poppers also always served at least two desserts and allowed their guests to follow their inclinations—a bombe or a pudding. Be-sides having a choice of a flourful or a flourless dessert, there was also a choice between a warm and a cold dessert. As I remember, I often ate both *Aprikosen Reis* and *Kastanien Torte*, or *Warmes Kompott* and *Kirschen Kuchen.*

The Viennese could hardly include more French in their language without actually speaking French. They solved the whole dessert problem by calling them *entremets* and ate *friandises* along with *Gateau Manon* and **Gelée Voltaire,** *Parfait aux Avelines* and *Soufflé aux Amandes*—but a *Strudl* was a *Strudl* and a *Knödl* was a *Knödl,* and by any other name Vienna denied their existence.

The Poppers always had a half a floor at the St. Regis Hotel in New York, and during one of the opera seasons a year or two later, Poldi's younger brother Fritz visited them. Sensation! A single, unmarried bachelor Popper, presumably as handsome as Poldi and, from all accounts, a magnificent dancer. I was then about seventeen, incredibly shy, still silent, and skinny. It was arranged that I would meet Baron Popper at tea at the St. Regis to discuss dancing plans. I have no recollection of the tea but a total recall of the dancing plans. I had expected that we would go to a *thé dansant* at the Ambassador and that, depending on my abilities, we would possibly go on to one of the Assemblies or a ball during the winter. Not at all—Herr Baron had a reputation to maintain, he could not be seen in public with an unworthy partner. It appeared that if I showed promise there would be a period of *eintanzen* (this cannot be translated since it means "in dancing," which means, I suppose, that two people dance with each other until they are "danced in" together). A team appeared to be what the Baron had in mind; we were, it seemed, going to wow New York with a certain professional proficiency which would make all other couples slink from the floor and leave us doing solos—a sort of amateur Irene and Vernon Castle or De Marco act.

The only reason for the tea at the St. Regis was to determine my height, weight, color, expression, conformation, angulation, action, and carriage. Since I did not have to open my mouth I could relax. The problem seemed to be (after I passed the initial tests) where we could go for the tryout. The St. Regis was carpeted wall to wall and no small rooms with a hardwood floor were available. It was decided by Baron Popper that we would make the necessary arrangements at my home. I was to produce a polished hardwood floor, a gramophone, certain specified records, and complete privacy on an afternoon in the following week. Up to the first step I had passed the test. He had, of course, not come anywhere near passing mine. He was not as tall as Poldi; he wore heavy glasses and was thickset and *old,* probably thirty. He never smiled and he took his dancing seriously.

With very limited cooperation from Mother and the maids, I was allowed to roll up the carpet in Mother's dressing room and have Grandmamma's old gramophone moved, and Mother promised to go out. When the day came, the Baron was more than satisfied, since the dressing room had four mirrored walls and he was able to see himself into infinity and enjoy the vision—from all sides—of his grace and proficiency in doing the tango, the waltz, the fox-trot, the hesitation, the polka, and a sort of Viennese cross between an Apache dance and the Death of the Swan. We had a short action test to see whether I was a born follower, whether I responded instantly to signals, was pliable, could be bent over backward, and whether I was able to waltz in one direction for forty-five minutes without getting dizzy. The dressing room adjoined Father and Mother's bedroom and Mother's chaise longue was so situated that it commanded a full view of the dressing room and all its reflections. It turned out that after being weighed and found satisfactory I was to be taught all the Baron's numbers before we would make our first public appearance in New York. After about three hours of strenuous instruction he dropped me on the chaise longue, took a large bed pillow from Mother's bed and continued the lesson solo—showing me what lay ahead when I, and not the pillow, would swoop around a ballroom in his arms.

Mother came home to find me exhausted on her chaise and the Herr Baron dancing with her bed pillow. After we had had about a month of lessons we had a period of reconnoitering—we had to evaluate the strength of the competition. We went to nightclubs, balls, and hotels, and I sat quietly (no pearls before swine for the Herr Baron) while he gave his critique. We ate lightly; after all, we were in training.

One day Herr Baron came with an announcement: we would make our debut at the Beaux Arts Ball at the Hotel Astor. I tried to tell him that it was not a suitable place for our talents, but the costume possibilities appealed to him and nothing would change his decision. I do not know whether the period was specified, but he decided on something romantic from the court of Louis XIV. He would be not Louis himself but surely someone close to the monarch. I was given samples so that I could be glamorous along the same lines and match his color scheme as harmoniously as his dance steps. We both went to infinite trouble and, I suppose, expense, since I recently discarded a pair of knee-length green leather boots of softest glove kid, which were part of my costume. I think the suggestion came from Léon Bakst. I was not the powdered wig, panier, and patches type, and in any case I could not have followed Herr Baron's signals in an encumbering skirt. My costume provided nothing in the way of pockets or pouches, so off I went to Broadway and Forty-third Street, to Times Square—defenseless, practically penniless, and dressed as Bakst's idea of a young huntress in the gardens of Versailles. We left our coats in one of the bedrooms which participants rented so that they could drink while others danced below. They were friends of the Baron's and I did not know their names or the number of their room. Then down we went to perform.

Exactly three minutes after we hit the crowded dance floor a young man from Yale, who was feeling no pain and was belligerent besides, cut in. Herr Baron brushed him off, but to no avail. We progressed around the ballroom in a *pas de trois* that threatened to become a punch on the Baron's nose. Suddenly he stopped and said to me in a loud voice (which stopped all adjoining couples), "I have trained you for two months, shaped you, taught you everything you know about dancing, had this costume made, I have fed you and sent you flowers, I had a massage and I showered, I was shaved and I rented a car, I picked you up, paid for your ticket, brought you here—and now you propose to dance with this young man who has neither bathed nor shaved, with whom you are not danced-in, who did not bring you here, who is dressed as a pirate, and can't dance." No doubt about it, the Baron was not enthusiastic about this product of old Eli.

I never heard the end. The young man from New Haven was apparently on the football team. He pushed the Baron Friedrich Popper Freiherr von Podrazy aside and dove into the crowd with me as though he were making a dash for the goal line. Someone else cut in and in a matter of minutes I realized I was alone at the Beaux Arts Ball—not exactly alone, but without my original escort. I told the unknown man I was dancing with that I was alone, penniless, coatless, carless, to which he said, "Good." I lost him in another few minutes— I never even knew either of their names. If the Baron was still there I could not find him, nor the room where my coat was. I tried borrowing a nickel for a telephone, but everyone was "tight" and thought my predicament extremely funny. Ben Webster, the director of the Woodstock Theater, cut in, but I lost him in the crowd.

I came home at dawn, after hours of hiding in corridors, peering into the wrong rooms (at the wrong moment), dancing with strangers, powdering my nose, and standing around in the ladies' room. I was too shy and it was too cold to go out on Times Square in my costume, and for a time I still thought I might find the Baron. I finally found a sober undergraduate in a monk's cowl from Princeton, who gave me breakfast at Childs and brought me home. I never saw the Herr Baron again—or the Yale undergraduate.

Ziegfeld, the Spas and Bads

*A*FTER THE MURALS for the Ziegfeld Theater were completed, I went to Vienna without waiting to see them hung. The Gerickes wanted to go to Italy and sublet us their apartment, complete with Sophie the maid and Frau Toni the charwoman. Doris and Mrs. Beck and Mother came to spend the spring with me and we ate ourselves through it, sitting in the sunshine of every café and restaurant that put its "garden" out on the pavement when it was warm. By then Doris was in love with Charles Lindbergh, who had just landed in Paris, and both our mothers were kept busy turning down the proposals we received from young Austrians who could come to America only by waiting endlessly for a quota number or by leaving instantly as the husband of a born American.

Doris and I ate *Aufschnitt* and **Linzen Salat Leopoldi** and *Grinzinger Torte* in the Heurigen gardens and went overboard at Demel's every afternoon. I once watched a budding romance progress through every torte on the counter. The man was ardently pleading his cause while they both ate a *Nuss Torte,* and only interrupted his eating to put a hand on his heart at intervals. As soon as the torten were gone he left off to fetch them each a wedge of *Dobos Torte,* and this went on until they were glassy-eyed. We went down the Wachau for weekends in country inns and ate dangerously. I remember a terrace luncheon of ice-cold cucumber salad and red-hot fried chicken, a combination that meant instant death in Father's menu book, without remarkable consequences.

I had acquired an old (about thirty-six) and heavy Viennese

admirer, and while I was thinking about reversing the migratory trend and living in Vienna, Father arrived to take Mother and me off for a cure. He believed that all ills (especially pallor) needed fresh air and a bath in some substance other than plain hot water. The only time that Father ever walked farther than across a pavement to a car was when he was doing a cure in a *Kurort*. That summer we took long walks, and every time we reached a place where the air looked as though it might conceivably be a little better than the air we had just come through, he stopped and said *Tief atmen* (breathe deeply), which we both did with mouths open. What I did about breathing at other times could be as shallow as I liked, but when we had traveled to breathe promising air, near trees or near water, we had to breathe it in to the point of dizziness.

It was the sort of breathing that Dr. Steel used to ask us to do when he pressed the prickly side of his goatee into our backs—in-out-in When we had breathed enough we walked back to the sanitarium or hotel and neglected our health over dinner. It had been and still was a time of elegant hypochondria, and everyone had something fairly harmless the matter with them. The first question when we ran into acquaintances—and they were all there, from the Rothschilds to Matzenauer—was *"Was fehlt Ihnen?"* (What do you lack?). It actually meant what are you suffering from, and the inquiry was always answered in unabridged detail—after all, it was a health resort. There were baths and spas and *Luftkur Orte* (air-cure places), and each cured certain areas. The spas were for drinking waters with healthful properties (usually laxative), which miraculously helped to reduce weight. In Carlsbad this was assisted by Zwieback, palest Prague ham, and Blue Brook Trout. Matzenauer probably belonged in Franzenbad which was frankly a reducing bath, but the musicians were at Carlsbad and she stayed where the music was.

I remember hearing that she married her second husband, Floyd Glotzbach, in or near Carlsbad and left her wedding bouquet behind to be petrified in the lower *Sprudel Halle*. The *Sprudel's* efficacious properties might help the liver, but they coated and petrified anything that was left (for a consideration) in the petrification chamber. It was a favorite place for baby shoes and corsages, but Matzenauer was a very large woman and she carried a proportionate wedding bouquet. I saw a wedding picture and it was enormous. The processes of petrification were such that the object not only acquired the permanence of stone, it also acquired the weight of stone. Since the process took some time, Matzenauer cast about for a friend who would bring it back to New York for her.

When she heard that Artur Bodanzky, the light and unencumbered traveler, the totally unsentimental yet highly temperamental one, was going to be in Carlsbad, she had the crated stone bouquet delivered to him at the Hotel Pupp. Father told me that the crash of the shattered bouquet could be heard all across Carlsbad.

Father, who always consulted several doctors, did not go to one spa alone. After Carlsbad came a week of relaxed eating and no exercise in and around Prague, where **Karlsbader Gulyas** and *Brandteig Knödel* (Bohemian Beignets) and *Vogelnester* (Birds' Nests) were very good. After that came the Weisse Hirsch, near Dresden, Doktor Heinrich Lahmann's famous sanitarium for famous people. At the Weisse Hirsch, the guests not only breathed fresh air, they let it come in contact with hitherto unexposed portions of their bodies. I had dinner recently at the Hôtel Lancaster in Paris where I met a Mrs. Wood, who had been taken there when she was a child and had apparently been just as undone as I was by the adults in negligées.

It was Doktor Lahmann's theory that unhealthy, unventilated clothing and poor nourishment led to all ills. He recommended the wearing of loose cotton garments, woven especially to permit the constant passing of fresh air, and a vegetable diet. The ladies discarded their stays and corset covers, and in that day of the rounded figure they looked ghastly—unrecognizable. Father never took to these loose and ventilated ways; he wore white flannels and a Panama hat and always left after three days of seeing his Wagnerian idols from Valhalla breathing through their pores in slack poses. When he had eaten vegetables *"bis da"*—up to here—(which he said while he pointed to a spot over his head) we went on to Baden-Baden and the Schwarzwald. There we could eat fresh **Warm Smoked Trout** with Horseradish Whipped Cream and *Weinberg Schnecken* (Vineyard Snails) and black cherries and breathe fresh air, albeit not through all our pores. We drove to all the Schwarzwald resorts and I swallowed a fishbone at Titisee and had to eat delicious Schwarzwald bread for three days. We stayed at the Villa Stephanie and breathed fresh air in Baden-Baden's Lichtenthaler Allee, where it was further rarefied by royalty. (I was taken to Doktor Schacht, a brother of Hjalmar, in Baden-Baden in 1929, when I was still in my wheelchair, and young

Lincoln Washburn wheeled me up and down the *allée* at a breakneck pace, which he said was as much fun as the motorcycle he was wishing for.)

German is a language made for illnesses. Germans say, *"Ich bin gelegen für Drei Tage"*—I had to lie down for three days. The prone position automatically indicates illness; they never say "I had a cold." There is always an explanatory verb and an adjective, they *suffer* under a *mortal* cold. (Just recently the bank director's wife in Lunz said when she felt a draft, "Tomorrow I will be ill unto death.") A cold in German is a *Schnupfen*, which sounds the way it feels. Whatever ailment they have, there is a water somewhere they will either drink or sit in to cure it, to which is added the pleasure of knowing they can eat what they want and go to a *Bad* to take off weight in a few weeks.

Even reducing was pleasant enough; since everybody was doing it together, no one suffered alone. They went to check their weight on rather magnificent public scales on the *Bad's* largest square. The wooden scale chairs looked as though an Italian Renaissance bishop should be enthroned in it. The weigher-in weighed from the side or back and noted the figure on a discreet slip of paper. Ladies and gentlemen sat facing the passing promenade while he fiddled with weights.

We went on to breathe deeply for a short period at Doktor Hansi's Sanitarium in the Semmering, but Father found the cure too serious. What he wanted was a fun cure during which he could eat and drink to his heart's content while some magic process took away all the aches, pains, superfluous fat—although he managed not to have much of that—fatigue, and what he referred to as his pockets (of gas).

Carlsbad, where both Father and Mother were born, was a major *Bad* (bath), while the Semmering, Homburg, Spa, and Baden were the resorts for the tapering off, or *Nach Kur* (after cure). The after cure was a gradual regaining and rebuilding of general strength, weight, and pockets of gas which the real cure had eliminated. The cures were strenuous and enervating and they frequently proved fatal. When Father's second cousin died in his box at the Vienna Opera, the cause of death was diagnosed as the cure . . . *"Er ist von der Kur gestorben"* ("He died from the cure") wrote his bereaved wife. The Carlsbad cure was more sensational than most and had elements which we enjoyed. For one thing it occupied Father until dinnertime. An attendant brought Father's hot *sprudel* and hot compresses at dawn—we could trust him not to get up and follow the routine—and then he went for his mud baths. When I once had to locate him I asked the new attendant, who didn't know Father, to take a message to the man with the mustache. I was told that there was no way of seeing the mustache when gentlemen were in the mud bath. In the meantime, I rode and learned to jump and went to the Zander Institute.

Zander meant my exercises were done for me. We either lay down on, sat on, or put our extremities into machines that rolled and wiggled us, turned and twisted us while we did nothing except walk from machine to machine. There were saddles and pounders and bouncers and white-coated attendants who attached us to the machines. I cannot remember why I made the cure, unless it was thinness, phlegm, or what Father called laxadaisicality—which was, in fact, too much Father.

As the summer wore on I decided that life in Vienna with an old husband would be a mistake, and since I had reached an age of relative congeniality with Father, we decided on a togetherness motor trip— just Mother, Father, and I, through the Pyrenees.

Father was reading a book called *Meine Pyreneen Fahrt* (My Pyrenean Drive), and was so impressed that he sent for the car, a huge Delage Landaulet, and made his plans. There were no wines or storeroom supplies of distinction to buy in the Pyrenees and it struck Father that what Mother and Marie and home needed most was a new approach to that great French dish the poularde. He organized what became a total Poularde Crusade that late summer. Starting from Avignon, rooms were engaged, poularde dinners were ordered, and wines were iced. Maps were marked and poularde recipes were studied. Each evening when we arrived at our destination, we were greeted by a different poularde.

Sometimes the *Poulardes de Bresse* were roasted; sometimes they were steamed a blameless white or browned and poached in a casserole. They were boned or unboned, in full or half mourning, or combined with anything from cucumbers to truffles. Father wanted to keep our palates unsmirched and his newly trimmed waist unwidened, so we sat down each evening to the poularde while entrancing hors d'oeuvre carts and other goodies went to other tables.

Mother and I ate only what agreed with Father, and our own iron digestions were never taxed. The dessert that became Father's "interior" best was a simple compote—so it was a simple compote that we had after each poularde. I need not stress that my poularde could have been followed most agreeably by any sweet of France—*Crêpes Georgette, Beignets Soufflés, Gâteau Mocha. Si vous le nommez, moi—je le mange*—but I went off to my room each evening with an unsatisfied craving for sugar.

At Carcassonne, at Superbagnères, at Font Romeu, wherever we stopped at the ends of high serpentines or the bottoms of gorges, we ate *Poularde Archiduc* or *Poularde Châtelaine*, or **Poularde Basque** or *Poularde Windsor*. I liked them best when they were beautifully browned and then coddled in a casserole with mushrooms and vegetables *à la Bonne Femme* or *Chasseur*, or a Pyrenean **Poularde Pharao.**

When we reached Pau and Biarritz, we had a last wild fling with *Poulardes Demidoff* and *Suvaroff*, and there, the home of wine and truffles, we went back to purchases and tastings and testings and cures, and poulardes were forgotten. At that time I had decided on a career and no Coming Out and certain foreordained achievements. I was going to have, among other things, the *Légion d'Honneur*. In Périgord I found the little red rosette, sewed onto its inverted black button, in the drawer of my night table, and after studying its anatomy I crossed it off my list—it would mean buttonholes in all my dresses.

All final plans for a return to Vienna were abandoned when Urban wrote that there was a nightclub in New York, a hotel in Pennsylvania, and other places needing murals—and there was also a new job, costume-designing for the Metropolitan. Father sailed off in his usual single state, and Mother and I stayed in Paris, where Seymour Fox and Ralph Jester had a studio in the Hameau Boileau, and all of us prepared for work and one-man exhibits in New York and I studied the costume periods of the operas that lay ahead. We stayed a few weeks and ate *croissants* and *fraises des bois* conserve for breakfast; a light lunch, croissants and the same *fraises des bois* conserve at tea-time, and each evening we went to one of Paris's great restaurants. Father had lived in Paris as a young man and Grandmamma had gone for the opera season, and their discoveries were the places we still go to today—the Tour d'Argent, the Escargot, Paillard, Marguéry, the Crillon, the Ritz, and many others that have improved or deteriorated, but they are still there. The only one that has disappeared was aptly called La Poularde and presented only two items, quenelles and a poularde that was skinless, white, and tender, steamed in brandy and eaten with rough salt. When Father cabled that the Anderson Galleries on 57th and Park would give me a show, we sailed on the *Homeric*. Seymour had his show at the Farragil Galleries and I had mine at the Anderson and an invitation to show in Chicago and we were off on our careers.

Mother had a telephone installed in my living room and I no longer suffered from Father's shut-off phone. Marie was in her kitchen, I had a schnauzer called Baldur and all was well—my only problem was the Metropolitan rehearsals, which lasted through the lunch hour and we again depended on the sandwiches we brought along. I could easily have gone without lunching, but the rehearsal sandwich was a reciprocal matter and I couldn't very well accept delicacies from Mrs. Ziegler and the other rehearsal-goers if I didn't have something as good to offer in return.

21

Rehearsals and a Wedding

M RS. EDWARD ZIEGLER, wife of the Met's business manager and Suzanne Gleaves' mother, had a special talent for sandwiches: hers were thin, English in their contents, watercress and mustard, lettuce, cucumber, and ham mousse, and she made lovely innocent egg salad sandwiches. They were fresh and always wrapped appetizingly in paper that didn't make thundering, reverberating sounds when she opened them in the middle of a quintet. In contrast, our Marie, left to her own devices, always ground down the legs of the Pheasant Suprême *au Vin* or the dark meat of the Roast Capon with Brandy or (judging by their flavor) Father's leftover cocktails, and produced an intoxicating paste that would have been more suitable, I thought, for a French *roué* (a very fashionable word at that time to apply to any foreign gentlemen over thirty). Mother and I worked over Marie, ordered special sandwich breads and achieved some improvements, but she still included some cold quail, a lobster claw, or a gull's egg whenever she could lay her hands on something exotic.

Rehearsal sandwiches were not by any means ordinary sandwiches. They had to extend the ambiance of the occasion and be a taste association with the opera. I remember that hard-cooked eggs (riced with cut chives and chopped cucumbers) spelled *Jenufa* for me, while an addition of caviar made them pure *Boris*. I couldn't sit through Wagner on frail lettuce sandwiches, nor through *Rosenkavalier* on cold roast pork. Rehearsals were a little like car races: while we don't want anything to happen, a race without a small accident is disappointing and a Met rehearsal in those days without

137

an interruption, a blowup, or one of Bodanzky's magnificent scenes wasn't really a successful rehearsal. Even though my participation started with the costume rehearsal, I loved to go to the earlier ones, where a tweed-suited Hans Sachs proved that costumes (at the Met) make the shoemaker.

Costume rehearsals were fascinating. Over a period of years I did the costumes for *Schwanda, Elektra, Notte di Zoraima,* Von Suppé's enchanting *Donna Juanita* (with Jeritza), and many others. I attended the rehearsals officially but still went to sit with Mrs. Ziegler, who had taken me in my *Backfisch* year and who still shared her sandwiches with me. Marie's technique with the bread knife improved, but she still used the most ill-assorted wrappings in the world. I invariably unwrapped her crinkly paper at the very moment when Gatti's silent silhouette would come looming up the aisle or rise unexpectedly from the row behind us. He moved about the rehearsals— a mighty bearded mass, restless, silent, monolithic, and magnificent. He always scared me to death. I remembered the Vienna dinner and avoided him whenever possible. I was able to go to all the Met rehearsals, if for no other reason than that chorus costumes were made to serve in related operas and I might have to help adjust *Schwanda* to *The Bartered Bride.*

First costume rehearsals were the most fascinating. There would stand a fully dressed, armored, and illuminated Brünnhilde, doing her bit in half-voice, and pale without makeup, while our friend and stage director, Herr von Wymetal, in his impeccable morning coat, and my friend Willi von Wymetal, his son, in sober gray flannels, threw themselves about in passionate and emotional attitudes, trying to inject animation where there was room only for concentration on cues and arias. No gesture carefully learned could take priority over the eye that must be kept on Bodanzky.

When all seemed to me to be going extremely well, Maestro Bodanzky (very different from the cozy Artur I knew) would rap like mad with his baton to ensure a silence into which he shouted, "What is this—a hotel for sows?" "What are you—*ein musikalisches Rind-fleisch?*"—literally, a musical beef animal—and similar endearments. We might be in the auditorium behind his back, but we cringed and cowered at his pleasantries. Gatti-Casazza and the Maestro would confer, the Siegfried in curls and bare legs would suddenly make a thoroughly New York shrug or put his hands on his hips. Lighting men came by with meters and Brünnhilde would chew on a lozenge. Next Gatti, the prowler, would suddenly clank the curtain rings as he pulled back the red velvet curtain in his box and listened from above.

Our dinner guests, Grete Stuckgold, Gustave Schützendorf, and Paul Bender, would walk about looking half human and half Wagnerian (while I exchanged more sandwiches with Ada Bodanzky and pretty Felicitas Bender, and we all slid down as Gatti came by again). Friedrich Schorr had come from Germany with Anna, his Junoesque wife, and always wore his glasses in rehearsal, giving Wotan a scholarly look. (I remember Schorr's tale of being asked to dinner at the Otto Kahns'—the invitation was casual; it was just a dinner at their house on 94th Street and Fifth Avenue. Schorr knew of Kahn's importance but had never met him. He and his wife drove to the house on the corner of 94th Street and were announced to a small group of guests. His host was delighted to see him, and dinner was excellent. The Schorrs were urged to come again and left in a rosy glow. The great Otto Kahn practically embraced them.

Next morning Schorr had a call from the irate Mr. Kahn. Where had he been the evening before? Why had he not arrived for dinner at Kahn's home on East 94th Street? Schorr discovered he had dined by mistake with Andrew Carnegie (who remained a friend). But Kahn remained offended.

I continued to paint murals, went with my parents to all the many pleasant dinners I had previously only viewed from above stairs. Maestro Toscanini was always at the Muschenheims and there were several young Muschenheims, a young Nikisch, young Toscaninis, young Deliagres and young Willi Wymetal, so the generations merged. That was a glamorous winter when we all entertained Max Reinhardt, the Thimigs, the dancer Harold Kreutzberg, and the Reinhardt troupe. Mrs. Toscanini had a lapdog who sat protected under her *poitrine* during dinner and then would cross the table to go to the Maestro. Mrs. Muschenheim had Yamanaka in New York do her floral decorations, usually just one spray of strange chrysanthemums or one exotic branch of cherry blossoms. On one occasion the little dog (who had probably never set foot on an ordinary street pavement) stopped to sniff at the single flower while the dinner party held its breath. Dinners at the Muschenheims were prepared by the chefs of the Hotel Astor and were masterpieces.

In the midst of all these innocent pleasures, in the winter of

1929, I went on my first winter-sport trip with four large and heavy young men. We tobogganed at Egremont, and when the young men turned to skiing, the lightest one and I decided on one last run on the toboggan. Someone called "Don't go down light," which was Latin to me—and the result was eight months at the Polyclinic Hospital. Part of it was in a curious baroque structure and part of it was in an armpit-to-toe plaster cast on which my large circle of celebrated friends wasted their bon mots and their autographs. Neddy Ziegler and Suzie stopped as they walked home from the opera every day and had a special telephone wire run in for me so that I could talk after the switchboard closed.

William Muschenheim was laid up at the Hotel Astor and we arranged to have his male attendant and my nurse (whose name was Miss Love) wave towels at each other from our windows across New York. Willy and I were on the telephone reporting on what the signals meant and on our limited view of the backsides of our waving attendants. Food at the Polyclinic was far from Lucullan, and I was promptly taken off of it by Father who had Maison Glass send in a jar of caviar every other day. I ate it—with enthusiastic assistance from guests—spread with classical simplicity on hospital toast. The caterer Mazetti sent frozen oranges filled with orange sherbet; Constantine sent glazed waffles; Mother brought **Chicken Jeannette**, and Ethel Saltus came in one day and—with me helpless to defend myself—strewed me, the room, and the bed, with baskets of rose petals.

When the mild summer evenings came around, Jack Janeway and Harry Eldridge snatched a long wheeled stretcher from another floor, transferred me onto it, and taking a back elevator, wheeled me out of the hospital. They rushed me up Seventh Avenue to 57th Street and were so wildly stimulated by their success that they stood on the frame and we coasted down the incline to what was then Sixth Avenue, singing all the way. When we got back, Miss Love was in hysterics and the authorities were extremely stern.

When I presented problems of non-knitting, Father had me packed, rigid and horizontal, and gave me to the Red Cross, who shipped me via Baden-Baden to the Sanitarium Bühlerhöhe. Suzanne Ziegler the elder and Suzie Ziegler the younger came and read to me. Finally we moved down to the Villa Stéphanie, where the **Chicken Stéphanie** and Baden-Baden Peaches helped. Doktor Schacht, brother of financier Hjalmar Schacht, did the rest and I made plans to return to New York in late autumn and be married.

Clarence Whitehall was another friend who combined a voice with distinguished good looks—a great relief from some of the well-voiced but pudgy-faced German singers. He also spoke proper English and perfect German and behaved, on the whole, as I felt a gentleman and a baritone should. For years he used to say that he would sing at my wedding, and Jeritza, not to be outdone, said *she* would sing at my wedding. When the time came, calendars and engagement books were assembled, Father Rogers, who had been transferred to Massachusetts, was consulted, and when it had been narrowed down to two weeks—in mid-January—we took the Metropolitan Opera's schedule of performances and went down to the offices of St. Patrick's Cathedral.

It turned out that there was not a single day that didn't conflict with either another wedding at the cathedral or an opera at the Metropolitan, and we were forced, with the priest frowning, to select a day that was convenient for all except Maria, Clarence, and Artur. I do not remember the opera with which we clashed, but presumably it was Wagnerian, and the wedding was arranged in such a way that we would follow it with dinner at the house and the three Wagnerites would come from the performance, and two of them would sing while the third accompanied.

I remember that Mrs. Whitehill came in a festive evening dress, since—being a woman after my own heart—she always wore her latest acquisition. She came into Gatti's box one evening when Mrs. Ziegler was entertaining us there, in a magnificent bright-red skating costume trimmed with white fur. She said she knew it wasn't opera gear, but it was new, ergo she had to wear it.

As I was still on crutches, it was decided that there would be only about thirty guests at the wedding and dinner, and that there would be a large reception when we came back from Hot Springs, Virginia and Washington. I had a pinkish-ivory satin wedding dress from Bendel and—since I could not walk with a veil—a small toque of the same satin. A bride in a hat was so sensational that I came out in a commanding position in the next Sunday's rotogravure section of the *Times.* (Maria Jeritza wore a cloche—which would have delighted Father's heart—when she was married to Mr. Seery at the cathedral some sixteen years later.) Bendel made me a lovely pale-blue dress for the reception. Mr. Schling made me the largest bunch of violets ever seen, and for the wedding he gave me boughs of incredible white lilac.

Before we had wound through cocktails and caviar and Marie's most sensational dinner, there was the music—Clarence, Maria, and Artur. Maria sang a beautiful Czech folksong, perfect for a marriage, and knowing that wedding guests cannot wait to have the bride and groom depart, we left immediately after Clarence sang "Drink to Me Only with Thine Eyes" so beautifully that we were all in tears.

Sophie from Vienna, who had come back with me, became cook and maid on 79th Street, from where she walked up to Yorkville to do her German marketing. We continued to eat **Wiener Huhn** with **Risi Pisi, Trude Hudler's Kaiserschmarren** and *Heurigen Salat,* and Florence Steinway, Julia Janeway, and several other talented young women came for drawing lessons, since I was not yet walking well. After two years of unbroken New York, we went to Europe for a winter in Taormina, spring in the Château de la Galère at Théoule, and summer in Aix and later in Switzerland. We returned to live at the house, and I went on with costume designs and work for the Urban Associates. Memory here is stirred again by pictures and a hideous one of me with Laubenthal reminds me that *Elektra* opened in what was by then a depressed period for everyone.

We built a house (which Urban had just started to design) and the Urban Associates took over in New Milford, Connecticut. Maria Jeritza married director Winfield Sheehan and moved to Hollywood, and we gave the New York house away (it became a Greek church). In New Milford we had a couple, or rather a trio, Hans and Käte Hess and little Hans. They drove, mended, packed and unpacked, cleaned and cooked, butlered, and took care of the kennel. They gardened and marketed and made the menus and we ate Maltese Rice, *Ente* (duck) with sauerkraut, *Schweinebraten mit Brauner Kartoffeln*—Pork Roast with Brown Potatoes—and wonderful hams in various forms. The Hesses took over while I worked in New York and New Milford, and I had a recurrent nightmare that they would leave and I would be helpless. We trundled back and forth to Europe and they did not leave until 1943, when I was able to cope very well without them.

22

Food by Land and Sea:
America Discovered

THE ERA OF American history that made the least impression on me, although it affected Father most profoundly, was prohibition and repeal. I remember that all conversations were spiked with references to adventures in speakeasies (to which Father never descended) and everyone had a personal bootlegger. Cartier and Cross and Tiffany did a thriving business in silver flasks and cups and fitted cases for carrying about one's illegal or even home-brewed refreshments. The silver flasks were saped to conform to the body on the same principle as the Eames chair, and pockets were made correspondingly large. I now have a little cache of silver flasks that do me no good in the world; one of them even has an inlaid glass strip, which enabled Father to see how much precious brandy was left.

The only apparent effect on Father was that he prolonged his European trips and never went to American hotels or restaurants and he stopped going to some homes. I recently found a small envelope among his papers labeled "Recipes, Drinks." Inside there are recipes for eggnog and Ward 8 and **Kalte Ente,** and a second envelope, labeled "Prohibition Remedies," which contains a group of frightening notes. A typical recipe starts with 1 gallon of grain alcohol, 1 gallon of water, and 144 drops of flavor, and goes on to end with *Shake Well*. A note is written in longhand at the bottom: "You observe that I don't put my name on this—or my address! Or yours! Or the date—or any other incriminating data!" Another one is dated Tuesday, December 7, signed by Mrs. Paul Gallico (mother of the writer and wife of the musician), and calls for 1 cake "east" with sundry raisins.

After nine days suspended in cheesecloth, this brew was further enhanced by 1 quart grape juice (Welch's, no doubt). The formulas for beer called for a fish kettle. Most precious of all is the recipe for Carlsbader Becherbitter. The last recipe was written by Father's podiatrist on his card, which only goes to show the extremes to which prohibition led. It is a combination of gin mixture and various flavorings and a final dollop of glycerine. I remember that when we came back to New York after a year abroad in 1933 all our friends had their cars plastered with REPEAL stickers.

We continued the old circle to Italy on the Italian Line and home on the North German Lloyd, and following my parents' custom we took the car, although it was only a lowly Packard and later a series of Fords. The first station wagon was almost as sensational as the old Stevens Duryea had been. On the *Vulcania* we ate **Tagliatelle alla Genovese,** *Gnocchetti alla Napoletana,* and *Ossobuchi alla Milanese.* They had a lovely raspberry (my eternal weakness) dessert called *Bacconcini Capriccio* (a little fancy), which is best when it is made with Italian *amaretti.* Coming back on the North German Lloyd we had *Artichoken Maltaiser Art* (Maltese Artichokes) and **Kartoffelpuffer** (Potato Pancakes) with lingonberries and apple sauce, and while the great gastronomes remember the *ballottines* and the *galantines,* I always remember the Potato Puffer.

When we were in Europe we always added new places and restaurants, new dishes and new acquaintances, and we went back to our old loves—Brioni, the Dolomites, Rothenburg and the Hotel Eisenhut, Vienna and the Bristol, and the Danube. I remember when Father's distant cousin, the one who later died of the cure, came to lunch with us on the sunny terrace of the Schloss Hotel in Dürnstein, the *maître* had our long table placed on an extension of the terrace so that we had privacy and the phenomenal view of the Danube (it always flows in the opposite direction from the one I expect). Our kinsman was punctual and we went to the terrace to await our other guests. The *maître* took this to be a signal and waiters brought out the anise-flavored Wachauer Rolls (Butter Curls), and presently they placed the first course on the table—two enormous platters of **Serbian Asparagus,** which glistened in the sun. Herr Minister, cousin Friedrich, had been Chancellor Seipel's other right hand and had written the definitive work on financial equilibrium in postwar Europe, *Geld und Geld Entwertung,* and on top of that he loved asparagus.

He paced up and down the terrace, while we sat on the sunny parapet, telling us about the world of valutas and financial manipulations and absently helped himself to a spear of asparagus every time he passed the table. He interrupted his dissertation at each turn to say a word in praise of asparagus—excellent, outstanding, splendid, *hervorragend, vorzüglich, ausgezeichnet, vortrefflich,* and so on. When the other guests arrived there were a few weary stalks of asparagus on the platters and apparently no replacements in the kitchen, since the waiters appeared with an unsolicited platter of **Karfiole mit Dillsosse** (Cauliflower with Dill Sauce).

The only other thing about cousin Friedrich that I can remember is that he asked Chancellor Seipel to officiate at his wedding. Seipel agreed and stunned the bride and groom and guests by presiding in his full bishop's robes, something that his closest lay ministers did not know about him.

We often go to Schloss Hotel in Dürnstein and climb up to the ruin of the castle or, better still, let our guests climb up to the ruin where Hadmar held Richard the Lion-Hearted in a deep dungeon for Duke Leopold II of Austria. Richard miraculously heard—and answered—the voice of his minstrel Blondel, singing on the road hundreds of feet below and was ransomed for 150,000 marks, of which only the first installment was paid. German history maintains that Leopold delivered Richard to Emperor Henry VI and that he was held at fortress Trifels in Germany until he was ransomed; they go on to say that Richard's freeing by the singer Blondel "is for the legends."

All of it is nothing compared with Austria's second historic ransom, that of Baron Louis de Rothschild in 1939 which involved millions. The suave Baron Louis later married Countess Auersperg, and both became enthusiastic Vermonters at East Barnard near Dorothy Thompson and Maxim Kopf. I remember sitting next to him at dinner one evening in New York when he took the first and only piece of costume jewelry I have ever worn (a hideous affair of great baguettes and gray pearls) for the real thing; he bowed to the Baronne across the table and said, *"Ma chère,* I regret that I dissuaded you from wearing your important jewels this evening, they would have been perfectly proper as I now see."

Actually the great parties were over. At one time we had almost lived on the second floor of the St. Regis or on the Roof, where I loved Crab Meat Remick and still go back to eat their Ice-Cream

Macaroon Cake sitting in Egg Nog Sauce. Jeritza's parties were fabulous, especially when Mrs. Greenough and I both wore the same dress and sat on either side of Mr. de Casanova—with a difference of a good fifty pounds and thirty years between us. There were dinner parties all up and down Fifth Avenue in homes that are now embassies or have been taken down to make room for apartment houses. The Crystal Room at the Ritz and the Plaza's Ballroom were our second homes, and men like Paul at the Plaza's Persian Room were our friends. I remember sitting next to a vice president of the Guaranty Trust Company when Paul presented us with menus; he couldn't resist telling me that Maître Paul's account was more substantial than that of any of the guests in the room.

Every time we came back from Europe, New York seemed emptier. Gatti-Casazza retired from the Metropolitan, Maria Jeritza married director Winfield Sheehan and moved to Hollywood, where Lauritz and Kleinchen Melchior also spent much of their time. One winter we drove to Florida and drove back to New York because in those days we didn't think that the Westminster Kennel Club could possibly get on without us, and then drove back to Florida, eating all the way. They were my first trips farther south than Hot Springs and I enjoyed what Father would have considered death-dealing combinations—hot breads, fried foods, cold beverages, and warm spices— and I celebrated every possible occasion with pompano. There was Pompano en Papillote, Baked Pompano, and lovely Broiled Pompano with Limes. We found a little place where they made Green Corn Griddle Cakes, and I was perfectly happy. Whatever room I had left over for a second love was filled with shrimp. I had Shrimp Creole, Shrimp Jambalaya, and **Shrimp in Grapefruit.** (When I think about America now from our *Jagdhäusl* in Austria, I miss—immediately after my family and a few friends—shrimp. I long for Shrimp in a Melon, Broiled Shrimp and, more recently, Shrimp Seviche marinated in lime juice.)

I worked in New York, but we lived more and more in New Milford, where life became, very gradually, competitive. We went to each other's homes for dinner, and all unconsciously, with the best intentions in the world, tried to outdo each other. At the same time we showed dogs, which is basically only one elegant step removed from manslaughter. Even our children competed for something somewhere —the honor list or something called the 100-meter butterfly—and I worked in New York as a designer and mural painter, which meant one long competition. Our friends, with whom we had pushed clouds around the sky, all became remarkably accomplished and passed with us from a great lack of interest, not to say scorn, of all things to do with the table to a growing delight in eating well; they even started to talk about wines, and many of them had to take to their kitchens as servants departed for wartime factories.

Jane Grant and Bill Harris in Litchfield had their devoted Eckhardt, and with a combination of all their talents (including Bill's eye for a piece of beef) and their White Flour Farm's herbs and Tellicherry Pepper, were the latter-day Luculluses of Litchfield County. Bill's salad dressing and Jane's applesauce cake were accomplishments. Clint Barker's couple invented a Cold Tomato Soup, and Elliot Pratt grew Housatonic Valley wines and arranged wine tastings. We were all preoccupied with food, and after dinner we played games within games. Bea and Allan Grover shone at "No, I Am Not Nebuchadnezzar," and the Toni Miners were unbeatable on the theater. The Stokowskis played a game in which everyone had to say what they couldn't get along without, and when it was Stokowski's turn and we awaited the gratifying revelation that he could not get along without Evangeline, he said "Asparagus." Later Evangeline remarried, and one day some years later I had a telephone call from a woman with a deep and vaguely familiar voice who said, "This is the Princess Evangeline Zalstem-Zaleski." I had a friend at that time—Natalie Lewis—who was given to telephone greetings along the lines of "This is your cousin Anatol from Moravia speaking," or "Mata Hari here." Knowing that she liked her openings to be greeted as extremely witty, I laughed and said, "Natalie, you have outdone yourself," to which the voice repeated "*I am* the Princess . . ." and I said, "Natalie, come off it, no one in his right mind would be called Zalstem-Zaleski." When we were all straightened out I found I was forgiven because Evangeline thought I had taken her for Natalie Paley, who was another princess, and if she had to be confused with anyone, she naturally preferred another princess.

Actually, brilliant Evangeline and Alexis, who turned out to be real and Polish and delightful, were great fun and great food lovers, although we didn't see eye to eye about breakfast. We overlapped on a weekend at Doolittle Lake in Norfolk and we all hung our heads down over the side of the bed for twenty minutes because Evangeline swore that was what she did to make her hair so magnificent. We also drank boiling hot prune juice to start the day, because Evangeline said that was why she was so glowingly healthy and beautiful, but whatever else that did for the rest of the guests, it did not improve their hair or their complexions.

Evangeline's family was large and embraced all Stokowski's children, including Olga Samaroff's daughter by the Maestro, Evangeline's own two daughters, and Stokowski's later sons. She called us after a lapse of years, and asked whether Lans would come over to play with the Stokowski boys, who were visiting her. Time had stood still for Evangeline, who stays young, for Lans by that time was in college and Stokowski's younger children were probably five and six. Alexis somehow managed to train plain New England cooks into producing utterly superb Russian food. Apparently the New Milford weekends were so successful that many guests looked around for old farms in the neighborhood and settled in. Suzie Ziegler Gleaves built in Kent. The C. D. Jacksons went to Stockbridge. Sandy Calder, whose toy circus we had often watched when he was in college, came to Roxbury to invent his stabiles and mobiles.

We continued to go abroad and lead our double lives. On our last voyage to Europe before the war in 1939, I sat on the captain's desirable right hand for the first two dinners and then, with great bowing and scraping and hemming and hawing, was invited to shift to his less desirable left hand to change places with a rather domineering German woman. It was explained to me that she was older than I and was an industrialist—she owned an enormous plant which manufactured corsets. Some thought it was trucks, but no one wanted to say. She had given the captain to understand that she would sit on his right—*Da*. I was delighted to change, and thought of her when Maxim Kopf, then in Prague, told me the old story about the German manufacturer of baby carriages who sent his poor friend a baby carriage upon the birth of his first child. He met the friend on the street a few days later and was surprised to find him carrying his baby. When asked, the father explained that he had tried to assemble the baby carriage in every possible way, but no matter how hard he tried, it always turned out to be a machine gun.

We came back to New York, where I repainted my murals in the Plaza Hotel's Persian Room to conform with a new and lighter color scheme. The New York apartment was on 53rd Street, conveniently across from Voisin, halfway between the old Ritz and the St. Regis and the Café Chambord. Deprived of Europe, I began a slow discovery of America. The Bakers loved the Colony Restaurant, where I ate my first egg in a block of toasted bread, Eggs Encore (in cases), and the best oxtail soup since Holland. Mother found Giovanni and took me there for the **Clams in Aspic,** out of which I still make an entire luncheon whenever I am there. The onion soup at the Café Chambord, and the **Guinea Hens Radetzky** at the Mont d'Or were re-creations of Paris, and at Habsburg House there were murals by Bemelmans in the upstairs dining rooms, a zither player, and splendid *Wiener Schnitzel.*

We had come through our decade of weddings, and Frances Crawford had married Howard Houston in a Port Chester garden. It was a happy wedding, which we recelebrated in various places on many major anniversaries, culminating thirty years later when we were all invited to Kashmir to celebrate on a houseboat. There had also been a constant migration to Connecticut, Massachusetts, and Rhode Island, and seeing our friends and attending dog shows took us zigzagging from Washington to Maine with two sorties to Milwaukee and a growing familiarity with regional American cookery. In time it seemed wrong to feed a kennel of hungry dogs with meat when there were food shortages, so we divided them over households that could support one dog each. Because the last bitch with three nursing puppies was destined for Eve Jolly (Prudence Penny) in San Francisco, I combined a desire to see America, an invitation to judge a dog show, and the possibility of a job in Hollywood into what turned out to be a nightmare wartime trip to the Coast.

Never having traveled by train, I had once misread an advertisement for a roomette—I thought it was a luxurious stateroom in which the nursing bitch, with her puppies and crate, and fourteen pieces of luggage, a typewriter, and I would be perfectly comfortable. It turned out that I had to back out of the roomette to even let the berth down, and dogs were not allowed. I walked down miles of cars of soldiers carrying three large puppies while their dam spattered milk and every G.I. barked at the top of his lungs. The baggage car was occupied by trainmen who were terrified of dogs, and I had to go back down those endless barking aisles at intervals during the night.

In Chicago there were officers with priorities, and at the last instant I was shifted to a train across the platform from the one the dogs were on. I ran to an open door as the train started moving and threw a bag of canned dog food and canned milk, a can opener, and some money at a woman who was standing there and shouted, "Feed the dogs on that train!" pointing like mad. She was probably the world's most intelligent woman. She called one word to me—something like "Luncheteria." I appealed to various conductors, who asked me whether I didn't know there was a war on, and finally found one who agreed, for a small contribution to his children's education, to hold the train in Omaha until I had run down its length up to a bridge into the station, sent a telegram to Eve Jolly on Mr. Hearst's *Examiner* and run back. The telegram simply asked that all trains from Chicago be searched for dogs. Before I checked into my hotel in San Francisco I looked up the password "Luncheteria" in the telephone book and found it. I went over and located the woman of the platform. She was a waitress who had seen her soldier husband off as far as Chicago and had planned to sit up all the way back to San Francisco. The dogs had lent her a certain prestige on her train, and the money had enabled her to bribe herself a very comfortable berth. She was grateful and the dogs were well fed and happy when she turned them over to a Hearst agent at the station. Eve Jolly was imprudent with her pennies and fed me a superb **Pot Roast** on a blacked-out hill behind San Francisco. I judged the dog show and went on to Hollywood and Laguna Beach.

Having accumulated gas coupons, I was a popular guest, and drove the Swami Pavra Venandra, Christopher Heard, Christopher Isherwood, and a strange assortment of people on their errands. Stokowski was there and Aldous Huxley, and I planned to stay and work but had to come East to fetch the car. When I arrived in New York, Dick had been evacuated from North Africa, and because he spoke the Scandinavian languages, sent to Saint Bonaventure and later to Cornell to learn German. I became a camp follower and learned a large repertoire of dishes that could be prepared on a single burner. I even enrolled in Cornell's art department and had a lightning promotion (because the freshmen's roof leaked and the sophomores' radiators were broken) to a sort of junior-senior class. I remember having a letter from a nice girl, only a few years older than my daughter, that she was going to be my Big Sister. We sometimes ate meat, but more often hoarded our coupons until we could buy a steak, which we broiled on the shores of Lake Cayuga.

Dick was transferred to G-2 school at Camp Ritchie, and after a stay in Washington with Mary Salomé Knabenshue Jondreau, later Mary Frank, I retired to New Milford.

23

Kate-eh

*A*LMOST ALL GASTRONOMES who have arrived in the upper circles of the American food-writer's world can remember making their first soufflé or omelette when they were still very young. The childhood recollections of most famous food experts sound as though their mothers had run small hotels or boardinghouses, so prolific was the cuisine and so deeply did the boards groan. The precocious children of these ladies apparently had a finger in every one of their melting pies. I had none of these advantages and didn't bake my first soufflé until I was well into my thirties. It was probably no better than any five-year-old food authority's first effort, but I had the advantage of being old enough to start out with a **Soufflé Vesuve,** and I was old enough to eat it too.

As for a real Lemon Soufflé, show me the promising child who will take the trouble to grate the rind from a dozen lemons—and the skin from his knuckles—or will bother to beat the egg yolks and sugar until they are thick enough to slash with a knife. Soufflés came to me, like beets, with maturity, and they led me (thirty years behind the experts) into writing about food. It all happened when Edith Evans came to New Milford for a weekend when we were long on eggs and short on meat in 1945. I gave her a Mushroom and Onion Soufflé with a Spinach Salad on Friday evening and a Crabmeat Soufflé with Avocado Salad for Saturday lunch—the Bacon Dressing came after rationing was over. The Apricot Brandy Soufflé on Sunday put her in such a mellow mood that she offered me the job of doing the food pieces for her *Living for Young Homemakers* magazine, and I started, quite naturally, with a piece on soufflés.

My first really successful omelette has not yet been achieved. It is not because I do not have a beautiful broken-in French copper omelette pan, or because I have not tried, but because there is a terrible telepathy between my omelettes and my friends. I no sooner bring an omelette up to that crucial instant before the first fold than the telephone rings. It almost seems as though my friends start to think about me at the very moment I start to think about making an omelette, and the result is always the same. Even if I do not answer the telephone, the moment of concentration is interrupted, and no one wants to repeat an omelette or eat a cold one.

Marie had given me cooking lessons one afternoon each week as part of a correct Austrian upbringing, and I had taken automatically to every phase of cookery that depended on manual dexterity, color, design, and architecture. I was never able to draw a fine line between art and cookery, color and taste, or a palette knife and a spatula. My paint brush was interchangeable with the pastry brush. I took my drawing materials to the kitchen and used my very best sable brushes for glazing the cold salmon with aspic and the cheese sticks with egg yolk. I used the tools of architecture to draw the precise circles for the layers of *Dobos Torte*, the Spanish Wind Torte, and the **Vacherin**. I was just as tempted by a jar of strawberry jam as by a jar of carmine. Everything that I knew about cookery was exactly what I didn't need when the time came to cook. That was in 1944.

After our Bridget departed to be near her husband at an army camp, I was left alone in New Milford with Nana and young Lans. Nana cooked for Lans, but I had to cook for Nana although every now and then, in desperation, she made **Queen's Pudding** for me. Cooking for Scotch Nanas, as everyone knows, is a little like cooking for a cross between Adelle Davis and André Simon. I could draw out an apple strudel dough to the thinness of tracing paper—with my hat on. (Mrs. Montant still reminds me that I came to the *Gourmet* kitchens, in the Hotel Plaza Penthouse, to draw out a strudel for the picture in *Gourmet's Old Vienna Cookbook* and that I never took my hat off.) But Nana did not want to share wartime isolation in Connecticut with Lans and me and the Hotel Bristol's *Pêches Ninette* or a platter of *Amuse-Bouche* or, for that matter, a replication of the *Exposition d'Art Culinaire's* gold-medal-winning **Saumon Porte-Bonheur**; what she really wanted was just a good square meal. She didn't care whether I could lard beautiful designs or marinate with genius or whether I had a light hand with **Heidesand** (Heath Sand); all she cared about was basic proper nourishment presented with a flourish. It was only due to her great fondness for Lans that she put up with me and my cookery.

When the combination of my cooking and rationing became too much for her, we went again in search for a cook. This time Nana unearthed a treasure called Christl, a retired German cook who had worked at Schrafft's for many years. While we had all gone through our sundaes-at-Schrafft's periods, we had outgrown them long ago, and being faced with triple-decker toasted tomato sandwiches at noon each day, creamed anything for dinner, and an enormous Extra-Hot-Fudge-Special-Ice-Cream-Cake on Sundays was—even for Nana—an astonishing epicurean experience. It completely extracted any latent sweet teeth in the family. Lans rarely eats sweets to this day, although I still go to Schrafft's for a butterscotch sundae with toasted almonds whenever I am tired and sorry for myself. We didn't have a serving platter that was wide enough for the ice-cream cake and deep enough to hold the ice cream and whipped cream that melted under the hot fudge, and there was always a disastrous dark-brown deluge before dinner was over.

The war came to an end, Dick came out of uniform, and Mother put her heart into parcels that went off to our scattered friends and relatives in Europe each week. We kept on sending them until Father's cousin in Vienna wrote that she would rather have *Vogue* than food—after all, one *had* to know what to wear. At the same time a Bavarian friend ordered shoes in assorted German sizes, bicycle tires in assorted German sizes, and a specified number of dekagrams of raisins, currants, candied peel, almonds, vanilla, baking powder, sugar, and glacéed cherries. All of it was to be used for herself, her children, and her wedding cake at her impending marriage to their father. Mother, having assumed that they had been married twenty years earlier, was disenchanted.

John Easton, who was still at our embassy in London, went to the Continent and Karlovy-Vary (Carlsbad) with messages and vitamin pills for Tante Therese and the shadowy Kate-eh to distribute among our friends and relations. In 1948, by strange postwar processes, the Sudeten Germans (including my family) in Czechoslovakia were repatriated to Bavaria. They left with only the clothes on their backs, and settled into rural German homes which had neither food to feed them nor any wish to have them. Kate-eh, who had been Grandmother's and Tante Therese's maid, was in an educational and age bracket that assigned her to field work, to which she had to walk several kilometers each day. Mother and Tante Therese decided it would be best to bring her to America.

After the decision was made, there was a period of waiting which I filled with dreams of everything we would eat after Kate-eh arrived. Visions of *Kaiserschmarren, Backhendl,* and **Gugelhupf** danced in my head, and at the end I even postponed a visit from the Otto Teegens so that they would be there to taste the first *Schinkenfleckerl* and *Spritz Krapfen.* I had read about Herman Smith's beloved Stina, about Rumer Godden's refreshing Mrs. Manders and her love of parties and guests. Most of all, I visualized Kate-eh as Phineas Beck's enchanting *Clementine in the Kitchen*—Austrian instead of Burgundian, but nonetheless cheerful and rosy-cheeked. I reread *Katish, Our Russian Cook* and rounded out my dreams of the impending Kate-eh with *Blini.*

I remember that when Kate-eh had her permit we wrote to ask whether she wanted to sail or fly and she answered, "Either," which seemed to me to promise well for her adaptability and enterprise, since she had rarely been in a car (and continued to be car-sick for years), let alone a plane. She came on a ship and Mother met her in New York. After a few days she put her on a train and we met at New Milford, where we took up our lives together, through upheavals and storms, sunshine and serenities, for the next fourteen years.

Curiously, though I had visited Grandmother in Carlsbad, I had always missed Kate-eh. She was either on vacation or with her parents. Her name was a household word, but no one had ever described her to me or told me exactly what she did. I had no picture of her but that didn't really matter, since I had such a clear picture of her Clementine-Stina-Mrs. Manders-Katish composite charms and took it for granted she would cook as well as they. We had eaten the good Irish cookery of Bridget and Christ-cum-Schrafft, and I longed for the Austrian specialties we had missed for ten years. On the day before Kate-eh's arrival, I bought a beautiful piece of boiling beef, a horse-radish root, mushrooms, and all the makings of a *Wiener Tafelspitze Fein Garniert,* and lots of butter and sugar.

I had expected a large woman; my first surprise was that she came barely to my shoulder. She had on a flat black peasant hat with a straightforward elastic band that secured it under her reddish bun. She looked exactly like a peasant on her way to church on Sunday, and later New York purchases never changed that look. I made friendly conversation on the station platform and then worked around to the things she was going to cook. It turned out that she had never been a cook, since that task fell to her only after there was little food to cook and no cooking processes other than boiling. She dealt me the first of two great gastronomic blows when she told me they had not had enough fat to fry a potato, least of all a chicken, in the last few years. Before that, she had always been the chambermaid. In short, she couldn't cook.

Actually Kate-eh took to cooking (though not to guests) as naturally as breathing. She had a peasant's instincts for food and developed a great talent, particularly for cooking game. Even the transition to an electric stove was painless, and within a short time she learned all that was necessary. She was a natural cook with a feeling for baking. Her short strong hands were just the right temperature for kneading smooth doughs, and she could cream butter, in a bowl on her knees creamier than I have ever seen it done. She made everything grow: The house plants hit the ceiling, the garden flourished, and the dogs had their day.

She was a small smooth fox terrier of a woman, who worried our heels, stood guard over us, sulked, flew into rages, and loved us as we loved her. She developed a sort of retired-nanny hold over us which must inevitably develop in someone who mended and darned our clothes, kept all the buttons and hooks on, knew where everything was in the house, remembered where I'd put the recipe for Shad Roe with Scrambled Eggs and always had a plate of fine baking waiting for us when we came home.

She exposed us to her nerves, her depressions, her moods, and angers, but she was loyal, unassuming, honest, untiring, and devoted. When she first came we sent her to New York each week for her English lessons. She became an American citizen and treasured a small American flag in her room. To compensate for the long periods when we were away and she was alone with the dogs, we sent her to Europe to see her family or to Lake Minnewaska for her summer vacations.

She resisted and always reported the job offers she received from strangers or from our acquaintances, ostensibly friends. These rained in upon her especially when we were away and ladies were doing their own chores while they thought enviously of Kate-eh's idle hands. There is very little honor among friends where cooks are concerned, and I remember being particularly annoyed by an offer she received from Chicago from the son of a Carlsbader who suggested that Kate-eh come to them, where she would be "a member of the family" instead of a servant (there were three small children and a baby in the family and a working mother). She supposedly told a Washington friend of ours who surrounded her with blandishments that she was being paid to rest and she had to fulfill her obligations—so she rested, gardened, mended, cleaned, and out-watchdogged the dogs.

Mrs. Manders, Stina, Clementine, and Katish were so busy making their kitchens smell divinely of baking bread, herbs, and preserves that they never seemed to concern themselves with their biographer's guests. Not so with Kate-eh; her loyalty to us was unswerving, but she turned a critical eye on many of our acquaintances. She accepted news of impending guests with such a marked lack of enthusiasm that she was soon released from making personal appearances at the table. We engaged some of New Milford's waitresses or I would do it myself, waiting until a slight tremor of the pantry door gave me the signal that the next course was ready. Nothing was ever said about our friends, but I heard later that terribly discreet letters had gone to Tante Therese, foreboding a bad end for Mr. D. or the worst for Mrs. X. She never spelled out their names.

When we had single guests, Kate-eh invariably suspected romance. When they were married, she either suspected that they were not or that they soon would no longer be. She loved some of them but took a dim view of anyone who came with children or pets or had a loud voice. I only heard some of this recently, and while I deplore such concerns, in view of later developments, she seems to have been right in most of her dire predictions. Young girls, who might conceivably have an early eye on Lans, made her bristle, but she liked Debbie Pierpont; she retired only after she was sure she was no longer needed to discourage undesirables.

Kate-eh's *Topfen Palatschinken* (German pancakes) and *Hasenpfeffer* were unsurpassed. She cooked a lovely *Rot Kraut in Rot Wein* (Red Cabbage in Red Wine) forever, and I still miss her **Apricot Turnovers** and the *Spritz Gebäck* we absorbed by the thousands. After fourteen years in America during which we took her as far as Arizona and Maine and during which she persisted in slicing onions up and down and sharpening our knives on the stone step in front of the kitchen door, Kate-eh retired to live with her sister in a small town on the Main in Germany. We went to visit her there, where she dealt me my second gastronomical blow. We turned off the Autobahn near Würzburg and headed, with a growing sense of anticipation, toward Miltenberg, where the Ruppert sisters lived. It was the middle of the day and we had breakfasted lightly in order not to spoil the lunch which swam before our hopeful eyes. We wondered about what Kate-eh would cook for us: Dick was sure of game, but if worst came to worst he knew she would make him his favorite peasant bacon—*Bauern Speck*—with beautiful widespread fried eggs. I leaned toward **Paprikahuhn** and apples in their dressing gowns, which she knew I loved. We were in a frenzy of expectation, and when a man directed us to the *Amerikanerin*, we found the sisters as happy and excited as we were.

They lived in the second story of a very nice old stone house facing the river Main. There was a bedroom with an oil painting and a kitchen-sitting room with divine, unidentifiable smells coming out of the oven. It was quite obvious that there had been great preparations. We stood, first in the hall, then in the bedroom, and later in the kitchen. Kate-eh was far too excited to ask us to sit down and she apparently forgot that she had a wonderful meal cooking in the oven for us. We were taken back and forth upstairs and downstairs to see everything. It was an extremely happy reunion for all of us, and we talked and talked while the fire in the stove died down and the good smells faded away. We were headed toward Bremen and our sailing, so we had to leave—on empty stomachs. We never knew what was in the oven, and I don't suppose the sisters realized they had not fed us, let alone let us sit down, until after their excitement died down. The first thing our friends in New Milford asked us when we came home, was to describe in detail exactly what Kate-eh had cooked for us.

With the retirement of Kate-eh came a series of unenlightened cleaning women and nice waitresses and the development of a style of cookery which would enable us to entertain our friends even though I was an isolated-dish cook and couldn't make the various dinner dishes come out at one and the same time. To this day I am only able to cook those dishes which require time and effort. I love to bake or produce meals that take three days to prepare. I want the time to make stocks and sauces, pâtés and pastries, *pains* and unlikely potatoes, and I want to cut flowers out of vegetables for the last garnishments.

But I cannot do such simple things as roast a bird in such a way that I can lift it out of its pan to make the gravy there, and have it timed to coincide with the completion of vegetables at their greenest perfection. I cannot whisk hot breads out of the oven with one hand while I produce crisply fried potatoes with the other and (*Gott Behüte*) a hot beverage and hot plates too. So now I have learned to fudge and I make menus that enthrall our guests, who never know that the whole thing is an evasion. They never know that they are being served a meal which has been sitting in a whole battery of double boilers or in my favorite utensil, the *bain-marie*. I make only independent sauces that have nothing whatever to do with the fat (and those brown particles) that are left in the pan.

Vegetables are always disguised and potatoes turn into a *Mont Dore*, or princess, or *Vésuve*. Eggplant becomes **Aubergines Irma,** and green peas turn into **Purée de Pois Verts** under a bonnet of browned onions and croutons. As cooking became a necessity and our work took all our waking hours, we shipped back crates of utensils from all our trips and more and more helpful major and minor appliances were added at home. I found that the heavy reinforced Austrian Riesswerk pots helped where I didn't have the time to stir, and Flammfest dishes took half the hazard out of recipes for baked delicacies. And dessert worries were saved with a combination of Austrian bombe molds, with blowholes on the top, and a large efficient American freezer. I learned to make *Appareil de Bombe* and filled the top shelf of the freezer with every imaginable combination of ice creams, with biscuit centers. All I had to do was fetch the mold, invert it on a doily, unscrew the little brass valve and blow into it (our guests never knew), and the bombe slid out with smooth and unflawed perfection.

We enjoyed the unserviced years, and while I too was tempted to write a book about our beloved cook Kate-eh, the hardships of cooking (at least part of the time) were mitigated by the pleasures of a life unblemished by the sniffs and sighs we always heard when we told Kate-eh there would be guests for dinner.

My Quadruple Life

*D*OUBLE LIVES ARE, they say, hard to maintain, but quadruple lives are impossible. I had been the child of two countries and grew into a fractured adult with a piece of my heart in four places. I had children, a profession, two homes, possessions, friends, and all the ice cream I wanted in America—but there were relatives—somewhat Baroque—more friends, waltzes, and a strong feeling for Viennese pastry in Austria. Grandmamma's home, still painted a Maria Theresa yellow, was in Czechoslovakia, and I had a close in-law relationship with Scandinavia and its food. In those days, before we took to the air and learned to alight directly at our destinations, we had additional transitory favorites, and I don't think I could have loved Vienna half so much, had we not gone via Italy, France, or Germany (stopping off in England) on our way.

My life became one long greener pasture, and wherever I was not, that was where I wanted to be. Nothing could be completely enjoyed because it always evoked other charms. The most delectable crisp shrimp salad in New York only served to remind me of red crayfish in the Tyrol or a pyramid of pink shrimp laced with dill on the Oslo fjord. Vienna's tenderest *Lungenbraten* (filet) was nothing compared with an American steak, but rice in New York couldn't hold a candle to a *risotto* in Milan. I couldn't enjoy chicken anywhere for thinking of *Paprika Huhn* (to gypsy music) along the Danube; on the other hand, there wasn't a baker on the Continent who knew what a muffin was, let alone a corn muffin with lime marmalade. Father always said of me, when I spent long periods looking into space, *Sie ist wo anders*—She is somewhere else. Actually I was always well away on the next trip to Europe or to America or deep into the next menu.

Blood was beginning to out and everything I had ever deplored in Father started to stir in me. Father had spent part of the First World War pacing about and muttering over the certain neglect and possible devastation of the vineyards of Europe. He longed for his aimful meanderings from restaurant to restaurant and worried over the fate of favorite chefs who had probably become army cooks. Later I thought of all this as having been in the worst possible taste, but I spent the Second World War conjecturing and dreaming in much the same way. I longed for the first blue trout and first nostalgic whiff of baking bread and roasting coffee that hangs over Vienna in the early morning. I wanted more than anything to wake up at the Hotel Bristol under a modernized feather bed, with a view of the horsemen on the Oper roof and Kaiser rolls on the breakfast tray.

But when the war finally ended and Dick came out of uniform to look extremely odd in a Wetzel suit, we turned our backs on all our dreamings and drove to Arizona (for health), paving the way with an assortment of doubtful tunafish-salad sandwiches and mediocre cube steaks. We reached rock bottom low with a bottle of non-vintage New York State champagne in a mop bucket, complete with mop wringer, while the mop stood in a corner and a huge propeller fan revolved slowly on the ceiling. It was on New Year's Eve in Shreveport, Louisiana, and I don't think our faithful companion Kate-eh spoke again until we were back in New Milford. I would, as usual, rather have been *wo anders*.

On our last evening before Arizona we ate good steaks in Texas, complicated by having to sit astride Western saddles along a sort of chic counter arrangement in an atmosphere of Spanish mission fathers. In Tucson my careful *gastronomische Erziehung* (gastronomic training) had not prepared me for prairie oysters (Father would have gone into shock), and I turned into the tenderest tenderfoot ever to reach Arizona. Easterners were bad enough, but a New Yorker with Austrian overtones, a diamond here and there, and a non-sporting dog (a boxer) was beyond the pale. One morning we ran into the largest, sleekest, and most magnificent mountain lion, who treated us exactly as the Arizonans did—with disdain. He slowly and deliberately crossed our path looking through us while he made a lovely

woosh with his tail. I was sorry when we reported him, since everyone laughed uproariously and told us about large hares, small deer,
pet cats, stray golden retrievers, and, especially, about optical illusions
and mirages—which gave him time to do considerable and concrete
damage before the Arizonans stopped laughing at us long enough to
track him down.

It was a winter of feeling pale-faced and ignorant, but there
were compensations.

For instance, Jo and Richard Reeve on the Bellota Ranch. We
arrived on the day they brought in the mighty elk that Richard had
just shot and we stayed to eat it right up to and including the last
(faintly, faintly high) scraps, ground into chuckwagon elkburgers, in
the late spring. From first to last it was superb, and considering that
the elk was Rocky Mountain and José, the cook, was Filipino, it seems
remarkable that he turned it into a series of delectable roasts, ragouts,
and salamis. But for eating our way through that almost endless elk
and **Maybelle's Western-Way Salad,** which the Reeves served before
the movie on every Sunday evening (it was usually *The Lives of a
Bengal Lancer*), food in Tucson was barely average.

We rented the small stone homestead on the Tanque Verde
Ranch. Sardonyx, the boxer, learned to stay out of the cactus, and
Kate-eh's silence became ever deeper—she didn't even clear her throat
disapprovingly. Mrs. Seth Thomas, Jo's mother, lived opposite the
Arizona Inn, just as though she were still at Redgate in Morristown,
and she continued her delightful teas just as though her guests had
not been dressed in various stages of pioneering and cowpunching.
She served *Sables Normand,* warm **Miniature Fritters,** and Turkish
bread, and she too had an Austrian cook who spoke occasionally in
purest Viennese.

In Europe we had been accustomed to restaurants wherever there
was an *Aussichts Punkt* (a place with a view) and they became better
as the panorama widened and the view became more magnificent.
But when we drove up through beautiful Rock Creek Canyon, there
was nothing whatever to eat. We visited Daphne and Carl Brown in
Sedona and ate cottage cheese with canned pineapple salad on the
brink of the stupendous Grand Canyon, thinking about restaurants
the Europeans would build if only they had a canyon like that. I
didn't take personal offense, as Father used to do, when food was less
than Escoffier-ish but I would have preferred something worthier than

a jellied dessert. We returned to Tucson and Kate-eh's long face.

Dick made a trip East and brought me back a horseradish root, the sort of thoughtful gift I appreciate. We planned an Austro/Arizonian farewell dinner around it, to which we invited all our old and new friends. Unaccustomed as we were to high altitudes and desert ways, we served our guests martinis, a red wine, and champagne. The Homestead kitchen was not up to anything more complicated than a *boiled dinner*, so Kate-eh made a bright-green *Kalte Spinat Suppe* (Cold Spinach Soup), laced with sherry; *Rindfleisch mit Kren* (Boiled Beef with Horseradish Sauce); and *Aprikosen Pudding*, simply saturated in apricot brandy. After dinner there were completely superfluous and totally inappropriate stingers, only because Dick came across a bottle of white mint. There is little to say about that well-intentioned little boiled dinner party. In no time at all the doors were taken off the hinges and flung down the mountain. One of the cars hung with its front wheels out over space and several of the guests had managed to get into a clump of cholla cactus with disastrous results. Kiefer Meyer and Jim Converse fought water duels that doused down the entire house, and Roy Chapman Andrews, indoctrinated in the wilds of Borneo, advised an icy calm when the shooting began and the party really got into its stride. Jo and Richard had invited us to come back and make our life on one of the outlying ranches on the Bellota, but now they made a proviso—we were never again to give a small Austrian dinner party. But there was work to do in New York and a job to return to.

Those were my designing years. I had moved from murals, stage settings, and costumes into designing everything from clothes to stained-glass windows and fountain pens. For a time I had worked for an industrial designer who exuded charm—with a flower in his lapel—in a lavish conference room signing contracts while I, who had never so much as heard of a "residential" organ, designed a whole line of them. Whatever came along I streamlined it or teardropped it, from candy boxes to better-looking floor tiles, and deeper carpets, to diverting dish towels. My employer was carried away by what he called my *Versatilität* while I worried about the clients, who paid large fees, not knowing that they were putting their products into the hands of a woman in the back room—who was always thinking about food.

I left to do sachets for Mary Chess and Elizabeth Arden, murals, steamship interiors, and textiles. By the time I had done an atrocious Mexican fabric that was called something like "Dipsy Doodle," which went into the highest known yardage, I met myself wherever I turned. I had been the gray mouse, the child who never opened her mouth and the woman who never stayed to sign her name or reap the harvest. I was still shy and retiring and suddenly I found myself with what Father would have called "the modesty of a bedbug" in almost every home in America. So we went back to Europe with recovered health and zest for the first trip after the war.

Mother had gone to spend a year, to gather and assist our relations who, along with three million other Sudeten Germans, had been transferred, in cattle cars, to Bavaria under the Potsdam Agreement. They were indigenous Austrians who had been turned into Czechs, then after ten years under Nazi occupation, they were shifted to Bavaria, where they belonged like the proverbial Austrian *Faust aufs Auge*—fist in the eye.

As always, the ultimate destination was going to be Vienna and, as always, we went via someplace, usually Norway, to get there. We landed in Oslo and after waiting a week for a lost Citroen, eating *Smörrebröd* and *Fiskeboller* the while, drove through magnificent country and memorable *Silde Salats* and *Faare Frikassée* to the fjords. It was late October, and coming south we raced the snow across the tundra straight to the Hotel d'Angleterre, and *Crêpes au Chocolate* in Copenhagen. We spent a sleepless night in Flensburg, and several years later had a letter from the hotel, whose bookkeeping ground slowly but thoroughly, stating that we owed them for two breakfast rolls and would we remit 80 Pfennig *Postwendend*—by return mail— which we did, in dimes.

In Munich, where we picked up Mother, we found Herr Walter-spiel, a little chubbier at his Vier Jahreszeiten. He still spoke of all his rich and filling dishes as *klein* (little) with such loving tenderness that I was invariably carried away into overordering tiny *Hummer Salat* (Lobster Salad), which he made with melon, small Chicken Cutlets Pojarski, and a bagatelle of an *Orangen Soufflé*. The Barons Panz and the Greek royal family went in and out and in spite of all the little things I had eaten for lunch, I always went down to tea in the lounge to eat plain biscuit slabs and listen to long-forgotten *Thée-Konzert Musik*, such as "The Indian Love Call" and "*L'Amour, Toujours L'Amour.*"

After years of visiting Tante Therese and cousins and the more distant relatives in Austria, I found they were all in their new milieu in Bavaria. While they didn't belong as thoroughly as they had in the part of Bohemia that was named for them, they were mercifully transplanted into the midst of Bavaria's most resplendent Baroque area. That year we made the first visit—repeated over twenty years—to a combination of Tante Therese in Garmisch-Partenkirchen, the Reindl Grill, the Wies Kirche, **Côtelettes de Veau en Papillote, Souffle Camargo,** and *Kaiserschmarren,* the Emperor Franz Joseph's and our favorite omelette, all torn up into sugary rags and pieces.

We went to stay at the Benediktenhof in Ettal to awaken opposite Zuccalli's curved and rotundaed Benedictine Abbey, highlighted with the first snow. We discovered the pink rococo parish church in Rottenbuch, overflowing with fat stucco putti and gold convolutions, and we found (which isn't easy even now) Ludwig's secret Schloss Linderhof hidden in the Graswangtal. It was the smallest of his castles and consequently the only one completed in his lifetime. He lived there often and for long unpeopled periods, facing its splashing water garden and sitting alone at the famous table that came up, fully set, through the floor. We went to unbelievable Neuschwanstein, more for the almond **Sevastopol Schnitten** at the café than the Wagnerian castle, and to Oberammergau.

Not from any sentimental *Recherche du Temps Perdu,* but more from a feeling of "Could it possibly have been true?" I went back to Schloss Ellmau under the Wetterstein Wall, where I had gone in 1922 with Professor Wimmer of the Wiener Werkstätte to visit the pianist Elly Ney and her husband, the Dutch conductor Willem van Hoogstraten. It was a long trip then. Professor Wimmer came from Munich, picked me up in Partenkirchen and we went via several changes on benighted railroads to Mittenwald and then by rickety taxi to Ellmau. When we arrived (I remember we were very hungry), Mme. Ney could not be disturbed—she was haying—Herr van Hoogstraten was cavorting about with the handmaidens and his children, and Herr Johannes Müller, the cultural philosopher, founder of the movement, was thinking beautifully in the shade. We had to walk down to a distant *Molkerei* (dairy) for a bread-and-milk lunch. Late in the afternoon the starry-eyed participators (barefoot and brown) in Johannes Müller's dream were able to give us a few minutes, but their minds were not on the prosaic outside world. They were preparing for the evening meetings, a forerunner of group therapy, at which profound problems were brought into the open, and souls were bared, culturally and philosophically. A friend in Vienna told me she had attended a meeting at which the leader asked for guidance, his followers asked for guidance, and finally one woman asked: *"Gott gebe das ich meinen Anschluss in München treffe"* (May God grant that I make my train connection in Munich).

Schloss Ellmau was there, beautiful and serene. It is still served by intrepid handmaidens, and with the passing of Herr Müller, is now ably administered by his daughter. It no longer tries to reconcile the traveler's hotel with the philosopher's retreat, but it has retained a sunny disposition and an inclination toward group dancing.

In Vienna we couldn't stay at our beloved Hotel Bristol, which was still partly army-occupied, and the floors were being renovated one by one as the military released them. We saw my cousins and school friends the von Demels, and then went to the Cobenzl (which was no longer there) and to a *Heurigen* in Grinzing. Dick asked for the *"Annenpolka,"* and the three musicians, incredibly, regretted that they didn't have the music. But the *Backhendl* was wonderful and there were little glimmers of Vienna as it used to be.

Considering the daily news we had read of Europe during the war years, it never occurred to me that there had been time for progress. But the Americans had been there, and with them had come self-service (the smallest shop had to snarl itself up with at least two marketing carts and a checkout counter) and the ice-cream cone had come to stay. The roads were full of vehicles, and the Europeans who had walked or wagoned or bicycled were now riding in three-wheeled bubbles or in the bug-like forerunners of the compact cars. We had planned on Norway and Vienna, but the urge to revisit favorite spots was so great that we turned south to Venice, where we were baffled by the new currency and mistakenly bought a speedboat instead of hiring it. We saw, we remembered, and we ate. After having dreamt about the most elaborate concoctions, I invariably ordered the simplest —*gnocchi, pesto,* or *fidelini.*

In Rome there was no longer a Hotel de Russie, but in Paris the Bristol was still there on the Faubourg St. Honoré and they gave Lans a little speech about fourth-generation guests before we returned to New York. Europe was back in our blood, and the following spring when we asked ourselves Father's old question, "Where shall we go this year?" the answer was still the same—Vienna, via England, France, Italy, Spain, or Scandinavia.

In New York I continued designing and did a spread for *Liberty* magazine each month that led to *Living for Young Homemakers*, where I finally shifted from the surroundings and decoration of our lives to food. On each European trip we extended our researches to places we had loved and memories of those earlier trips with Father and Gostike Kotti.

On Lago di Como all was well, the Grand Hotel Villa d'Este at Cernobbio was more beautiful, and the food, which was always special, was even more so. At Bellagio the Grand Hotel Villa Serbelloni was still all that Father had ever asked of it in its overstuffed royal way. I followed in Father's footsteps and rejoiced in each place that had not only lived up to his standards but had the fortitude to survive. At Abano his 1913 notes indicated that he had found the mud (*fango*) baths as efficacious as he found the Hotel Orologio's food delicious—it now had a red castle classification in Michelin. And Abano has had the wits to stay just as it was, with the usual improvements in plumbing and technicalities. At Montecatini—even in Italy Father's way was paved with good cures so that he could sin gastronomically all the more in between—he underlined the Grand' Albergo della Pace and forty years later we found it changed to Grand Hotel e la Pace but it was still an *albergo di gran lusso*.

We crossed on the *America* and *United States*, the *Leonardo* and *Kungsholm*, the *Bergensfjord*, and late one March we crossed on the *Berlin* from Bremerhaven. Sailings were fewer and further between and the S.S. *Berlin* was the only ship not off on a frivolous cruise. On our first crossing there were thirteen other passengers and Kapitän Heinz Vollmers; on the second crossing there were fewer, but Obersteward Reiner never relaxed. We sat at the captain's table (I had now reached an age and Germany had reached an industrial sophistication where nothing would have induced me to cede my place on the captain's right hand). At the captain's dinner the dining room was set with a single table and Captain Vollmers behaved exactly as though he had several hundred first-class passengers on board. We had Beluga-Malossol-Kaviar with vodka, Pheasant Consommé, *Hummer Ragout* with *Johannesberger Untere Holle*, and an ice. Captain Vollmers, no mean gastronome, had always loved the refreshing sherbet interruption and introduced a small glass of something that tasted like frozen champagne before we ate **Grenadins von Kalb**—veal—with Beaujolais and *Kirschen Jubilée* with *Henkell Trocken*. It ended, I remember, with *Schwarzwalder Himbeergeist* (Raspberry Spirit), the only thing made of raspberries that I can resist. The captain was not one to break with traditions, so he and I led a *Marsch Polonaise* into the ballroom with four couples following us, brought up by two bachelor gentlemen, and Dick and the ship's pastor in the rear.

When we came back to New York I clipped my traveling wings down to one trip a year for four years and went to work for the architectural firm of Shreve, Lamb & Harmon Associates and condemned myself to five hours' commuting a day in order to put in an eight-hour working day in New York. On my first homeward trip I ran into Willis Conner and asked him what in the world I should do with the more than twenty hours of each week I was going to spend on a train. His answer was, "Write a book, of course."

I had written occasionally through the thirties on how to train dogs, and there had been *Liberty*, *Living*, and other magazines; I had put in a part of each summer at a hotel or restaurant training school, and a book on food seemed preferable to a book on dogs, and much as I love dogs, food was in my blood. My double life between design and travel became a quadruple life and I wrote my first cookbook.

In the middle fifties New England was no longer the wilderness that Father had found it, with *"Nichts zu essen,"* and still less to drink. We had friends there and others moved in. Daphne and Carl Brown came back to Winstead from Sedona, and Pete Street was still in Norfolk; the Houstons came back from India to Meriden and Quisset, and a whole new group of young people took to their kitchens as though they descended from generations of *haute cuisine*. We might travel as far as the Hotel Eisenhut in Rothenburg and the Auberge du Père Bise in Talloires for game, to Pappagallo in Bologna for Rembrandt-Brown Chocolate Ice Cream and the Stadt Krug in Vienna for *Salzburger Nockerl*, but in America most of our friends had either turned into cooks *malgré-eux* or they had learned enough to train their cooks. In Camden the McLaughlins' cook, who had never been out of Maine, produced *Crème D'oseille* (Sorrel Soup) and a *Soufflé de Pruneaux* worthy of France. At the Houstons in Quisset we ate orange biscuits and lemon bread and had our first superb corned beef. In New Milford (still in competition and pleasant rivalry with Roxbury and Washington) we all set standards that meant planning, preparations, marketing in distant places, and menus that were a swingback to all my memories. We sent for utensils, imported fondants and farfetched ingredients, and re-created dinners as Father liked them. Old New Milforders said that life had been strictly Roast Turkey and Mince Pie until we all came there—and now look at us.

25

The Near East, the Far East,
and All Around the World

*A*FTER THAT FIRST commuter-train-written, weekend-tested cookbook, someone took my life into his hands and sent a piece of it up to *Gourmet* magazine. The then editor asked me to come to talk about doing a piece for them. I had read (and saved) the magazine from the first issue and had even carried *Gourmet's* cookbooks all the way to Arizona and back. It did me little good, as it turned out, with the Homestead's two-burner oil stove, but it provided splendid reading. *Gourmet's* Hotel Plaza penthouse address had always sounded unattainable to me, a little like getting to heaven, which I did with the help of two elevators. They proposed a series of pieces on Vienna and suddenly brought me face to face with my past and what was to become my future.

All Father's foibles, his frequent preachings on *was sich bei Tisch gehört*—what is proper at the table—suddenly stood me in good stead. I remembered how he had pounded the vintages into me, drop by drop, like making mayonnaise. I remembered his admonitions and dissertations on wine, his dinner catechisms (which usually ended in tears), and his assumption that if *he* wanted Sauce Alexandra on his Hearts of Palm, so did his small children. I had grown up thinking that when I was old enough I would eat broiled lamb chops and hashed brown potatoes forever and never again let an overdone *Gigot d'Agneau à la Bayonnaise* come between me and my family. But I was glad—in retrospect—that I had been forced to eat *Salade Demideuil* (Potato Salad in Half-Mourning) with thin slices of black truffles,

170

when my tastes ran to the sort of potato salads I saw in the school cafeteria.

I met once and was deeply impressed by Mr. Earle MacAusland and entered into that most enviable of all occupations, the ability to work for someone and toward something that was dedicated to good living with absolute integrity. All this was on one hand; on the other hand and at the same time, I was working for Shreve, Lamb & Harmon Associates as their color consultant and interior designer. It was probably the least well-assorted combination of work in the world, but for me it was a perfect balance. I coordinated colors and materials all day and settled executives into their suites, in what was then New York's least gourmet district. We had a lamentable sandwich shop across the street, a crowded Brass Rail around the corner, and the Epicurean delights of a clattering cafeteria in the building.

After eight hours a day in the warehouses, executive suites, and decorator's buildings, I came home to write about *Mousse de Jambon* with a *Salade Royale,* and for all I know, *Bananes à la Niçoise.* On weekends we ate the tests, and on Mondays I came back to doing yet another office in green. My work at S. L. & H. entailed exciting, in tensely creative short periods when colors and materials were selected; clients (who were going to occupy the offices or premises) were consulted; and work was organized. After that it often deteriorated into long months of dreary prodding and pushing and battling. Hours were spent on the telephone, inspections were made, and I learned to do battle for every deadline. When offices were finally occupied, people sat at their desks, pupils moved into schools, and doors were opened for business. I often thought it would be easier to weave the carpets, paint the walls, and hang the fixtures myself than it was to get others to do it.

After a time I could have taken anyone up the length of Manhattan—not that I would expose anyone to such a journey—from Broad Street to Columbia, and from Princeton to Groton, and pointed out the hundreds of jobs I had fought over. But even on this side of my life, there were lighter moments; the executive who wanted a carpet that matched his secretary's blue eyes, and sat by, perfectly seriously, while I held wool samples up to (but not into) her eyes; the executive whose offices were arranged with every safety device and possible precaution against air raid, fire, theft, lightning, or a stray airplane, but who gave his top-secret plans to a toy manufacturer.

The color sense of my clients was phenomenal: Some said I could do their offices in any color so long as it was green, and others asked the bootblack to help with the final choice. I worked for men who could make lightning decisions involving (I like to think) millions, who were where they were because they had the ability to think clearly and evaluate precisely, but they couldn't make up their minds about their draperies, let alone the upholstery of their executive chairs. I have often thought about the years of study with Professor Hoffman in Vienna, the Academy, the League, the careful training, the long experience with Joseph Urban, the research and the preparation— plus the high fees paid to S. L. & H. for an hour of my time—and then some of my executives would call in whomever was passing in the corridor for his opinion and advice, and make their decision accordingly.

There were executives who didn't really care how their offices were decorated, just so long as they were bigger and deeper (and had one more window) than the one across the hall. Others weren't happy until they had taken the presentation home for a week so that I could arrange their offices according to the tastes of their families always well represented by photographs on the desk.

My non-gastronomic days continued in what Father would have called the *Gott verlassene* (God-forsaken) wilderness between Sixth and Vanderbilt avenues on 44th Street. The Algonquin was there, but so was everyone else from the whole area. There were a few luncheon clubs, but any lunch based on filling a number on an order slip comes off with a bad start. So I went lunchless through the years and concentrated on real or written delicacies for dinner.

The clients were usually more approachable and human in direct ratio to their positions. The chairmen of the board were much easier to deal with than those who wanted to be. Curiously the two clients who were proud of their humble beginnings had the unerring taste and understanding that we always think results from generations of training—General Sarnoff and that PR genius and art collector Ben Sonnenberg.

There were a few murals to paint, fabrics and carpets to design, and some assignments for residences and churches, but most of the work was for office buildings, banks, plants, schools, and public buildings. The president of one college did not permit a color he didn't care for even in any of the dormitories he would never enter.

In the meantime work went on for *Gourmet*, and the pieces were made into *Gourmet's Old Vienna Cookbook: A Viennese Memoir*. In the summer I took cookery courses. Dick and I established first one, then two, and finally four European trips a year. We followed the same pattern, crossing by ship to Italy in November, with other trips fitting into the work schedule. Every time I saw Mr. Bernhard, the boss, at the office he asked, "When are you going to Europe again?" But they kept me on at Shreve Lamb & Harmon Associates for fifteen years in spite of longer and longer absences and two slow trips around the world. Although my work was for RCA, U.S. Rubber, Western Electric, Columbia, the Irving Trust Company, the First National City Bank, and other prestigious firms in New York, my heart had remained, so to speak, in the kitchen and on the move. And then Jane Montant, the gifted editor of *Gourmet*, called with that most musical of all questions, "How would you like to do a travel piece for us?" That sentence made all the pieces fall into place—it opened both an old and a new perspective on travel with gourmet interests that had not been fully enjoyed since the days when we had traveled so much with Father.

There were changes. Now we flew, instead of boarding those dignified ocean liners, and there were times when we went to lengths which Father would have frowned upon. There was an evening when we ate a full dinner at the Restaurant Vier Jahreszeiten in Munich (we had planned on a *Vorspeise,* but Herr Klaus Walterspiel had inherited his father's persuasive charms for all the tiny little specialties and we ended with liqueured raspberries hiding a heart of ice cream and buried under crushed Italian *amaretti*—macaroons). We then went on to eat a second dinner at Restaurant Humplmayr, which ended in **Ananas Helena** with **Bavarian Cream** and then, since it seemed the only way to stay alive, we walked poor Mrs. Montant back to the hotel. It was probably a good mile, although she says we described it as just around the corner.

There were beautiful meals, wonderful discoveries, markets before dawn, and always—at the other end of the work—the same man who spared no effort to make his magazine beautiful, with unerring taste and integrity. I may have been envied for the banks and executive offices, the law firms and the brokerage houses that came my way at Shreve Lamb & Harmon, but I consider myself really fortunate now, because I am doing exactly what I love to do for people who are doing the same.

I remember hearing a clear American voice behind me saying, "So this is how it's done," at the moment when I was tactfully trying to get a baker in Taormina to let us see his delightful marzipan fruit and not his marzipan Moon Landing group—a horror. The voice turned out to be an ardent subscriber of *Gourmet* magazine who never dreamt she would see an article in the making.

Whenever we were back in Connecticut and New York, Dick painted and I worked. Weekends were a concentration of friends, entertaining, and as the years went by, doing more and more of it ourselves. The great transition from employing the cook to being married to the cook took place all around us.

Into the midst of our partially servantless life, Maria Jeritza came back to New York to live at the Plaza with Liesl, her companion. As it turned out she began to sing again. She came to dinner with Dorothy Thompson and Maxim Kopf, Jane Grant and Bill Harris, making three gifted women who retained their maiden names for their careers, although only Jane Grant was a Lucy Stoner.

A little later Jeritza came to New Milford for the weekend, a delightful echo of the past. She turned up alone in a glorious creation by Adrian of Hollywood—dark brown with inlaid purple under the arms, a highly dramatized jockey's cap, flapping galoshes, and a leather coat made by Grünbaum in Vienna twenty years before which had all the protective properties of a small, well-insulated tepee. Liesl, her companion, was told to follow by train. A whole drama ensued, worthy of our prima donna guest.

In New Milford it turned out that Maria was an energetic house guest. She could only sleep behind locked doors; when she heard we had no keys to the bedroom doors, she said we must push the bureau across the door and then leave by the window; we explained that the windows were barred by immovable screens, whereupon she said *she* would push the bureau across the door after we left; then she discovered there was no movable loose furniture, so she finally barred herself in with a spare tire, a mound of Britannicas, and my lignum-vitae head by Isamu Noguchi. On the next day we witnessed the meeting of Jeritza, back in her traveling ensemble, and Valentina, who was dressed as a young Robin Hood; both behaved exactly like fighting cocks taking each other's measure. During the entire visit we were hanging on telephones and meeting trains in all kinds of places until we finally located Liesl at the station in Milford, Connecticut, where she had gone by mistake, instead of coming to New Milford. Dick drove over to pick her up in the middle of the night.

There was a Saturday dinner party for Maria for which we had made every effort, and Maria expressed herself as enchanted with the guests, but what she really wanted was *Ein Gulyas.* So all the guests were later invited by her to dinner at our apartment in New York for Liesl's special *Echtes Gulyas.* Jeritza also invited Emmerich (Countess Maritza) Kalman and an assortment of Hungarian *gulyas* eaters. Liesl sent a marketing list with the most alarming amounts of onions and cooked a lovely peasant-kitchen *gulyas*, suitable for a winter's night on the Hungarian *puszta*, which we ate, however, in uncomfortable evening clothes on the hottest night of the summer.

Shortly after that, Maria met her present husband, William Seery, and early the following spring, we were invited to their wedding at St. Patrick's Cathedral, followed by a reception on the St. Regis Roof. Maria had always filled every house and she filled every inch of the cathedral. I had never expected to see cathedral wedding guests stand on the pews, but they did, to see Maria in pink, and beautiful as ever, walk down the length of the center aisle to the high altar. Later, at the St. Regis, the bride and groom stood in a bower of flowers, and Met singers Martinelli and De Luca were handsome added attractions.

Some time later Mr. Seery engaged the Newark Opera House for a performance with the settings, costumes, orchestra, and artists of the Metropolitan, including Raoul Jobin. Maria appeared there again as Floria Tosca to send the same cold shivers down our now slightly aging backs. We went with a party and sat in the second row. All those who had not seen her waited for the *"Vissi d'arte,"* which those of us who knew had said would be sung from the floor and in a partly raised position, supported by her arms, to allow for necessary breathing. But this time she sang it flat on the floor, face down. Her voice came ventriloquially from under her armpit and we all held our breaths in fear of the expected cough from the dust that had to be there. Thanks to Mr. Seery, Maria and all of us enjoyed a memory come back to life. We had lost Jeritza (and Farrar and others) too early, but this evening brought back the last Golden Age of the Met.

Hanging on to and maintaining the golden age of travel and dining was still possible. The annual November crossing on the Italian Line took us to Naples or Genoa (with *Pesto* at the Hotel Columbia Excelsior), and Christmas shopping in Milan with Savini's **Filet Mignon Rosemary** and Restaurant Gourmet's **Risotto con Scampi,** followed by a beeline for Kitzbühel, where Lans met us for skiing and great comforts at Johann Harisch's Goldene Grief or at his restored medieval Schloss Munichau. From there, in the manner of homing pigeons, we went on to the Hotel Bristol in Vienna and to the ministrations of Chef Portier Franz Smirmaul.

Next to home, I am happier in the satin-paneled Bristol in Vienna than anywhere else, and there are moments when I might even reverse this preference. From the warm greetings when we arrive to the last bow when we depart (which I have heard favorably compared to that given to minor royalty) it is a hotel of the old school. Father always said, "The way you shout into the woods is the way they echo," which I apply to hotels. Admittedly, hotels reflect the nature of their guests, and the Bristol isn't half as nice when it isn't appreciated. If the floor waiter cannot bring you your breakfast and the elevator man cannot tell you about the weather and his tooth, if Chef Portier Franz Smirmaul cannot struggle to get you the last two seats at the Oper, then all is not well. In this respect we live up to the Bristol: Franz Smirmaul leads our life for us, squeezes us into the Spanish Riding School, arranges, coordinates, banks, and says, *"Dafür sind wir da"* (That's why we are here) when we ask for the impossible.

One evening we went out to the Poldi Kurz Heurigen in Grinzing, where we had recaptured a little of Vienna on our first trip after the war, and found it unchanged. We had spoken of it so often, with suitable nostalgia, that we were undeniably disappointed when their memory of us did not appear to be as vivid as our memory of them. Soon the three musicians played *Fiakerlieder* at the request of guests and finally came around to our table. The violinist sat down opposite us and the guitarist and accordionist stood behind him. The violinist said, *"Eine kleine Uberaschung"* (a small surprise), and they played Dick's request of years before—the *"Annenpolka"*—for us. I decided then that it could only happen in Austria and that we would one day have to live in a land where memories were long and music was lovely.

They say that as we grow older we are happiest with friends who share our memories, and the same can be said for hotels. The Bristol and I share our memories from my childhood, through the period when the then Prince of Wales looked startled when people sat down in the elevator in his presence. I remember it when whole floors were occupied by the Maharaja of Kapurthala, his entourage and his prayer rooms, and all other guests were relegated to half a floor. I once received a sensationally embossed, engraved, and unexplained invitation to one of the Maharaja Jagatjit-Singh's receptions at the palace in Kapurthala, and can only attribute it to some kindly soul at the Bristol.

It now turns out that our retired friend in Lunz, Herr Julius Eckle, was *Küchen* Chef at the Bristol during those years and created the menus I ate with such pleasure. Both being collectors, we recently compared old menu cards, and found we had kept the cards for the dinner that followed the world première of *Die Agyptische Helena*, by Richard Strauss, on June 11, 1927 (I did the costumes for the later Metropolitan production), and for his dinners for the American ambassador Albert Washburn and luncheons for Mrs. Washburn. It seems there was suitable Rhubarb Pie, but I only remember agonizing shyness. We shared our memories of his **Selle d'Agneau Richelieu** and **Fraises Sarah Bernhardt** and the lovely salads *Lorette* and *Trianon*. In March 1927 the Bristol's Beethoven centenary dinner ended with *Le Parfait Moonlight Sonata*, the name being expressed with the two opening measures, so that only musicians knew what the connection was. The Bristol has not changed; it is as it always was, and I now believe with Father that all hotels echo their guests. If you call the Bristol properly, the echo answers clearly—*luxus*.

In 1964 after our son Lans and Debbie were married, we began to lay plans and pull strings to fulfill an old wish—a box at the Vienna Opera Ball and eight good friends to share it with us. The fact that we and six of the friends lived in America, while two lived in Hamburg and the ball was in Vienna, did not deter us. We have always been blessed with venturesome and mobile friends and they accepted for a 1965 weekend at the Bristol in Vienna and the ball. Fran and Sam Houston came early and we picked them up in Munich to retrace our annual steps and meals at the Benediktenhof in Ettal, the then fabulous Postkutsche in Kitzbühel, the Goldene Hirsch in Salzburg and Vienna. In Vienna we did a dry run, eating at the Bristol, Franziskanerkeller, Stadt Krug, Schloss Laudon, and Poldi Kurz's

Heurigen, with Schloss Auersperg for birdsong and Demel's for Demel's own sake. Jo and Earl Tasman came in from Italy, where they had debarked; Esther and Edward Jonas flew in from New York; and Hanni and Pui Koch called from Arosa to say that Pui, who, with the Vienna Opera Ball ahead, had kept off skis, had broken her ankle doing the Charleston at home. Since Dick would not accept a refusal and a ballgown had been made, she was put into plaster and a maneuverable chair, and came, cast and all.

We had engaged the two rooms on either side of the green-satin-lined corner salon and three more rooms running down the Oper side, and the Bristol was so carried away with the whole project that they decked the rooms with even more than the usual fruit, flowers, and mineral water, and Sam sent corsages and more flowers (a thoughtfulness we reciprocated four years later—disastrously). Our first dinner was *Rehrücken* at the Stadt Krug, with dancing at Palais Auersperg later. The second dinner, before the ball (Franz Smirmaul had made five afternoon hair appointments for us months in advance) was **Filet Mignon Opera** at the Bristol and the most invigorating *Gulyas Suppe* after the ball was over. The next evening we went to Mozart's *Entführung aus dem Serail*, so that everyone could see how the Oper really looked, and late dinner was *Crêpes Mancelle* at the Franziskaner Keller. We lunched on Blue Trout and *Salzburger Nockerl* at Schloss Laudon and went to Demel's in the afternoon. For our last evening we had engaged the ancient cellar and cells (for recalcitrant nuns) below Poldi Kurz's Heurigen in Grinzing. We all sat at a great table under an arm of the ancient wine press, while the few gentle snowflakes we had welcomed on the drive out gathered into a formidable snow and ice storm which immobilized all cars, taxis, and other means of transportation. We danced, we ate Viennese Fried Chicken with our fingers. We drank Heurigen wine with all the pleasant effects for which it is famous while the Three Grinzingers played *Wiener Lieder* and the "*Annenpolka*." It was the perfect end of a perfect weekend, but when we came up out of the cellar there was only a cold, bleak, empty Heurigen restaurant and no transportation. The ladies each took a long hard bench and waited while the ever-intrepid Sam and Edward and Dick went out into the night to find a way to get back to Vienna. Earl and Hannie did the same, but they only went next door, where they warmed themselves with a bottle of *Himbeergeist* (raspberry soul), the deadly sister of *fram-*

boise. The gentlemen found two owners of VW's who, for a fee, ferried seven of the guests back to the Bristol, while Sam and Dick and I, in the spirit of the captain and his ship, waited to be picked up later. When Heurigen owner Poldi Kurz came home in tails and white gloves from a hunt dinner, he skidded us back to Vienna and we fell into our beds quite unaware that our guests were having champagne nightcaps—just before breakfast was due.

Next morning the Houstons, Tasmans, and we left in two cars with a rendezvous planned at the Goldene Hirsch in Salzburg and gave explicit orders for luncheon to anyone who got there first. We met at a halfway station, and Earl Tasman changed his order from **Pheasant in Sauerkraut** to a large portion of mashed potatoes. We completely forgot to show our friends Vienna, but they were mollified when the *National Geographic* magazine came out with its piece on the Vienna Opera Ball and there we were, tiny but distinguishable, in the first box on the Chancellor's right.

In 1966 we flew to Japan, where we met the Houstons, and under their magic guidance came around the world. Sam had been minister to India for six years, where he is now stationed again, and both of them have a deep understanding and love for the East. It was one of those trips that can happen to a fortunate traveler but rarely do— a convergence of events and beauties, unpredictable phenomena, and rare occurrences.

As we came down in Tokyo the moon was rising and the sun was setting and Fujiyama stood, clear and unhazed, against an apricot sky. It was the moment when every chrysanthemum in Japan, unexpectedly pleached and cultured into ordered forms, came into simultaneous bloom. Everything was intentional, and the food was an extension of the entire habitude—it was impossible to draw a line between its exquisite presentation and its taste.

I remember our first **Tempura** dinner, which consisted of one perfect shrimp on a long green leaf, clear soup, delicately flavored by a single pine needle, and a thimbleful of grated radish salad to refresh the palate. Afterward we saw diners fresh from the Tempura restaurant eating what I am sure they considered a "square meal" in the Miyako Hotel's Grill Room.

We had parted from food made to be eaten with forks and knives on the plane and come into a world of new foods, new tastes, utensils, implements, and attitudes. In Korea the food was too highly spiced and garlicky for my taste, but our visit coincided with that of the Berlin Opera Company's season and the most spellbound (often two to a seat) audiences I have ever seen. Food fluctuated as we moved south and west: It became milder or more ornate, hotter or blander and sweeter.

At the Grand Hotel in Taipei I finally understood why Chinese cookery is rated with (and sometimes ahead of) French cuisine. In Hong Kong touches of the United Kingdom were interwoven with Chinese food, and in Macao we might just as well have been in a suburb of Lisbon. We flew to Cambodia, where Thanksgiving dinner opposite the Angkor Wat was designed to follow French traditions and yet please the American palate. They called it *Dindonneau à l'Américaine* and it was undoubtedly some large dry bird. Dick, the determined optimist, went on to the dessert, vanilla ice cream with hot fudge sauce, and what they gave him was white and dark brown but had no other resemblance to America's favorite sundae.

Thailand was a dream of strange fruits and flowers, some carved beautifully out of vegetables, and a milder cookery with the fruit and fish and rice combinations I love. We had arrived in time for each feast and festival, and in Bangkok, on the full moon of the twelfth month, we launched our little *Krah-tongs*, little leaf boats filled with flowers and a light, on the Chao Phraya, the night of hundreds of thousands of floating flickering lights. On the flight to Katmandu we passed Everest and Annapurna, ice clear and overwhelming, a view which had been hidden by clouds on all the Houstons' previous trips. The surprisingly comfortable hotel gave us a different delectable soup each day: *Potage Cressonière, Crème Normande, Velouté, Dieppoise, Purée à la Flamande,* and *Consommé Lillienne.* The chef must have had a book from which the names were composed, for actually it was the same broth each day and the flowery sounding main courses were always the same stew.

In India, especially in the homes, curries were hot and we learned to eat them with the right hand. I loved the fabulous breads, Mulligatawny, and all the cauliflowers and eggplants, but I took to cold sliced chicken when the curries began to burn. Which left me pleasantly hungry in Teheran, Isfahan, and Shiraz, where we lived very simply on caviar, and I interrupted whole meals of pistachio nuts, melons, caviar, and yogurt only long enough to have dutiful tastes of lamb, rice, sturgeon, and pigeon and to see the most beautiful of all the ancient cities, Persepolis. Seeing the world and tasting its foods serve one purpose—we know what to look forward to when we go back.

As we travel we come to fall in love with things (mostly food) which we associate with certain places, and when we return we repeat a meal or occasion and we revisit our memories. I could never go to New Delhi without seeing the white tigers, any more than I could go to Lübeck without eating a meal at the Schabbelhaus, or to St. Gallen without repeating the cold shivers that the cathedral there always gives me.

My returns are complicated because the memories cover two generations. I go back not only to eat my favorite dishes but I go back to Father's haunts and *Leibspeisen* (body dishes), which is the German way of saying favorites. There are a great many that still exist but the long travel preparations and anticipations are gone.

I remember that in my father's day, before we sailed, Mike and two assistants carried enormous innovation trunks and hatboxes to our rooms which stood open in the corner, and which over a period of several weeks we filled with riding boots and inflatable traveling pillows, a light and a heavy plaid throw, and (in my trunk at least) one drawer was devoted to packages of Life Savers. Mother always took her green motoring parasol, which could, with great pinching of fingers, be turned from an open horizontal to a closed vertical position. I almost forgot to remember that Mother always put in the shoe trunk her Gold Staub, gold-dusted evening shoes, high-laced and embroidered with bronze beads.

Once when Father admired the Matterhorn from a train to Zermatt a man who stood next to him asked if he would like to climb it. Father and Mother, she still in her Gold Staub evening shoes inside a pair of borrowed mountaineering boots, climbed the Matterhorn with three guides from the Zermatt side by way of the Matterhornhütte— believe it or not. We were left with Fraülein in Zermatt, and Father sometimes said without enthusiasm, "Do you remember when your Mother climbed the Matterhorn in Gold Staub *Schuhe?*" What he never knew was that the aftermath is one of my earliest memories: Father and Mother bandaged to their eyes in separate darkened rooms in the Zermatt Hospital, where Fraulein took us to visit them. Father always said the *Aussicht* (view) was magnificent, and Mother always said that Father ate a bitter chocolate bar on the *Gipfel* (summit), which was more than he ever allowed us to do.

In these later years, whenever we returned to New Milford we began to follow a second prescribed pattern of things to eat and memories to relive. It would have been impossible to travel so much without coming to rest in Roxbury now and then on the Vestals' terrace with one of their wonderful arrays of hors d'oeuvres, or basking in Lil and Harry Skirm's warm hospitality—and the best Baby Lamb Chops in the world. We began to develop as many beloved places and meals in America as we had in Europe. On my last trip I filled a year's lobster deficiency in one evening in Essex, Connecticut, at our son's home there.

Lunz-am-See

DURING THOSE LUNCHLESS footsore years, I once stopped for a cup of tea in one of the drugstores that cater to all aspects of life —including literature and sports—and boast a tiny prescription department as large as a telephone booth in the rear. I sat wedged between a counter and a revolving wire bookrack with a book staring me in the face which was especially aimed at people who were born between June 22nd and July 23rd—people called Moon Children, or Cancerians. Naturally, as my birthday fell on July 5th, I bought it and discovered that I was sympathetic, full of insight, loyal, sincere, hospitable, and kind, and that I remembered everything. It went on to say that my understanding of others was phenomenal (not always including bosses, clients, or food experts, alas) and that I should use green in my home, my dress, and my house plants. It ended with the revelation that Cancerians could never under any circumstances throw anything away.

It struck me immediately that if more prospective parents would procreate in late September and October, there would be more nice, quiet, amenable children in the world and nothing would ever be discarded. Mankind would settle down to a peaceful clutter of possessions and a happy and harmless preoccupation with cookery. No one would ever waste time with activities that could possibly interrupt the amiable pleasures of the table. I read on and found—at last—that I could attribute to the stars above a houseful of green plants and the accumulations of a lifetime spent in avidly throwing nothing away. New Milford was not only full of everything that had ever come into my life (and not gone out of it again), but it was full of everything that had been part of Father's and Mother's and even Grandmamma's lives.

I discovered myself—over an indifferent teabag cup of tea—as an arch-Cancerian, a true Moon Child, not just a casual hoarder of string and old Mason jars but a serious and dedicated non-thrower-away. It was no wonder, considering the stars, that I still had a Scheherazade-like dress designed by Léon Bakst, a Baumé sugar scale, some clingingly snake-like negligées by Mariano Fortuny, a curved fish mold into which Marie had once glued black truffle scales with liquid aspic, a box of devastating feather boas and a slinky, long-trained Gallenga gown, vintage 1926, from the Via Tornabuoni in Florence. I also had vintage opera programs, Princeton prom programs, and so many letters that even a Cancerian memory could not always remember who they were from, even though they were signed "With love."

I toyed with the idea of buying additional books for Leo and Gemini, but I knew what I would find: that I am surrounded by people who are star-fated to throw everything away instantly. I suddenly realized that a giant step had to be taken, that disposal was essential before departure and that *the time had come*; I turned over a new leaf in my life and dropped the *Astrological Guide* along with my year's handbag squirreling (precious paper clips, unidentified keys, cartridges for a deceased fountain pen, a jar of poster green, some SAS air-baggage labels, a dried leaf of the flower of immortality, mints, matches, and ten aluminum groschen) into the nearest trash basket. I stripped myself down to an unencumbered mobile change purse, three chestnuts, a pencil sharpener, and my passport.

I think the decision to live near Vienna had probably been made long ago when I went to art school there: No one could love the Oper, Baroque art, and the blooming chestnut trees, the Bristol, Demel's, Austrian food, Austrians, the country *Gasthäuser* (inns) and Dürnstein as much as I did without having to end up there. The only thing I had not taken into account was what I would be capable of accumulating over the thirty-odd years between. The balance was tipped that day, from living in Connecticut and New York and going abroad several times a year to living abroad and coming to America twice a year. We had our toehold in Austria; why not set up a *pied-à-terre* and live where Father always said *"Sie wissen wo Gott wohnt"*—They know where God lives. (He probably meant Gambrinus or Bacchus.)

We had barely taken the first step when in 1966 a cousin I had never met called on us in Vienna at the moment we heard we had lost an apartment we wanted. He comforted us in the spirit of sour grapes, maintaining we hadn't really wanted it at all when we could buy a whole house in Lunz for the same money. We said, just as everyone says to us now, "You mean Linz?" But it was a quiet different place called Lunz-am-See—on the lake—a very small town in Lower Austria about eighty miles from Vienna, and now our home.

Cousin Hans apparently looked around, and a few months later he sent three little transparencies to New Milford: one of a very small house in a clearing with a blooming fruit tree and a fat white hen; one of a very narrow lane with a large post carrying one wire (evidently it had electricity of sorts); and one with a view of a snow-clad mountain (which we can see by taking a short walk from the house). It was the hen that decided me and the mountain that decided Dick, so we sent a deposit, not knowing that no such thing as a sight-unseen purchase existed in Austria. The upright woodsman who owned the place refused to sell until we had inspected it.

The years 1967 and 1968 were full of decorating and traveling, doing pieces for *Gourmet* magazine, painting, and writing books, so we rented the little house in Lunz for two years, and when we finally had time to see it, it was buried so deep in snow that I had to drop out at the nearest neighbor's because there was still a mile of waist-high snow to get through. Dick, the mayor of Lunz, and Cousin Hans made it to the buried house, and when they came back Dick said, "It's ours." I never saw it until it had been ours for half a year.

Lunz, it turned out, had a Biological Institute to which cousin Hans's father had been called long ago, an Apiary Institute which Hans heads, a very good bakery, and an unusual double-transepted Gothic-Baroque steepled church. For the rest it devotes itself enthusiastically, tirelessly, and to the exclusion of everything else—including the completion of our house—to hunting. When the season is open the local cabinetmaker, the electrician, the mason, and the plasterer go into the mountains, and but for the uncanny bellow of an occasional stag, everything at our *Jagdhäusel* (little hunting house) comes to a standstill. It has stood still now for several years, and when we went to neighboring Gresten, where the paperhanger is more interested in a faith-healing and divining-rodding sideline than in hunting, our Lunzer friends were deeply wounded. We now have paper in one of the mini guest rooms, and they who hunted while they should have papered have their antlered trophies. When the season closes, the Lunzer artisans converge on Grubmayer's, where they stand each other *ein grosses Dunkles*, or *ein grosses Helles*—a large dark or a large light beer—and beetling at each other over the foam on their steins they recall the hunt, and when that palls they electrify themselves with the mad, mad *Amerikaner* who have put in an unbelievable *vier Klos* (four toilets).

But back in 1969 when Lunz was ours but still unoccupiable, nothing seemed to dovetail at any point. The center of gravity had changed but I had a last bank and a last insurance company in New York to finish decorating, and hunting was even more entrancing for the Lunzers, since it could be done (we strongly suspected) on our time. It was finally decided that New Milford would be emptied (by me) and rented, and I would work in New York while Dick went to Lunz to vie with the hunting instincts of the workers, to have a road built, and to turn the cow stable into a master bedroom.

Dick flew off with our Baroque Madonna on the seat beside him, and I stayed behind to finish my various jobs. On weekends I worked at the Great Disposal, beginning by offering my American treasures to various charitable organizations who accepted winter clothes (albeit they were by Poiret), only in October, summer clothes only in April, and no high-heeled evening slippers—from Perugia or otherwise. They were not interested in foreign-language theater programs, and the very man whom I had paid up to five dollars for a single back issue of a magazine offered me one dollar for a whole year's issues, packed and labeled and delivered to the Bronx.

I finally engaged a nice man with a large truck and disposed of my treasures—load after load—over weekends for four long months. I think now of those nameless people who sit at the receiving end of what is placed (I won't say dumped) into the large metal containers marked "Goodwill Industries" that stand on Connecticut corners. There they were, getting along perfectly well on old egg-beaters and broken watches and old clothes when suddenly they were confronted with a slightly rusted *batterie de cuisine* (the paraphernalia of cookery), from graduated larding needles to truffle cutters, and everything with which to create an epicurean dinner for thirty-six. I can just see them tut-tutting over dariole molds, a picture of Margarethe Matzenauer as Ortrud, and dozens of oblong fluted pans in which Marie had made her little *Barquettes Regina.* They cannot possibly have known why they were swamped with small wooden half-rounds on which they could—provided they first soaked them in water—make perfect meringue shells, or lots and lots of rather dry long white kid gloves. I imagined them leafing through old opera librettos, tossing seductive pink feather boas around their necks, and staggering around on shoes that only Perugia could have designed.

In Lunz Dick started to rebuild the house and put in the road, and besides the working crews who all "slept in," an incredible number of people climbed up the mountain from the village to stand silently outside the windows looking in at him. They did this even when he was bathing in the primitive stone bathtub (now full of geraniums). When he couldn't stand being watched he went outside to say *"Grüss Gott,"* and they invariably explained that they just happened to be passing by—a lame excuse, since there is nowhere beyond to pass on to.

His daily letters reminded me of diplomatic security measures, since he invented obviously false and absurd names for everyone—*Etzletzbichler, Plankenbichler, Wildschnick,* and *Schweighofer.* One day it occurred to me that they would soon be raising the roof tree and Dick wouldn't know that a sort of party was expected of him. Actually Dick knew exactly what was needed. The workmen had long since given him a rundown on just how many cases of beer and how many rolls and how much *Gulyas* they would eat, but on the day when they were going to raise the tree they took out the kitchen floor and left Dick isolated on one plank in front of the ancient wood stove. Word had apparently gotten about, and men turned up whom Dick had never so much as seen near the job, and the first ten kilos of beef and seven kilos of onions (Dick did not give in to Lunz's traditional equal-parts-of-beef-and-onions) were not going to be enough. He rushed to town and bought as much again and rushed down a second time to get four more kilos of thick **Lunzer Gulyas** from the local *Gasthaus.* As it was, Dick himself got only a ladle of sauce, and when I came to Lunz I found we owned a hotel-sized dark-brown enameled *Topf* (pot), in which we put the burlap-balled Christmas tree.

My part in this party was entirely by proxy, and my letter to remind Dick about the essential lemon peel in the *Gulyas* came too late; by that time he had been pronounced the *Gulyas König von*

Lunz (for his *Gulyas* with caraway seeds and rosemary, but without lemon peel), and the roof, which had actually been there ever since 1746, was considered *up*. When I came to Lunz on one of my later trips, I met Herr Etzletzbichler and Herr Plankenbichler, and Garnweidner, also Toritzbacher, Eichwalder, Eppensteiner, Latschbacher, Gallhuber, Leichtfried, and Tallhammer (a sort of Austrian Big Chief Long Feather type of name common in Lower Austria).

The little hunting house in Lunz was still in the orange-crate stage when I went there for the first time, two days before our first guests, Dot and Spence Miller, were scheduled to arrive. We had all been invited to celebrate Fran and Sam Houston's thirtieth wedding anniversary on a string of houseboats in Kashmir. The Millers, who were coming from Connecticut, planned to break the long flight to Srinagar by stopping at Lunz-am-See. We had beds, four rickety and extremely straight chairs, presumably left from the first resident, four plates, two forks, and two knives (used alternately), and had a hilarious time. Dick had cased the surrounding country for *Konditorei* (confectioners' shops) and had a different one in which we could store energy each afternoon.

We drove to Rome via our now deeply grooved route, Salzburg (*Nockerl*), Benediktenhof (**Rohes Rindfleisch**), Garmisch-Partenkirchen (**Almond Pudding**), Leermoos (Crayfish), Innsbruck (Flatbread) at the Goldene Rose, Verona at our beautiful and beloved Hotel Due Torri (*Gnocchi*), and Rome (Fried Artichokes). From there we flew to Athens (**Avgolemono**), Istanbul (*Tarator*), and New Delhi (Mulligatawny). We overlapped with the Houstons for two days in Istanbul before they hurried off to ready the houseboats for eighteen of us. We stayed on to make some unwise purchases (the gold turned black for keeps) in the bazaars and spent two days in New Delhi.

At the New Delhi Airport we took a good look at the passengers for Srinagar and selected a couple who were obviously "one of us," and introduced ourselves as fellow anniversarians. A second couple seemed to feel the same way about us and introduced themselves, and so we deplaned in Kashmir, as pleased as eight freshmen who had found friends on the way to school. At Dal we boarded the Clermont Houseboats of Haji (pilgrim title) Gulam Mohamed Butt and embarked (though moored) on the most fabulous week of our lives.

We each had half a houseboat, which meant bedroom, bath, and salon, and we converged on the Houstons' boat, complete with a drawing room and dining room, or on the garden (which had once been a small Mogul garden with mighty Chenar trees) whenever we met. Our houseboat was by far the most distinguished, as framed and autographed photographs indicated that Adlai Stevenson and members of the English nobility had all been happy in it. It was further enhanced by an Indian triumph of plumbing which gave us cold water in the bathtub and a geyser of boiling water when we flushed the john. Kingfishers somersaulted out of the air, lotus blossoms and lilies floated around us, and across the lake the Himalayas changed in every light and merged into their own reflections.

It was a week of unforgettable enchantment, *shikaris* took us under Srinagar's nine bridges and across the azure lakes. We picnicked in the mountains on freshly caught and sautéed brook trout and suppered on an island accompanied by haunting music. We walked through Shalimar and went to a wedding feast prepared by the itinerant cookers of lamb who hand down their secrets from generation to generation. We ate a series of incomparable lamb dishes, with our right hands, knowing that they could never be enjoyed again unless we attended another Kashmiri wedding. (The incredibly beautiful young bride and the redheaded groom had never seen each other; the wedding had been going on for only three days; and they would not meet until it was over.)

As the Houstons' anniversary drew near we remembered the gift of flowers in Vienna, and asked Haji Butt to decorate the dining room with flowers. It contained one long and two small tables, a stuffed bear standing upright extending a card tray, some large engravings of stags at eve, stags in mortal combat, and stags at bay, an upright piano and a clerestory of stained glass. We went off to see the Awantipur Ruins and had a beautiful lunch at the Oberoi Palace, and when we came back young Fred Houston came to our houseboat. He was almost too hysterical to speak—he had seen the flower arrangements in the dining room. Mr. Butt like all of us loved the Houstons and he had expressed his affection with flowers, in a land of flowers. A solid ceiling of garlands was festooned to the side walls while curtains of green hung between the guests. We couldn't see each other or the Houstons, and we had to grope about among the flowers in order to find the cutlery. It was a new sport: deep-flower diving.

Then Dick and I went on to Japan for *Gourmet* magazine and to see the almost completed Expo 1970. Again we ate the beautiful still-life food and the instantaneous dishes that are prepared at the table while you watch. I sent back articles from Japan, Hong Kong, Thailand, India, and Iran, and when I later met the Turkish ambassador he said, "If you are doing a piece on Istanbul and its food, I wager that hard as you may try, you will not be able to write about our food without mentioning our traffic." And I couldn't; the market of a million bright-green grapes, the snow-white smoked sturgeon, and the yard-long Shish Kebabs were eclipsed by the bizarre meanderings of grotesque vehicles. It cannot even be described as bumper-to-bumper traffic, since cars are often bumperless, hoodless, and hornless, and they are as apt to be up against a donkey's tail as ahead of a horse's mouth. We picked up our car in Rome and came back to Lunz, where we invited our close friends—the Eastons, Kevin Curley, Elizabeth and Malcolm McLaughlin, and the Jonases—never really thinking clearly about how uncomfortable we would manage to make them.

There were a few more decorating jobs for S.L.&H. and stimulating work with architect John Pruyn, and another year of commuting between Lunz and New York. Then finally the tables turned. We moved with what turned out to be, in spite of all the discarding, the largest non-corporate, non-diplomatic-container shipment ever made. Far more than our small Austrian hunting house could hold.

We now live in that inaccessible pinewood, and when there are great exasperations with minor bureaucrats or with the paneling in the hall which is still waiting for the end of the hunt, I go into the kitchen and bake. Any land that produces such finely milled flours, such enormous eggs with orange yolks, the heavy lifetime utensils, and the yellow cream cannot be *ganz schlecht*—all bad. The only thing we originally specified was that the house had to be small—an outcome of the ever-increasing difficulty in finding the Glorias and Georginas, the Henriettas and Gloxinias, who have skimmed through our lives with a dustcloth. We might just as well have specified a large house for all the Resis and Trudes and Gretels that are available here. Life in Lunz is heavenly peace, and if the birds hadn't discovered that those crazy Americans were putting out—of all things—birdseed in winter, there wouldn't be a sound. We are surrounded by fat, red-chested bullfinches who make extra swoops and joyful circles because they know they have found *eine gute Sache*—a good thing. And when I hear a giant coughing irritably outside the window in the middle of the night I now know it is just a stag passing by.

Dick had to apply for an Austrian driver's license, which meant studying a large book, an appointment for an eye and ear examination, a deposit, and the great test. Though both eyes and ears are located on the head, all applicants have to strip for an all-day major physical checkup, including a urinalysis. Many apply but few are chosen, and when they now race and cut in or pass on the left, we know that at least they are perfect physical specimens. But sometimes I think a speed limit would do more good.

Lunz lies in the heart of three hunting domains—Habsburg, Kupelwieser, and Rothschild—and the descendants of all three families still live on the properties. We are on the Habsburg land under the ancient proviso that we maintain gates on each side of the property so that no Habsburg would ever have to *go around* us. So far the Emperor Franz Joseph's great-granddaughter, who lives in the house where I waited on the first snowy day, has not had to "go around" us because she comes *in*, instead, to that most pleasant of all functions, afternoon tea.

I remember that when we lived in New Milford we had guests who were surprised that we could spend a whole evening in conversation, of all things, without having to resort to bridge, television, or games. In Lunz we were surprised that our neighbors could spend a whole evening in conversation without having to resort to gossip, casting stones, or scandalmongering. Their enviable capability for carrying on well-tempered talk, peppered with bon mots and learned communications in various languages, is endless. Which is more than can be said for the next step down the social scale, the villagers. Not only are they limited to one language, but that language is incomprehensible Lunzerisch. They call themselves the *haute volée* (a phrase that I thought had gone out with my grandmamma), and they fly high between the aristocracy, the intelligentsia, the two *Amerikaner*, and the peasantry. Their life is uncomplicated. Some have never been to distant Vienna, two hours away, and as the Herr Bürgermeister goes, so goes Lunz. As the stag bellows, as the trout jumps, as the *Auerhahn* cries, and the chamois leaps, so life in Lunz weaves its way through the hunting seasons.

We have unpacked our memories and our mannerisms, and added

yet another sport to the Lunzer's life—*Amerikaner*-watching. But alas, not *Amerikaner*-copying. While we were aware that there were those who said we overfed our guests, our dinners were mere diet pills compared with a Lunzer *Abendessen*. The absolute cream of the *haute volée* pauses in the living room for an aperitif, allowing about ten minutes for bottoms up, but the proper procedure is punctual arrival, a hanging up of coats in the front hall, and a lightning streak to the dinner table which coincides with the arrival of the soup (which has the equivalent of a whole meal floating in it, in the form of a dumpling). Dick always looks bereaved, sighing over his lost happy hour, and course follows course in rapid succession. Wine bottles are opened and emptied as everyone devotes himself to eating—time enough for conversation *nach de Nachtisch*—after the "after table."

All meals in Austria are eaten in an aura of anticipation of the moment supreme when everyone heads for dessert. The last course has various designations: *Süssspeisen* (sweet dishes), *Mehlspeisen* (flour dishes), *Nachtisch, torten* (elaborate cakes), and *Kuchen* (cake). There are also *Obst, Kompot,* and *Käse* (fruit, stewed fruit, and cheese). In a restaurant we can choose between a *Süssspeise,* which is an ice or a mousse, and a *Mehlspeise,* which is any dessert other than a *Torte* or *Kuchen* which contains flour (strudels, tarts, and *beignets* fall into this category).

The Lunz hostess of any strata below the cream but above the salt does not rack her brains about which of these desserts to prepare: She simply falls to and prepares one of each. (We still live to remember a pork roast with cabbage and potatoes—I won't even go into the dumplings in the soup—followed by gigantic cream puffs, a gargantuan punch cake, and stewed fruit buried under a high hat of sweetened whipped cream.) After the table is cleared, the guests remain there until they go home, although the hostess usually takes the ladies on a small sortie to show them her kitchen and her flowering house plants. No other part of the anatomy of the home is shown, and when they return to the table it has been cleared to make room for the *Bäckerei*—petits fours and cookies. More wine is opened and conversation begins.

Now, forty years later, I remember all Father's forebodings when he was asked out to dinner in New York, but nothing he ever dreaded can compare with dinners in Lunz. After accepting an invitation we go on a week of deprivation and starvation, and we arrange the calendar to give us at least a week of rehabilitation after the dinner. Two Lunz dinners a month would be disaster.

I am reminded of Father's sudden departures from New York when he said that matters were pressing in Carlsbad, but what was really pressing was his hunger for a familiar menu card and a sommelier with a *Tastevin* cup hung around his neck and an impressive *cave* below. He missed his European cuisines when he was in America as we, who now have everything we love within eating distance, miss fresh Maine lobster, Susan Emerling's Sausage Rolls, Dot Miller's **Cocktail Spareribs** and Five-Rib Standing Roast, Lil Skirm's Baby Lamb Chops—and *shrimp*.

The Lunz census-taker came up, and while I wanted to give her details, I was a bit taken aback that she only cared about whether we really had those four johns in the house. I still love Austria, and every now and then we see something that endears it to me even more. There is a window of modern built-in kitchens on the Ring in Vienna, which to all intents and purposes looks as though G.E. had been there, but the salesman proudly pulls out a very large bottom drawer on gliders, and reveals a full-sized bathtub. Mother's favorite Matauschek, for kitchen utensils, is still on the Rauhensteingasse, and Julius Meindl is still on the end of the Graben for marketing.

I now read the old Baedekers with Mother's and Father's footnotes, and find that he recommended a dinner then costing seventy cents which today would cost seventy dollars. And, while I heed Mother's note: "Remember to take along Ruskin and Vernon Lee," I disregard the part about "Spiritus Lamps and Menthol." We retrace their steps, meals, and enthusiasm, and when we are at home in Lunz we relive their enjoyments. Everything reminds me of Father, from his knives to his glasses. I remember when we were home alone and he carved with knives that he had sharpened himself (no one else ever knew how). There was always the first critical incision—the pleasure of finding the roast perfect or the wrath with which it was commanded back *zur Kuche*—to the kitchen—for one more minute in the oven, or never to be seen again if it was overdone. Fathers wineglasses remind me of the critical frown with which he tasted his wine, of his concentration, and of the relief and pleasure with which he gave Oscar the signal that the glasses were to be filled—and his contented *"Prosit"* as he raised his glass.

PART II

RECIPES

Page numbers following recipes refer the reader to the author's mention of the dish in Part I. Unless otherwise indicated, all recipes yield 6 servings.

Appetizers
Soups
Fish and Seafood
Poultry and Game
Meats
Vegetables and Pasta
Eggs
Salads
Sauces
Bowles and Drinks
Desserts and Baking

Appetizers

Caviar aux Crêpes de Pommes de Terre
Caviar aux Tomates
Cocktail Spareribs
Cucumber Slices Filled with Crab Meat
Fonds d'Artichauts au Caviar
Lachs Imbiss
Warsaw Tartlets

CAVIAR AUX CREPES DE POMMES DE TERRE
Caviar with Potato Pancakes
(page 199)

3 medium potatoes
2 tablespoons stale bread crumbs
1 tablespoon sour cream
1 egg, beaten
1 teaspoon grated onion, or to taste
  Salt to taste
  Butter for frying
1 pound ice-cold caviar
1 cup sour cream, whipped

Peel and grate potatoes quickly before they turn dark. Mix grated raw potatoes with all other ingredients except the whipped sour cream and caviar. Fry by the tablespoonful and turn once to brown both sides. The pancakes should be lacy and crisp. Place them on an absorbent paper towel in a low oven until all are completed. Keep them hot and serve on hot plates with ice-cold caviar. Sour cream should be passed separately.

Blender Method:

Peel potatoes, cut them into cubes. Put ¼ cup milk in container, add potatoes and blend until they are grated. Mix with other ingredients and add bread crumbs if mixture is too moist.

CAVIAR AUX TOMATES
Caviar in Tomato Boats
(page 80)

Select tomatoes large enough so that a slice cut from each side will yield, when emptied of seeds and pulp, a small oval saucer. Count on 12 such saucers to serve 6.

6 large ripe tomatoes, peeled, cut into saucers and emptied
1 14-ounce jar fresh Malossol Caviar
2 hard-cooked eggs, yolks and whites riced separately
1 small onion, finely chopped
1 recipe Blender Lemon Mayonnaise, page 297
¼ cup finely chopped parsley
   Boston lettuce leaves
2 lemons, cut into wedges

Prepare the tomatoes, fill 6 of them with caviar and garnish them with a border of riced egg whites, a circle of yolks, and a center of onion. Fill the remaining 6 tomato saucers with Blender Lemon Mayonnaise and sprinkle with parsley. Arrange one of each on lettuce leaves on 6 plates and add lemon wedges.

COCKTAIL SPARERIBS
(page 201)

1 side trimmed spareribs (about 4 pounds)
2 lemons, sliced
4 medium onions, sliced
2 tablespoons finely cut chives
3 tablespoons red currant jam (if not obtainable use red currant jelly)
1½ tablespoons brown sugar
1 tablespoon Düsseldorf mustard
1 orange, juice only
3 lemons, juice only
3 tablespoons soy sauce
½ to ¾ cup strong tea

Lay spareribs in a small roasting pan and add all other ingredients except the tea and let the ribs marinate for 2 hours, basting them frequently. Place the pan in a 350° F. oven and roast them, basting and turning them twice, until they are brown and crisp but not dry, about 1¾ hours. As the liquid in the pan evaporates, add tea. Split the ribs into portions and serve with the strained sauce.

CUCUMBER SLICES FILLED WITH CRAB MEAT
(page 50)

1 long narrow cucumber of even thickness
1 6½-ounce can king crab meat, all cartilage removed and meat
    flaked
3 gherkins, chopped
2 tablespoons finely chopped onion
2 tablespoons black caviar
¼ cup Blender Lemon Mayonnaise, page 297
¼ cup minced parsley

Cut the ends from the cucumber and peel it down the length with a fluted knife. This leaves small ridges of dark green on the light-green surface. Cut the cucumber across into ⅛-inch slices and place them on a paper towel to drain. Press out the crab meat in a kitchen towel to remove all moisture. Combine crab meat, gherkins, and onion. Combine the caviar and Blender Lemon Mayonnaise. Add more mayonnaise to bind if necessary. Top the cucumber slices with mounds of the mixture and completely cover them with minced parsley (which keeps the mixture from running). Do not prepare too long before serving, and keep them cool until they are served.

FONDS D'ARTICHAUTS AU CAVIAR
Caviar in Artichoke Bottoms
(page 80)

This is very much nicer in 6 small freshly cooked and trimmed artichoke bottoms than it is in canned Fonds d'Artichauts.

6 small artichokes, cooked and chilled
1 tablespoon lemon juice
2 lemons, cut into wedges
1 10-ounce jar fresh Malossol caviar
1 small onion, minced
2 hard-cooked eggs, yolks and whites riced separately
    Boston lettuce leaves

Trim the stems from the artichokes, remove leaves and scrape the flesh from the bottom of the larger leaves and put into a small bowl. Discard scraped leaves and chokes. Trim the bottoms; mince the flesh from the leaves with lemon juice and divide it over the 6 bottoms. Cover with cold caviar. Carefully arrange a line of minced onion across the caviar. Arrange riced egg whites on one side of it and egg yolks on the other. Serve on lettuce leaves with lemon wedges and pass the Mayonnaise (page 296), thinned with Dick's French Dressing (page 295), separately.

LACHS IMBISS
Salmon Snack
(page 62)

1 large package of cream cheese, at room temperature
3 to 4 tablespoons sour cream
   Salt to taste
2 teaspoons minced onion, or to taste
3 tablespoons freshly grated horseradish, or to taste
6 large slices mildest smoked salmon
2 tablespoons finely cut chives
   Smallest capers

Cream the cream cheese with the sour cream until it can easily be piped; add more sour cream if necessary. Add salt. Divide it in half and combine one-half with the minced onion and the other half with the grated horseradish. Cut the salmon slices in such a way that you can make at least 12 very small cornucopias out of them. Secure them with wooden picks and pipe the onion-flavored cheese into six of them through a small fluted tube. Pipe the horseradish cheese into the second six. Sprinkle the first half with chives and decorate the second half with small capers. Refrigerate the cornucopias until the cheese is set and the wooden picks can be removed. Serve with the folded side at the bottom.

WARSAW TARTLETS
(page 50)

24 smallest Tart Shells (see below)
2 anchovy fillets, minced
3 tablespoons butter, at room temperature
1 boiled beet root, chopped and drained
2 hard-cooked eggs, yolks and whites riced separately
1 medium dill pickle, seeded, finely diced, and drained
1 medium sweet gherkin, finely diced
3 tablespoons finely minced parsley
1 small jar of Malossol caviar

Prepare Tart Shells. Stir anchovy fillets with butter and spread a little in the bottom of each tart. Combine chopped beets with egg, pickle, gherkin, and parsley and fill the mixture on top of the anchovy butter. Center with a little black caviar and chill before serving.

Small Tart Shells

For Warsaw Tartlets and wherever recipes require small tart shells, use the ingredients for making the crust in one of the following pastry recipes: Apricot Raisin Pie, page 309, Onion Tart, page 273, or Spinach Tart, page 281. Roll the pie or tart paste out thin, and cut it into rounds, which can be used either to cover inverted muffin pans (standard or miniature) or to line muffin tins or small molds. *To cover inverted muffin pans:* press the paste down over the inverted cups of the pan. Trim and prick it on the sides and top with a fork. Bake in a 450° F. oven for 6 to 10 minutes. Cool and lift carefully from the pan. *To line muffin pans or small molds:* press the paste into the molds very carefully so that no air remains under the paste. Prick them all over with a fork and bake them in a 450° F. oven for 6 to 10 minutes. Cool for a few minutes before taking from the tins. Small Tart Shells may also be filled with dried peas or cherry pits to keep them flat, but pricking them well is usually sufficient.

Soups

Avgolemono
Cold Senegalaise Soup
Consommé Sir James
Lake Placid Corn Chowder
Potage St. Hubert
Potage à la Steward
Potée Lorraine
Purée Soissonnaise
Sénégalaise au Kari
Smaragd Suppe
Sour Cherry and Plum Soup
Ungarische Fischsuppe

AVGOLEMONO
Egg and Lemon Soup
(page 188)

8 cups chicken broth
½ cup rice
4 eggs, beaten
3 lemons (juice 2 and slice 1)

Make a strong chicken broth and strain it into a bowl. Let it cool and chill it until all fat congeals on the top. Lift off the fat and strain the broth through cheesecloth (doubled and moistened) into an enamel saucepan. Bring it to a boil, add the rice, and cook, uncovered, until the rice is tender, about 20 minutes. Remove from the heat, beat the eggs well with a rotary beater,

205

and gradually beat in the lemon juice. Continue to beat and gradually add two cups of hot—but not boiling—soup. Beat the lemon soup into the remaining soup and heat, but do not allow it to boil. Serve at once with a lemon slice on each serving.

SERVES **6** TO **8**

COLD SENEGALAISE SOUP
(page 52)

1 **3-pound chicken, quartered**
½ **garlic clove**
½ **teaspoon peppercorns**
  Salt to taste
1 **onion, stuck with 2 cloves**
1 **carrot, scraped and quartered**
3 **sprigs parsley**
11 **tablespoons butter**
¾ **cup flour**
2 **tablespoons Madras curry powder, or to taste**
1 **cup milk, or to taste**
1 **cup heavy cream**
1 **cup unsweetened coconut or shaved almonds**

Put chicken pieces with garlic, peppercorns, and salt in cold water to cover and bring to a boil. Skim the foam from the surface, and add onion, carrot, and parsley. Cover and simmer for 25 to 30 minutes. Take the meat off the 2 breast pieces, return the skin, giblets, and bones to the stock, adding enough water to keep the remaining chicken covered; continue to cook for 1 hour longer. Strain it into a bowl to cool and chill. Retain remaining chicken meat for a chicken-almond sandwich spread or a mousse and discard the bones. Retain the liver for the soup. When soup has been chilled, lift off the fat and strain it once more. Heat 8 tablespoons butter in the top of a double boiler, over simmering water, stir in flour and moisten the roux gradually by stirring in the chicken stock. If there are more than 5 cups chicken stock, reduce it to 5 cups by boiling it un-covered before adding it to the roux in the double boiler. When the soup is smooth and thickened, put curry powder in a cup and stir ¼ cup soup into it. Stir the mixture back into the soup and add more curry powder in the same way until the soup is as strong as desired. Add milk to taste to obtain at least 6 cups of soup. Chill the soup until just before serving. Cut the chicken breasts into long strips and chop the liver. Whip the cream, add a pinch of salt, and fry the coconut (note that it browns easily and quickly) or almonds in 3 tablespoons of butter. Set enough whipped cream aside to top each portion generously and beat any remaining whipped cream into the soup. Pour the soup into 6 soup plates or wide cups, top each portion with whipped cream, and divide the chicken and liver over the cream. Sprinkle the toasted brown nuts over the top.

CONSOMMÉ SIR JAMES
Cold Turtle Soup
(page 125)

  4 cups clear turtle soup (canned)
¾ cup Madeira
¼ cup Cognac

All three ingredients have to be of excellent quality. The amount of wine and Cognac may be changed to suit the taste. Chill the soup and serve it from iced cups or from cups bedded in shaved ice.

LAKE PLACID CORN CHOWDER
(page 58)

  6 large ears fresh corn, or enough to yield 3 cups scraped corn
     kernels
½ cup diced bacon
  2 tablespoons butter
  2 medium onions, chopped
  1 large potato, cooked, skinned after cooking, and diced
½ green pepper, seeded and finely chopped
  2 cups stock, vegetable, chicken, or beef
  2 cups milk
    Salt and freshly ground black pepper to taste
  1 pint heavy cream
  1 roast red pepper, finely diced
½ cup chopped parsley
  1 cup fried bread croutons
and 1 decanter whiskey

Cut kernels from the ears into a large bowl. Turn the knife blade and scrape what is left on the ears into the same bowl. In a wide pan, fry the bacon in the butter, stirring frequently until brown. Take it out with a slotted spoon and drain it on absorbent paper. Add the onion to the bacon fat left in the pan and stir it over medium heat for about 5 minutes; add the potato and green pepper, and stir for 3 more minutes. Add stock and simmer until potato dice are tender, about 10 minutes. Transfer the contents of the pan to a heavy kettle, add corn and milk, and season with salt and pepper to taste. Simmer until the corn is tender, about 4 minutes. Add the cream and cook only long enough to heat the chowder through. Serve it with four little bowls of the crisp bacon dice, red pepper, parsley, and croutons, and pass a decanter of whiskey separately.

POTAGE ST. HUBERT
Game Soup
(page 51)

 1 old pheasant or 2 pheasant carcasses with all remaining scraps
13 tablespoons butter
 1 medium onion, quartered
 1 carrot, scraped and quartered
 4 mushrooms, coarsely chopped
 2 stalks celery, chopped
 8 cups stock (vegetable, chicken, or beef)
 ½ teaspoon peppercorns
   Salt to taste
 1 bouquet garni
12 large chestnuts
 2 truffles, peeled
 1 cup sherry
 ⅔ cup flour
 ½ cup red currants, fresh or lightly stewed

Cut pheasant or carcasses and scraps into pieces and simmer them gently in 5 tablespoons butter with the vegetables for 30 minutes, stirring frequently. Add stock and bring to a rapid boil; skim the soup thoroughly, lower the heat, and add pepper, salt, and bouquet garni; simmer the soup for 1 hour. If a whole pheasant was used, remove half the breast for garnishing; if carcasses were used, remove any good meat scraps for garnishing. Simmer the soup for 2 more hours. Strain it well and set it aside to cool. Cut a cross on the flat side of the chestnuts with a sharp knife and put them in a low oven until the shells curl back, then draw off the shells (you may prefer to buy shelled chestnuts). Cook the meats in salted water until the inner skin can be drawn off easily (this may have come off with the shells) and the chestnuts are tender. If they have not broken during cooking and skinning, break them into medium small pieces. Simmer the peeled truffles in a little of the strained game stock for 10 minutes, remove from heat, add sherry, and set them aside. Lift the fat from the cold game stock and strain the stock again (there should be approximately 5 cups). Melt 8 tablespoons butter in a wide pan, letting it get slightly brown. Stir in the flour and gradually stir in the game stock until smooth and thickened. Simmer the soup, stirring frequently, for 20 minutes. Add the pheasant meat, diced, the broken chestnuts, and the truffles cut into short matchsticks. Continue to cook until meat and nuts are hot. Add the sherry in which the truffles cooled, and garnish with fresh or stewed and drained red currants.

POTAGE A LÀ STEWARD
American Game Soup
(page 122)

Prepare brown pheasant stock as for Potage St. Hubert, page 208, when 3 plump pheasants are available. Quarter the birds, brown them well in butter, and remove the 6 breasts from the stock as soon as they are tender. Return the skin and breastbones to the stock and hold the trimmed breast aside to serve in the soup. Omit the chestnuts, truffles, sherry, and currants, and reheat the pheasant breasts in the soup before serving. Stir ½ cup heavy cream into the soup, and if it is not a rich deep brown, correct it with a little dark-brown gravy color. Arrange 1 pheasant breast in each soup plate, pour the soup over each, and top the breasts with a julienne of ham and a sprinkling of freshly chopped herbs (parsley, chervil, basil, thyme) to taste.

POTÉE LORRAINE
Vegetable and Smoked Pork Soup
(page 17)

1 pound salt pork
½ pound streaky bacon, in one piece
1 smoked pork knuckle
4 quarts water, lightly salted
3 carrots, quartered
2 turnips
1 kohlrabi
1 small white cabbage, blanched and quartered
3 onions, sliced
3 leeks, sliced
5 potatoes, peeled and quartered
6 small smoked pork sausages, the skin punctured with a fork
½ loaf French bread, cut into thick diagonal slices

Put pork and bacon in the bottom of a large earthenware pot (from which the *potée* derives its name) and add water. Put it on the stove, bring it to a boil and skim. Cover and simmer for about 30 minutes. Add the vegetables and cook 2 hours longer. Add potatoes and pork sausage, and cook 30 minutes longer. Put the bread slices in a tureen and pour over the soup. Serve meat and vegetables separately.

PURÉE SOISSONNAISE
White Bean Puree
(page 17)

2 cups dry white beans
5 cups bouillon
Salt and pepper to taste
Milk to taste
4 tablespoons butter
1½ cups toasted bread croutons
½ cup brandy, warmed

Soak beans overnight in water to cover. On the following day set them on the stove with cold bouillon and bring them to a boil. Simmer until the beans are very soft, then put them through the blender. Depending on the saltiness of the bouillon, correct the seasoning and return the soup to the top of the double boiler over simmering water. Let it heat, uncovered, stirring at intervals, and add as much milk as needed to make the desired consistency. Melt butter in a wide pan, fry the bread croutons, shaking frequently until golden and crisp. Serve the soup, pour the warmed brandy over the croutons, flame them, and spoon croutons and brandy over the soup plates.

SÉNÉGALAISE AU KARI
Shrimp Curry Soup, Senegalese Style
(page 94)

1 pound shrimp, shelled, deveined, and cleaned (retain the washed
    shell)
4 cups boiling salted water, or fish stock if available
6 tablespoons butter
¼ cup flour
1 cup scalded milk
3 tablespoons curry powder
¾ cup grated unsweetened coconut
1 cup heavy cream

Add the shrimp to rapidly boiling water or stock and boil them for 4 minutes after the water returns to a boil. Take them out with a slotted spoon and keep them warm in a covered bowl. Add shrimp shells to boiling water or stock and boil them rapidly while preparing the roux. Melt 4 tablespoons of the butter in a saucepan, stir in the flour, and cook for 3 minutes without letting it brown. Stir in the strained shrimp stock and milk, little by little, and stir until the soup is thickened and smooth. In a cup, stir the curry powder with a little of the hot soup and pour it gradually back into the soup until the curry flavor is as strong as desired. Put the shrimp back into the simmering soup. Fry the coconut in the remaining butter over very low heat. Stir to prevent burning and take it off the heat as soon as it starts to brown. Whip the cream and serve the soup with a topping of whipped cream covered with browned coconut.

SMARAGD SUPPE
Emerald Soup
(page 58)

1 small cauliflower, with stem well trimmed
2 leeks, white part only, sliced
1 cucumber, peeled, seeded, and diced
5 cups stock
2 cups small tender green peas
⅓ cup butter
½ cup flour
1 cup heavy cream
¼ cup finely chopped parsley
1 hard-cooked egg, riced
   Salt and white pepper to taste

Boil cauliflower, leeks, and cucumber in stock until the cauliflower is just tender. Take it out and separate 24 flowerets from it. Set them aside and return the remaining cauliflower and stem to the simmering stock. Continue to cook until the vegetables are very soft. Drain off 3 cups of the stock, and blend the soft vegetables into a purée with the remaining stock. Cook the green peas in salted water, drain them well and combine them with the flowerets. Melt butter in a saucepan, stir in flour over low heat. Gradually stir in the 3 cups warm stock and continue to stir until the soup is thickened and smooth. Add the blended purée and half the cup of cream. Whip the remaining cream with a little salt. Correct the seasoning of the soup, bring it to a boil and pour into 6 hot soup plates. Decorate each plate with whipped cream, the flowerets, and green peas and sprinkle with parsley and riced egg.

SOUR CHERRY AND PLUM SOUP
(page 33)

2 **pounds sour cherries, pitted**
1 **pound ripe blue plums, stoned and quartered**
6 **cups very lightly salted water**
8 **tablespoons butter**
6 **tablespoons flour**
  Sugar
6 **slices white bread, trimmed and cut into triangles**
1 **2-ounce jigger or ¼ cup kirsch**
1 **teaspoon ground cinnamon mixed with sugar to taste**
½ **cup heavy cream, partially whipped**

Select about a third of the cherries and half of the plums and set them aside. Simmer the rest in salted water until very soft. Pour the fruit and water into a blender and blend into a smooth purée. Melt half the butter in a heavy pan, stir in the flour, and gradually add the blended fruit, stirring until smooth. Add the remaining fruit and sugar to taste and simmer very gently, stirring frequently until the fruit is just soft. Fry the bread triangles in the remaining butter until golden on both sides and sprinkle them very lightly with the cinnamon-sugar mixture. Add kirsch to the soup and stir it well. Place toast triangles in soup plates or cut the toast into smaller pieces and place them in wide soup cups. Pour the hot soup over the toast and pass a small bowl of the cream. Soup may be chilled before serving.

UNGARISCHE FISCHSUPPE
Hungarian Fish Soup
(page 114)

2 pounds fish scraps, heads, tails, skin, and bones
2 tablespoons pickling spices
2 quarts boiling water
2 pounds fish fillets (sole, flounder, and haddock, or other combination of three kinds of fish)
⅓ cup lemon juice
¼ cup butter
2 medium onions, finely chopped
¼ cup flour
2 tablespoons sweet Hungarian paprika
1 chicken bouillon cube
¼ teaspoon each, caraway seeds and black peppercorns
1 egg yolk
1 cup heavy cream
1 tablespoon cut fresh dill

Place fish scraps and pickling spices in a large kettle, add water and simmer, covered, for 2 hours. Season the fish fillets with salt and marinate them in the lemon juice for 2 hours. Heat the butter in a heavy soup kettle, stir in the onions and cook until lightly browned, about 7 minutes. Sprinkle flour and paprika over the onions and stir until they are browned and smooth. Gradually stir in the strained fish stock, add the bouillon cube, caraway seeds, and peppercorns, and stir over low heat until the soup is smooth. Set the soup kettle into a pan of boiling water and add the fish fillets, divided into pieces. Cover the kettle and let the soup *draw* for 15 minutes, or until the fish pieces are white and flaky. Beat the yolk into the cream and stir it into the hot soup; continue to stir until the soup is thickened, but do not let it come to a boil. Garnish with dill and serve at once with toasted hard rolls and beer. (The Hungarians drink Schnapps with this but Gatti-Cazazza didn't.)

SERVES 6 TO 8

Fish and Seafood

Clams in Aspic
Codfish Balls
Hering in Senf
Langouste Fra Diavolo
Norsk Fiskfärs
Risotto con Aragosta
Risotto con Scampi
Saumon Porte-Bonheur
Saumon Rothschild
Shrimp in Grapefruit
Solè Francine
Sole Valérie
Soufflé Vesuve
Tempura
Trout in Aspic
Warm Smoked Trout

CLAMS IN ASPIC
(page 149)

If you own a set of 24 scrubbed clam shells for various clam recipes, buy ½ pint of shucked clams or 1 7½-ounce can of minced clams.

    2 quarts unshucked clams
    ½ cup water
    2 envelopes plain gelatin
    ⅓ cup sherry
    1 cup clear consommé
    3 tablespoons butter
    ¼ cup flour
    1 cup heavy cream
    3 sprigs parsley

Place the scrubbed and washed clams in a kettle with boiling water. Cover the kettle closely and steam the clams over medium heat until they open, about 10 to 12 minutes. Take them out, separate the shells carefully and keep them for this recipe and for future use. Strain the clam broth and mince the clams. Stir gelatin into sherry. Heat the consommé to boiling, remove from heat, and stir in the sherry until the gelatin is completely dissolved. Pour it on a shallow platter and set it in the refrigerator as soon as it is cool. Melt the butter over low heat, stir in the flour and moisten the roux with a little of the clam broth—it must be very thick. Add cream and the well-drained clams, and cook over low heat, stirring constantly. Add a little more broth if necessary. Let the mixture cool. Place a spoonful in each cleaned clam shell and chill. Cut the aspic into small dice and cover the clams with aspic. Garnish each shell with a bit of parsley and serve with cocktails or as a first course.

CODFISH BALLS
(page 85)

1½ pounds salt codfish
3 cups mashed potatoes
   White pepper to taste
1½ tablespoons minced onion or finely cut chives
6 eggs (3 whole and 3 separated)
   Deep fat, heated to 375° F.
   Fresh lettuce leaves
6 sprigs parsley

Soak the codfish in cold water to cover for 6 hours, changing the water twice. Bring to a boil in fresh water until it flakes easily. Flake it, press out the moisture, and combine it with the potatoes. Season, stir in the onion and the whole eggs, beaten well with the 3 yolks. Whip the 3 whites until stiff and fold them into the mixture. Shape the mixture into 12 balls with floured hands and fry them in the deep fat until they are golden. Serve on lettuce leaves, garnished with parsley. Serve with tomato sauce or homemade ketchup.

HERING IN SENF
Herring in Brown Mustard and Dill Sauce
(page 104)

6 salt herrings, 1 to 1½ pounds
   Milk to cover
¾ cup salad oil
1 large egg yolk or 2 small yolks
¼ cup dill-flavored or white vinegar
¾ cup brown mustard, preferably Düsseldorf or Dijon
1 lemon (juice and grated rind)
¾ cup cut fresh dill
6 sprigs fresh dill
   Freshly ground black pepper to taste
   Fine brown sugar to taste

Soak herring in water overnight. In the morning, remove heads, tails, and skin, and soak them in milk for the rest of the day. If they are still too salty, leave them in the milk until the next morning. Fillet the herring carefully and lay them, as nearly intact as possible, in a deep casserole with a lid. Make a sauce as you would mayonnaise, by beating oil, drop by drop, into a beaten egg yolk. Add a little vinegar as you go along, until the sauce starts to thicken. Then add the rest of the oil in a thin stream. Stir in the mustard, the rest of the vinegar, the lemon, and the cut dill. Season with pepper and sugar. Spread the sauce over the fillets, add dill sprigs, cover and chill. Serve the herring in the sauce with sliced raw apples and thinly cut onion rings at any time after they have been in the refrigerator for 48 hours.

LANGOUSTE FRA DIAVOLO
Grilled Lobster
(page 42)

    3 2-pound lobsters
    7 tablespoons soft butter
    ½ cup brandy, warmed
    2 teaspoons English mustard
    3 tablespoons French mustard
      Salt and freshly ground black pepper to taste
    2 cups bread crumbs
    ¼ cup melted butter

Prepare the lobsters by inserting a pointed knife in the center of the back at the point where the head meets the carapace; quickly bring down the knife to cut through the length of the back. Spread out the 2 halves, discard the intestine and stomach. Take out the fat, the green liver (or tomalley) and the coral (or roe) and mix them with 5 tablespoons soft butter. Stir over very low heat for a moment, add the brandy, and flame it. As soon as the flame subsides stir in the two mustards, salt and pepper, and 2 tablespoons butter. Remove from heat and spread half the mixture over the 6 lobster halves. Split the claws and arrange the lobsters, shell side down, in an oiled pan. Bake them in a 400° F. oven for about 15 minutes, take them out and cover them with the remaining sauce mixed with the crumbs. Sprinkle with melted butter and put the pan under the broiler. Broil until the crumbs are brown. Serve at once.

NORSK FISKFÄRS
Norwegian Fish Ring
(page 65)

3 pounds whole fish, haddock, pike, or cod
1 pound fillets of flounder
  Salt and white pepper to taste
6 tablespoons flour, preferably potato flour
4 tablespoons soft butter
2 eggs
1 cup milk
1 cup heavy cream

(The reason for using the whole fish is that there is a gelatinous substance under the skin, which should be incorporated into the mixture.) Scrape the raw fish meat into a bowl, being sure to scrape the back of the skin carefully. Grind fish and fillets three times through the meat grinder with seasonings and flour. Beat in the soft butter and the eggs, one at a time. Beat in the milk and cream, little by little, until thick. If too thick, add milk; if too thin, add another egg. Spoon the mixture into a buttered and bread-crumbed ring mold, leaving space for expansion at the top. Cover with foil and tie it securely. Stand the mold in a kettle of simmering water (the water should not come higher than ¾ way up the side of the mold). Cover the kettle and steam the ring for 1 hour on top of the stove. Add water when necessary. Invert the ring carefully onto a hot platter and fill the center with cooked green peas or any other vegetable. Serve with tomato or curry sauce and parsley potatoes.

RISOTTO CON ARAGOSTA
Rice with Lobster
(page 25)

2 freshly cooked 1½-pound lobsters (or 1½ pounds ready-cooked
    lobster meat cut into large pieces)
1 onion, 1 carrot, and 1 celery stalk (if live lobsters are to be used)
1 onion, finely chopped
½ cup butter
½ cup dry white wine
3 cups Italian rice
6 cups broth from lobster shells or fish stock
¼ teaspoon dried oregano
2 teaspoons minced basil
1 tablespoon minced parsley
    Salt and pepper to taste

Cook lobsters about 20 minutes until red. Crack shells, take out meat and
return the shells to the water in which they cooked. Add the onion, carrot, and
celery, and boil uncovered over high heat until the broth is reduced to 6 cups;
strain and keep it warm. Sauté chopped onion in half the butter until golden.
Add the wine and simmer 3 minutes longer. Add the rice and stir until it is
transparent and glossy. Add the hot broth, 1 cup at a time, and continue simmering after each addition until the liquid is nearly absorbed (it will take about
20 minutes). After 15 minutes add the lobster meat and herbs and season to
taste. Stir in the remaining butter. Cover the pan to let the risotto steam for a
few minutes before serving it.

RISOTTO CON SCAMPI
Rice and Shrimp
(page 176)

- 2 quarts salted water
- 1 carrot, quartered
- 1 small onion, quartered
- 1 celery stalk
- 1 pound shrimp, shelled and deveined (rinse and retain shells)
- 6 tablespoons butter
- 1 clove garlic, chopped
- 1 onion, chopped
- 6 sprigs parsley, chopped
- ½ cup dry white wine
- 2 cups rice, preferably Italian
- Salt and pepper to taste

Bring 2 quarts salted water to a boil in a kettle with the carrot, onion, and celery. Add the shrimp, a few at a time, so that the water will not stop boiling. Boil for 3 minutes after adding the last shrimp. Take out the shrimp with a slotted spoon and set aside. Add the shrimp shells to the kettle and boil until the broth is reduced to 6 cups, strain it, and set it over low heat. Melt 4 tablespoons of the butter in a wide pan. Sauté the garlic, onion, and parsley in it until lightly browned. Add the wine and simmer 2 minutes. Stir in the rice until it is glossy and transparent. Add the simmering shrimp broth, one cup at a time, and cook over moderate heat until the liquid is almost absorbed before adding the next cup. Add the remaining butter and shrimp with the fifth cup. Test the rice and remove from heat as soon as it is tender but not soft. It may not require the last half-cup of broth. Cooking time will be about 20 to 25 minutes. Correct seasoning and serve at once.

SAUMON PORTE-BONHEUR
"Lucky" Cold Salmon
(page 153)

3 quarts Court Bouillon, page 224
1 6- to 8-pound drawn salmon
1 bottle dry white wine
1 egg white and 1 broken eggshell

Prepare a Court Bouillon exactly as for Saumon Rothschild. Put in the salmon and substitute 1 bottle dry white wine for the bottle of champagne. Cook the salmon at 10 minutes per pound after the bouillon has returned to the simmering stage. Take out the salmon and let it cool. Reduce the Court Bouillon to 6 cups and let it cool. Stir in the egg white and crushed eggshell, and continue to stir as the bouillon comes slowly to a boil. Reduce heat and simmer for 20 minutes. Strain the bouillon through a triple cheesecloth, wrung out in cold water, and set it aside to cool for the aspic. Refrigerate the cold salmon until ready to decorate.

Decorating and Garnishing:

Transfer the cold salmon carefully to a serving platter or tray. Gently remove the skin from the upper side and return it to the refrigerator.

2 envelopes gelatin
½ cup dry white wine
4 cups Court Bouillon, page 224
   Salt and white pepper
1 pound shrimp
1½ cups butter
1 bunch watercress
2 hard-cooked eggs, cut into 6 sections each
1 recipe Blender Lemon Mayonnaise, page 297
¼ cup chopped pistachio nuts

Stir gelatin into wine and set aside for 10 minutes. Heat 1 cup of the Court Bouillon to boiling and remove from heat. Stir in the gelatin until it is dissolved. Stir in the remaining Court Bouillon and season to taste. Set the aspic aside to cool but not to set. Shell and devein shrimp and wash the shells. Boil the shrimp in salted water for 4 minutes, drain and chill them. Crush the shrimp shells and pound them fine with the butter and any small or broken shrimp. Put the mixture in a low oven until the butter is melted, then pour it through a sieve and chill it to the proper consistency for piping. Brush the cold salmon with a coat of gelatin and return it to refrigerator. Repeat this process several times until it is well glazed. Break off watercress leaves and apply 4 evenly sized leaves, to resemble a four-leaf clover, and secure them with wooden picks along the side of the salmon. There should be room for at least 4 clovers. Apply the next 2 coats of aspic, and when the clovers are coated and adhere to the sides of the fish, remove the picks. If the aspic becomes too thick to use, soften it by setting it in a bowl of hot water. When the salmon is glazed draw outlines on its surface with the shrimp butter, piped through a flat bordering tube. Outline the clovers and chill the salmon immediately. Surround it with watercress, shrimp, and sections of hard-cooked egg and serve with Blender Lemon Mayonnaise, sprinkled generously with chopped pistachio nuts. Serve with a mixed vegetable salad.

YIELDS 8 TO 12 SERVINGS, DEPENDING ON SIZE OF SALMON

SAUMON ROTHSCHILD
Hot Salmon with Oyster Mushroom Sauce
(page 8)

Start by preparing the fish farce and refrigerate it until needed.

Fish Farce or Stuffing:

2½ cups dry bread crumbs
Enough milk to moisten crumbs
1 onion, finely chopped
3 shallots, finely chopped
2 tablespoons butter
8 medium mushrooms, chopped and pressed dry in a kitchen towel
½ small clove garlic
Salt and white pepper to taste
1 small pinch nutmeg
4 eggs

Soak bread crumbs in milk. Fry onion and shallots very lightly in butter and cool them. Put them in a chopping bowl with chopped mushrooms, parsley, and garlic, and chop them all together until fine. Add the well-squeezed crumbs and chop them into the mixture. Season to taste and beat in 1 egg. As soon as it is absorbed, beat in the second egg. If the stuffing becomes too soft, add more crumbs soaked in milk and pressed dry and omit the last egg. Shape a very small test dumpling with floured hands and simmer it in water until it is slightly puffed and firm. Take it out with a slotted spoon. If it is too soft, add more crumbs; if it is too hard, beat in the last egg. Shape 24 small dumplings, the size of a hazelnut, out of the stuffing and chill them. Use the remaining farce to stuff the salmon, and sew up the opening.

The next step is preparing the Court Bouillon.

Court Bouillon:

A 6-pound salmon cooked in a narrow fish kettle usually needs 4 quarts liquid to cover it (3 quarts Court Bouillon and 1 bottle champagne). If the fish kettle is large and more liquid is required, increase the quantities of bouillon proportionately.

> 2 large onions, sliced
> 2 carrots, sliced
> 1 celery stalk
> 1 bay leaf
> 4 sprigs parsley
> 1 tablespoon salt

Combine all ingredients in the fish kettle. Add 3 quarts cold water, cover and set the kettle over two burners on the top of the stove and bring it to a boil. Add vegetables. If the fish kettle is equipped with a rack or screen, lay the vegetables on it. Reduce heat and boil slowly for 1 hour. Cool the Court Bouillon, discard the vegetables.

Now for the Salmon:

> 1 6-pound salmon
> 1 recipe Fish Farce
> 3 quarts Court Bouillon
> 1 bottle dry champagne
> 6 peppercorns
> 1 fillet of sole or flounder, optional
> 1 pint oysters
> 1 pound large shrimp, peeled and deveined
> 3 large truffles, poached, peeled, and sliced
> 1 recipe Oyster and Mushroom Sauce

Lay the stuffed salmon on the rack or screen. If there is no rack in the kettle, lay the salmon on a wide double strip of cheesecloth, leaving two short ends to use as handles, and lower it into the cold bouillon. (Fold over the two ends, do not let them hang out of the kettle as they may prevent the lid from fitting closely.) Add the champagne and peppercorns and bring the bouillon back to a boil. Skim it, reduce heat to a simmer and cook the fish for 1 hour, or approximately 10 minutes per pound. While the salmon is simmering, prepare the Oyster and Mushroom Sauce. During the last 20 minutes of cooking the salmon, simmer the farce dumplings, "crimp" * the sole, and boil the shrimp for 4 minutes in salted water. Poach the bearded oysters in their own liquor until the edges curl. Set them aside for the garnish and hold the oyster liquor for the sauce.

Carefully lift the rack, or cheesecloth, out of the kettle and let it drain well. Increase heat under the kettle to high and boil the bouillon, uncovered, until it is needed for the Oyster and Mushroom Sauce. Transfer the salmon to a heated fish platter. Put absorbent towels around it and draw out the stuffing stitches. Take the skin off the upper side and quickly arrange the truffle slices on it in a graduated row, ending with the largest slice at the head. Take away towels and surround the salmon with drained dumplings, crimped sole, poached oysters, and shrimp. Serve it immediately with Oyster and Mushroom Sauce.

Oyster and Mushroom Sauce:

⅓ **cup butter**
⅓ **cup flour**
2½ **cups reduced Court Bouillon from the kettle in which salmon was**
    cooked
    The retained oyster liquor
1 **cup finely sliced mushrooms, sautéed for a few minutes in butter**
    Salt and white pepper to taste

Melt the butter in the top of a double boiler over simmering water and stir in the flour. Have this roux ready and stir in the reduced Court Bouillon and oyster liquor as soon as they are ready. Stir until the sauce is smooth and thickened, then set it over direct, extremely low heat and let it barely bubble while garnishing the fish. Stir in the well-drained mushrooms, season to taste, and simmer until ready to pour into a hot sauceboat and serve.

YIELDS 8 TO 12 SERVINGS

*To crimp fish: cut raw fillets into narrow diagonal strips and place them in ice water for 30 minutes. Then poach them in boiling salted water until white.

Salmon Hollandaise

Poach an unstuffed salmon as for Salmon Rothschild. Omit all garnishes except crisp watercress and lemon wedges and serve it, unskinned, with 1 recipe Hollandaise Sauce, page 295.

YIELDS 8 TO 12 SERVINGS

Salmon Valois

Poach an unstuffed salmon as for Saumon Rothschild. Omit all garnishes except parsley and lemon wedges and serve it, unskinned, with 1 recipe Béarnaise Sauce, page 291.

YIELDS 8 TO 12 SERVINGS

SHRIMP IN GRAPEFRUIT
(page 146)

    6 small grapefruit
1½ pounds shrimp, peeled and deveined
    2 tablespoons tarragon vinegar
    1 cup Mayonnaise, page 296
    1 tablespoon apricot jam
    3 gherkins, minced
    ¼ onion, minced
      Salt and pepper to taste
    3 tablespoons grapefruit juice
    3 tablespoons chopped mint or parsley

Cut grapefruit in half and scoop out the sections with a grapefruit spoon, reserving 6 shells. Set sections aside, collect juice in a bowl. Scrape membranes out of the shells and chill shells. Cook shrimp in rapidly boiling salted water, dropping in a few at a time so that the water does not stop boiling. When the last shrimp has boiled 3 minutes drain all and sprinkle with vinegar. Cool and chill. Make Mayonnaise, stir in jam, gherkins, onion, seasonings, and 3 tablespoons grapefruit juice. Divide shrimp and grapefruit sections among the 6 empty shells, pour the sauce over each stuffed shell and serve sprinkled with mint or parsley.

SOLE FRANCINE
(page 38)

8 fillets lemon sole
  Salt and white pepper to taste
2 tablespoons melted butter
3 shallots, finely chopped
4 sprigs parsley, finely chopped
1 cup white wine
1 cup fish stock or chicken broth
½ cup heavy cream
1 recipe Hollandaise Sauce, page 295
3 eating apples, peeled, cored, and cut into wedges
3 tablespoons butter

Season fillets to taste and lay them in the butter in a fish pan or roasting pan with a lid. Add shallots, parsley, white wine, and fish stock. Cover tightly and simmer 5 to 8 minutes depending on size. Carefully lift out the fillets and arrange them in an oval baking dish. Reduce the liquids left in the pan over high heat. When 1 cup remains, add heavy cream and boil 1 minute, stirring. Keep the sauce warm and make 1 recipe Hollandaise Sauce. In a separate saucepan, cook the apple wedges in butter for a few minutes. Arrange a few wedges on each fillet. Combine fish sauce and Hollandaise. Spread the sauce over the fish and place in a 450° F. oven until browned. Serve with boiled potato balls.

SOLE VALÉRIE
(page 6)

1 pound fish scraps and bones
3 cups water
1½ cups dry white wine
6 fillets of lemon sole (or flounder)
1 pound peeled and deveined shrimp
½ pound button mushrooms, stems cut off evenly with the caps
2 tablespoons butter
1 shallot, minced

Cook fish scraps and bones in water to obtain a strong fish stock. Reduce it to 1½ cups, strain it, and add the white wine. Arrange the fillets of sole in a slightly overlapping circle in a shallow buttered baking dish. Pour over the fillets enough of the fish stock to cover, and simmer them covered for 8 to 10 minutes, depending on their thickness. In the meantime cook the shrimp for 5 minutes in a small amount of salted water and sauté the mushrooms in butter with the shallots until they are glossy and darkened. Drain the stock from the fillets and return it to the remaining stock. Arrange the drained shrimp in a circle over the fillets and arrange the mushrooms in an inner circle. Keep the platter warm while making the Sauce Vin Blanc (recipe below). Pour the finished sauce over the garnished fillets. Glaze the fish under the broiler, with the oven door open, until the top is browned—a matter of seconds only. Serve with boiled parsley potatoes and a lettuce salad.

Sauce Vin Blanc:

>   4 tablespoons butter
>   6 tablespoons flour
>   ⅓ cup heavy cream, whipped

Melt the butter in a heavy saucepan over low heat. Stir in the flour, and moisten the roux gradually with the stock. As soon as the sauce thickens, let it simmer slowly for a few minutes. Season it to taste and cool it a little before folding in the whipped cream.

SOUFFLÉ VESUVE
Crab Meat Soufflé
(page 152)

>   4 tablespoons butter
>   4 tablespoons flour
>   1 cup milk, scalded
>   1 cup crab meat, fresh or canned, carefully picked over
>   3 gherkins, finely diced
>   2 tablespoons finely chopped onion
>   2 tablespoons finely chopped pimento
>   1 lemon (1 tablespoon juice and the grated rind)
>   6 eggs, separated
>   Salt and white pepper to taste

Place an *unbuttered* 1½-quart soufflé dish in a slightly larger frying pan filled with water. Melt butter in the top of a double boiler over simmering water. Stir in flour and gradually stir in the hot milk. When the mixture is smooth and thick, remove from heat and let it cool slightly. Stir in the crab meat, gherkins, onion, pimento, lemon, and beaten egg yolks. Add seasoning and fold in the stiffly beaten whites. Pour it into the souffle dish and bake in a 375° F. oven for about 40 minutes, or until puffed and brown. Serve with lemon butter sauce and a green salad.

TEMPURA
(page 179)

1½ **pounds shrimp, peeled and deveined**
   Flour for dredging
   Enough vegetable oil to be 3 inches deep in a large heavy pan
2 **egg yolks**
2 **cups ice water**
1½ **cups flour, sifted**
1 **bottle Teriyaki Sauce or to taste**
1 **jar lime chutney**

Rinse shrimp and pat them dry. Dredge them with flour and shake off any excess. Heat oil to 375° F. (If sesame oil is available, make a mixture of half vegetable and half sesame oil.) Prepare the batter just before using. Beat eggs into water and stir in the flour little by little. Stir until smooth. The batter should be thin but not so thin that it won't coat the shrimp. Add a little flour if necessary. Dip in the shrimp and fry them until golden; drain and serve them at once. Lime chutney is not an accepted accompaniment, but it is extremely good. Teriyaki Sauce may be added if preferred.

TROUT IN ASPIC
(page 50)

6 **fresh trout or 3 packages frozen trout (2 in each)**
3 **lemons (2 finely sliced and 1 juiced)**
3 **small onions, sliced very thin**
   Dry white wine
2 **envelopes plain gelatin**
1 **small jar red caviar**
2 **hard-cooked eggs**
3 **tablespoons chopped parsely**
2 **tablespons chopped onion**
4 **small tomatoes, peeled**

Arrange trout in a wide pan (do not wash or defrost frozen trout). Add lemon juice and cover the trout with half the lemon and all the onion slices. Pour ¼ cup dry white wine into a cup and stir the gelatin into it; pour the remaining wine over the trout. Set them over very low heat or on an asbestos mat so that they can simmer at the lowest degree. If the heat is low enough it will take 1 hour to simmer frozen trout, and about 30 minutes to simmer fresh trout. Remove from heat, draw off the skin while they are hot—leaving heads and tails intact—and put the wine broth back to boil for 5 minutes. Strain it and stir in the gelatin until it is dissolved. Pour it onto a platter and chill it. When the trout are cold, fill them with a stuffing of caviar, riced hard-cooked egg, parsley, and onion. Arrange them on a cold platter and chill them. Before serving, decorate the trout with tomato slices and fill the spaces around them with finely diced wine aspic. Garnish with remaining lemon slices and parsley and serve with thinned mayonnaise.

WARM SMOKED TROUT
(page 132)

6 small or 3 large hickory-smoked brook trout
1 cup heavy cream, chilled
  Salt to taste
3 tomatoes, peeled, sliced, and chilled
12 slices hot thin buttered toast
½ fresh horseradish root

Fillet the trout and arrange them on a lightly oiled baking sheet. Warm them in a 300° F. oven. Have ready a warm serving platter and warm plates. Whip the cream and refrigerate it until the last moment. When tomatoes and toast are ready, grate the horseradish on a grater or in the electric food grater, and fold it into the whipped cream with salt. Serve warm trout and warm toast with cold tomatoes and cold horseradish cream.

Poultry and Game

Chicken Hash
Chicken Jeanette
Chicken Rossini
Chicken Stéphanie
Dinde à la Provençale
Faisan Titania
Grinzing Backhendl
Guinea Hens Radetzky
Huhn in Riesling
Maxim Kopf's Paprikahuhn
Partridge in Casserole Madeira

Pheasant in Sauerkraut
Poularde Basque
Poularde Pharao
Poulets en Chaud-Froid Talleyrand
Rehrücken mit Kastanien
Saddle of Hare
Squab Chickens in Casserole
Squabs with Scrapple
Suprêmes of Pheasant
Wiener Huhn

CHICKEN HASH
(page 119)

4 whole breasts or 8 suprêmes (boneless halved breasts) of chicken
3 celery stalks with leaves
2 medium onions
1 carrot
3 sprigs parsley
3 peppercorns and salt to taste
5 tablespoons butter
6 tablespoons flour
1 cup heavy cream

Trim the breasts or suprêmes, and put wings, skin, and trimmings in 6 cups water with the vegetables, peppercorns, and salt. Bring to a rapid boil, reduce heat and simmer, covered, for 30 minutes. Skim off the foam and add the chicken breasts. Bring back to a boil, reduce heat again and simmer until they are done, about 20 minutes. (Do not let them dry out.) Take out the breasts and keep them warm in a covered bowl. Reduce the broth over high heat to 3 cups. In a heavy saucepan, melt butter over low heat, stir in the flour and moisten the roux, stirring constantly, with the strained chicken stock. When the sauce is smooth and thickened, stir in the cream and chicken, cut into small dice. Correct the seasoning and serve sprinkled with freshly chopped parsley. (It can also be served in a rice or pastry ring, or with a poached egg.)

CHICKEN JEANETTE
(page 140)

6 suprêmes of chicken (halved breasts with the first wing joint left
    on) or 6 pieces of white chicken meat
½ cup goose- or chicken-liver mousse or pâté
3 envelopes plain gelatin
¼ cup white wine
4 tablespoons butter
4 tablespoons flour
2 cups clear chicken consommé
    Salt and white pepper to taste
½ cup heavy cream
2 peeled truffles, sliced
¼ cup sherry
1 cup clear bouillon

Poach the suprêmes of chicken in salted water until white and tender, about 15 minutes. Trim them and spread the underside with the goose- or chicken-liver mousse or pâté. Place them on waxed paper and chill. Stir 2 envelopes of the gelatin into the wine and set it aside. Melt butter in the top of a double boiler over simmering water, stir in the flour and gradually stir in the consommé. Continue to cook, stirring until the sauce is thickened and smooth. Take it off the heat and stir in the gelatin until it is dissolved. Stir in the cream and set the sauce aside at room temperature. Arrange the cold chicken pieces on a wire mesh and place the mesh over a pan. Coat them with the sauce. (The sauce cannot be brushed on or patched, it has to be poured over the chickens in a wide stream.) Return the chickens to the refrigerator and return the sauce from the pan under the mesh to the top of the double boiler. Rewarm it to flowing consistency over simmering water. Let the sauce cool again and repeat the coating of the cold chicken pieces until they are smoothly covered and all the sauce has been used. Press truffle slices into the last coat before it sets. Soften the remaining envelope of gelatin in the sherry. Bring the bouillon to a boil, remove it from heat, and stir in the gelatin until it dissolves. Let the bouillon cool and then brush it lightly over the cold chicken. Repeat until all the pieces are well glazed. Serve the chicken with a salad of green peas and mayonnaise thinned with heavy cream to taste.

CHICKEN ROSSINI
Breast of Chicken
(page 6)

6 large chicken breasts, halved
2 tablespoons flour for dredging
   Salt and white pepper to taste
7 tablespoons butter
1 cup brown stock
½ cup dry Madeira
1 pound narrow noodles
6 slices foie gras
1 cup very small toasted bread croutons
1 recipe Sauce Madère, page 293

Dredge the chicken pieces lightly in flour seasoned with salt and pepper and brown them very slowly in ⅓ cup butter in a heavy casserole. Turn the pieces with kitchen tongs. When they are evenly browned, after about 15 to 20 minutes, add a little of the stock and wine and cover the casserole tightly. Let the chicken braise on top of the stove until tender, adding ¼ cup stock and wine as the liquid evaporates, but do not add too much at one time. Fifteen minutes before the chicken is done, boil noodles in salted water. Drain them well and arrange them in the center of the casserole. Lay the chicken breasts against the noodles and place a slice of foie gras, lightly sautéed in the remaining butter, on each chicken breast. Sprinkle the noodles with very small toasted bread croutons and pass the Sauce Madére separately.

CHICKEN STÉPHANIE
(page 140)

2 tender broilers, quartered
4 tablespoons butter
4 tablespoons oil
3 cucumbers, peeled, seeded, and cut into medium dice (If the
　　cucumbers are thick, the flesh can be cut into lozenges. Use more
　　cucumbers to obtain 3 cups lozenges.)
1 cup chicken stock
1 lemon (juice and grated rind)
　Salt and white pepper to taste
1 recipe Hollandaise Sauce, page 295

In a heavy casserole, sauté the chicken pieces in butter and oil until they are lightly browned on both sides. Add cucumber dice and stock, half the lemon juice and the grated rind. Cover the casserole and simmer the chickens for 30 minutes, or until juicy and tender. Arrange the pieces on a serving platter and keep them warm in a low oven. Strain the pan juices and fold the well-drained cucumber dice into the Hollandaise Sauce. Serve the chicken and sauce at once with steamed broccoli and parsley potatoes.

SERVES 4 TO 6

DINDE À LA PROVENCALE
Turkey Stuffed with Onions
(page 20)

1 8-pound young turkey
6 medium white onions, sliced
2 tablespoons soft butter
⅓ cup bread crumbs
3 tablespoons minced herbs: sage, basil, parsley, chervil, chives
3 peeled truffles, diced (optional)
　Salt and pepper to taste
2 eggs, beaten, just enough to bind the stuffing
2 tablespoons butter
3 cups tomato sauce

Boil wing tips, neck, and giblets of the turkey. As soon as the heart and liver are tender, take them out and chop them to add to the stuffing. Parboil the onions and drain them well. Mix softened butter and bread crumbs and add to the onions, together with the chopped liver and heart, herbs, truffles, and seasonings. Bind with the beaten egg. Stuff the turkey with this mixture, sew the opening with kitchen string and a large kitchen needle, and truss the bird closely. Rub well with butter, season and roast on a rack, breast side down, in a 325° F. oven for 1¼ hours. Then turn and roast breast side up, basting every 15 minutes until the second joint can be pierced with a fork and any juices that run out are colorless, about 1¾ to 2 hours in all, or 15 minutes to the pound. Take out the turkey, cut the kitchen and trussing strings, and serve with tomato sauce.

FAISAN TITANIA
Pheasant in Casserole
(page 85)

Do this when green seedless grapes are in season. Use a heavy enameled casserole or Dutch oven with a tightly fitting lid.

    3 young pheasant
        Salt and freshly ground black pepper to taste
    6 thin pieces of pork fat
    1 cup (½ pound) butter
    1 onion
    1 carrot
    6 juniper berries
    ¾ cup brandy, warmed
    2 cups seedless grapes
    2 cups orange sections
    ¾ cup dry sherry

Make a broth of wing tips, neck, and giblets with the onion and carrot. Truss the pheasant closely and tie pork over their breasts. Season them well with salt and pepper. Sauté them in ¾ cup butter in a casserole over medium heat, turning them carefully until they are evenly browned on all sides. Add the juniper berries and 1½ cups of the broth. Cover the casserole tightly, reduce the heat to simmer and cook the birds for about 35 minutes. Remove the pork and simmer uncovered 10 minutes longer. Take the birds out, discard the trussing string and keep them warm in a low oven. Skim the fat off the pan juices. Return the pheasant to the casserole, pour the brandy over and ignite it. As soon as the flame subsides, add grapes, orange sections, and sherry, and simmer covered for 10 minutes longer. Arrange the birds on a hot serving platter, garnish them with the fruit and keep them warm. Add 1½ cups strained broth from the wing tips to the pan juices, and bring the sauce to a rapid boil. Stir in the remaining ¼ cup butter and correct the seasoning. Serve the birds with the sauce.

GRINZING BACKHENDL
Viennese Fried Chicken
(page 92)

3 **tender young broilers, quartered**
1 **cup flour for dredging**
3 **large eggs, lightly beaten**
3½ **cups dry bread crumbs, sieved**
1 **teaspoon salt**
   Vegetable shortening for frying
¼ **pound butter**
1 **recipe Risi Pisi, page 279**

Trim chicken quarters, draw off all skin. Place a few pieces at a time in a brown paper bag with the flour and shake it to dredge the chicken with *just as much* flour as each piece will hold. Dip the pieces in the beaten egg and then into the bread crumbs, sieved with the salt. Be sure all of them are thoroughly coated. Set the pieces in a cold place. Fry the pieces, meat side down, in two large frying pans in vegetable shortening, 1½ to 2 inches deep, heated to about 350° F. Turn the pieces once to brown both sides. When they are brown reduce heat to about 350° F., and continue cooking until they are done, about 20 minutes. As the smaller pieces are finished place them in a roasting pan in a 325° F. oven. Do the same with the larger pieces. Pour the melted butter over the chicken and serve with parsley potatoes, Risi Pisi, and a crisp lettuce salad.

GUINEA HENS RADETZKY
(page 149)

    2 large or 3 small guinea hens
    ½ cup butter
    ½ cup Grand Marnier, warmed
    1½ cups port wine
    2 truffles, peeled and diced
    1 cup cream
    2 teaspoons potato flour

Make 2 cups broth out of the neck and wing tips of the guinea hens and mince the livers to a pulp. Rub guinea hens with butter and roast them in a 350° F. oven for 30 minutes, basting them frequently with butter. Take them out and flambé them with the Grand Marnier. As soon as the flames have died down, carve the hens into quarters and arrange them in a casserole with the wine, truffles, broth, and ½ cup cream. Cover and simmer in a 325° F. oven until tender. Depending on the age and size of the hens this can take up to 2 hours. Take out the birds, stir the remaining cream with the potato flour and add it to the sauce. Boil until it is thickened. Return the hens to the sauce and bake long enough to reheat. May be served with purée of chestnuts, beaten up with a little port wine.

HUHN IN RIESLING
Broilers in White Wine
(page 17)

    8 tablespoons butter
    3 small broilers, quartered and seasoned
    3 large shallots, chopped
    ¼ cup brandy, warmed
    2½ cups Riesling or other dry white wine
    ½ pound small mushrooms
    1 cup heavy cream

Heat 6 tablespoons of the butter, add the chicken pieces and brown them on all sides. This should take 5 to 6 minutes. Add shallots and sauté 2 minutes longer. Flame with the brandy, and as soon as it subsides add the wine. Cover tightly and simmer until tender, about 20 minutes. Add remaining butter, mushrooms, and lemon juice, and transfer the chicken pieces to a warm casserole. Reduce the pan juices. Quickly stir in the cream and cook 1 minute. Strain the sauce over the chicken pieces and add the drained mushrooms. If a thicker sauce is preferred, stir 3 tablespoons flour into the last 2 tablespoons butter.

MAXIM KOPF'S PAPRIKAHUHN
Paprika Chicken
(page 158)

    1 cup chopped onion
    ½ cup butter
    2 tablespoons sweet paprika
    1 tablespoon salt
    ¼ teaspoon pepper
    3 broilers, quartered
    1 tablespoon flour
    1½ cups heavy sour cream

In a wide pan or Dutch oven, cook onion in butter until transparent, combine paprika, salt, and pepper, and season the chicken pieces well. Add them to the onion and brown them carefully on all sides. Cover the pan or Dutch oven, reduce heat and cook very slowly, turning the pieces several times, until they are tender, about 30 minutes. Remove from heat and strain the sauce into a small saucepan. Cover the chicken to keep it hot. Beat flour into ¼ cup of the sour cream until smooth. Beat in the remaining sour cream and beat the cream into the sauce. Stir over low heat until it thickens. Transfer the chicken to a hot serving casserole and pour the sauce over it.

PARTRIDGE IN CASSEROLE MADEIRA
(page 94)

6 partridges
1 carrot, scraped and quartered
1 onion, sliced
4 peppercorns and salt to taste
1 pound evenly sized small mushrooms
1¼ cups melted butter
4 shallots, chopped
4 cups soft, stale bread crumbs
1 cup diced celery
½ cup toasted almonds or washed, dried, and chopped salted almonds
2 teaspoons each, minced tarragon, basil, and rosemary
Salt and freshly ground black pepper to taste
1 egg, beaten
½ cup Madeira, or to taste
24 small white onions, trimmed and peeled
¼ cup red currant jelly
1 cup heavy cream

Make a strong broth by simmering giblets, wing tips, and necks of the partridges in 4 cups water with carrot, onion, and seasonings. Trim stems evenly with caps of mushrooms and chop them. Sauté the caps in a heavy casserole in ⅓ cup of the butter until they are glossy, about 5 minutes. Take them out with a slotted spoon and set them aside. Add the chopped stems and shallots to the butter left in the casserole, and sauté them 5 minutes longer. Add bread crumbs, celery, almonds, and herbs; stir well and remove from heat immediately. Season to taste and stir in the egg. Stuff the partridges with the mixture and truss them well. Brown them in the casserole in the remaining butter; turn them carefully to brown all sides. Add 2½ cups of the giblet broth and ¼ cup Madeira, and cover the casserole. Bake it in a 325° F. oven for 45 minutes, then baste every 15 minutes. Add more broth if necessary, and Madeira to taste, until the partridges are almost tender. Depending on their age, this can take up to 1½ hours. Add the mushroom caps, shallots, and the remaining broth, and bake uncovered until the birds are tender and the shallots are soft, about 20 to 30 minutes. Take out the partridges and keep them warm in the oven. Put the casserole over medium heat, stir in the jelly until it is dissolved, add the cream and boil the sauce, stirring until smooth, about 3 minutes. Correct seasoning, return the partridges to the casserole, and return to the oven only long enough to heat through before serving from the casserole.

PHEASANT IN SAUERKRAUT
(page 179)

6 cups Brown Sauerkraut, page 268
1 teaspoon juniper berries
2 tart apples, peeled, cored, and sliced
2 cups brown stock
½ cup bacon (or other) drippings
3 plump pheasant
  Salt and pepper to taste
1 tablespoon dried marjoram
¼ pound butter, melted
6 tablespoons flour
½ cup Madeira

Simmer Brown Sauerkraut with juniper berries and apples in brown stock in a covered kettle for 6 hours, turning it over at intervals. Melt drippings in a heavy casserole, add the drained sauerkraut, and cook it covered over very low heat while roasting the pheasant. Prepare a broth of wing tips, necks, and giblets of the pheasant and reduce it to 3 cups. Rub the birds with salt, pepper, and marjoram, and truss them. Brush them generously with melted butter and roast them in an open roasting pan in a 375° F. oven for 40 minutes, basting every 10 minutes with the remaining butter and pan juices. Turn the sauerkraut and spread it out. Remove trussing strings and bury the whole pheasant or the carved breasts and legs deep in the sauerkraut. Add half the strained broth from the giblets and simmer the pheasant, covered, for 20 minutes. Place the pan in which the pheasant were roasted over low heat on top of the stove. Stir flour into the butter in the pan until it is well browned. Add the remaining stock and the Madeira and continue to cook and stir until the sauce is smooth; season it to taste. Serve the pheasant in the sauerkraut, and pass the strained brown sauce separately.

POULARDE BASQUE
Poached Chicken with Noodle Stuffing
(page 135)

½ pound small shelled and deveined shrimp
¼ pound butter
3 tablespoons chopped parsley
½ cup dry bread crumbs
1 pound narrow noodles, cooked
1 8- to 10-pound capon or roasting chicken
2 to 4 cups chicken broth, as needed
1 onion, sliced
1 carrot, sliced
Salt and pepper to taste

Fry the shrimp in half the butter only until they are almost transparent. Take them out of the butter, add the parsley and crumbs to the pan and fry until the crumbs are brown. Mix shrimp and crumbs with the cooked noodles and fill the chicken with it. Secure the opening and truss the bird firmly. Brown it evenly on all sides in butter and place it in a deep casserole not much larger than the bird. Add 2 cups broth, the onion, carrot, salt and pepper, and poach covered in a 375° F. oven. Add broth as necessary. After 1½ hours, take off the lid and let the chicken brown a little more. Test for doneness and remove from the oven as soon as it is tender. Test with a skewer in the thickest part of the thigh. If the juice that runs out is clear the bird is done; if pink, continue poaching, uncovered. Correct the seasoning of the pan juices and serve from the casserole with Brussels sprouts, or any preferred green vegetable, and a berry compote.

POULARDE PHARAO
Roast Stuffed Chicken
(page 135)

1 recipe Risi Pisi, page 279
1 onion, chopped
2 tablespoons butter
3 tomatoes, peeled, seeded, and chopped
½ cup raisins

½ cup pistachio nuts, coarsely chopped
1 8- to 10-pound capon or roasting chicken
6 tablespoons soft butter
1 cup dry white wine
   Salt and pepper to taste
1 cup chicken broth

Prepare the Risi Pisi, undercooking the rice. Brown the onion in the butter and add it with the tomatoes, raisins, and nuts to the rice. Stuff the chicken with this mixture; secure the opening and truss the bird firmly. Rub it well with half the soft butter and roast it for about 18 minutes to the pound in a 350° F. oven. Add the wine, season the bird, and baste it frequently. Cover the breast with foil after the first half hour. Remove the foil about 30 minutes before the bird is done and spread the remaining soft butter over the breast. Take the bird out of the oven, add the broth to the pan juices, and boil for 4 minutes. Strain into a sauceboat and serve the chicken with a tomato salad.

POULETS EN CHAUD-FROID TALLEYRAND
Cold Broilers in Aspic
(page 94)

3 tender young broilers
1 carrot
1 small onion
1 bouquet garni
¾ cup butter
8 tablespoons flour
1 cup cream
1 teaspoon brown coloring (Bovril or Kitchen Bouquet)
¼ cup red currant jelly
3 packages plain gelatin
½ cup Madeira
   Salt and pepper to taste
1 jar red spiced crab apples
12 slices truffle

Put the giblets, wing tips, and necks of the broilers in 4 cups cold water with carrot, onion, and bouquet garni. Rub the broilers well with half the butter, and roast or broil them on a rotisserie until they are tender, about 1 hour depending on size; let them cool. Brown the remaining butter in a heavy saucepan, stir in the flour and cook, stirring until browned. Moisten the brown roux with the strained broth from the giblets and stir it into a thick, smooth sauce. Add cream, brown coloring, and jelly, and let the sauce simmer over very low heat. Stir the gelatin into the Madeira and set it aside for 10 minutes. Remove the sauce from heat, stir in the softened lump of gelatin until it is dissolved. Add seasoning and set it aside to cool—but not to set. As soon as the sauce shows signs of setting, quarter, skin, and trim the 12 chicken pieces, lay them on a cake rack, and glaze them with the brown sauce. Continue to glaze them until they are heavily coated. Reheat the sauce as well as whatever sauce falls through the rack by setting the saucepan in warm water whenever it becomes too thick to flow. Mound the spiced apples in the center of a serving platter. Arrange the glazed chicken pieces in a circle around them and garnish the pieces with truffle slices. Serve with cranberry sauce and a salad of green beans in herb mayonnaise.

REHRÜCKEN MIT KASTANIEN
Saddle of Venison with Chestnuts
(page 19)

1 4-pound saddle of young venison, larded in 4 rows with larding
    pork
6 juniper berries
4 peppercorns
¼ cup butter
2 cups sour cream
2 tablespoons flour, stirred into ¼ cup water
1 cup boiling brown stock or bouillon, or to taste
2 tablespoons red currant jelly
    Salt to taste
1 recipe Browned Chestnuts, page 269

Place venison in an open roasting pan. Add juniper berries and peppercorns and season the meat with salt. Spread it with the butter and roast it in a 375° F. oven, basting it frequently with pan juices until it starts to brown. Add the cream and continue to roast and baste until done, about 1 hour. Transfer the venison to a hot serving platter and keep it warm. Skim fat from the sauce and stir in the flour and water over low heat. As the sauce begins to thicken, add boiling stock to taste. Dissolve the currant jelly in the sauce, correct the seasoning, and serve with Browned Chestnuts, red cabbage, and compote of fruit.

SADDLE OF HARE
(page 40)

2 well-trimmed and larded saddles of hare
  Salt and pepper to taste
1 teaspoon powdered juniper berries
2 small onions, sliced thin and separated into rings
1 lemon, slivered rind only
¼ cup melted butter
3 tablespoons tarragon vinegar
2 cups sour cream
2 tablespoons flour

Arrange the saddles in an open buttered roasting pan and sprinkle them with seasoning and juniper. Cover with onion rings and slivered lemon rind, and pour the melted butter over it. Roast the hare in a 350° F. oven, sprinkling it with vinegar. Baste it frequently with 1½ cups of sour cream. Roast until the saddle is brown and done, about 1 to 1½ hours depending on size. Stir flour into the remaining cream and continue to baste with it. Take out the hare and arrange it on a hot serving platter. Stir the sauce and blend or purée it with the onions, lemon, and cream into a smooth sauce. Season it to taste and serve it in a sauceboat. Accompany the hare with lingonberry conserve and mashed potatoes covered with browned, chopped hazelnuts.

SQUAB CHICKENS IN CASSEROLE
Baron Popper's Leibspeise (*Favorite Dish*)
(page 125)

6 squab chickens or Rock Cornish game hens
2 carrots, scraped and quartered
2 medium onions, quartered
4 celery stalks with leaves
4 sprigs parsley
10 tablespoons butter
⅔ cup flour
1 cup milk
1 pound fresh spinach or 2 2-pound bunches broccoli
4 egg yolks
2 cups heavy cream
   Salt and white pepper to taste

Truss chickens or hens loosely, just to keep the legs from sprawling in cooking. Place them in a large kettle with wing tips and necks, and carrots, onions, celery, and parsley, and pour over them enough boiling salted water to cover. Cover the kettle and boil gently until tender, about 20 to 25 minutes. Remove the trussing strings and skins, and keep the birds warm in a heated casserole with a little of their hot broth. Return the skins to the kettle and boil uncovered over high heat until the broth is reduced to about 3 cups. Strain it through a triple cheesecloth and set it aside. In the top of a 1½-quart double boiler, over boiling water, melt the butter, stir in the flour and gradually stir in the milk and 2 cups of the strained broth. Stir until the sauce is smooth and thickened; reduce heat to simmer. Wash spinach and discard coarse stems. Cook it in a covered kettle over low heat with only the water that clings to the leaves, until it is wilted and very green. If broccoli is used, trim off the stems, divide into rosettes and cook in salted water until just tender and green. Beat the yolks into the cream, add a little of the hot sauce from the double boiler and stir the mixture well. Return it to the double boiler and stir it over simmering water until the sauce is smooth, thickened, and very creamy. Season to taste. Heat the chickens in the covered casserole, pour off the stock, and spread the spinach or broccoli over them. Cover the birds with the hot sauce from the double boiler and serve them from the casserole. If preferred, enough broth may be added to ensure at least 6 to 7 cups of a thinner sauce, and then the chickens may be served from soup plates with the spinach or broccoli in the soup around them.

SQUABS WITH SCRAPPLE
(page 50)

  1 onion, chopped
18 medium mushrooms (chop only the stems)
  1 pound chicken livers
  2 cups Philadelphia scrapple
  3 slices fried bacon, crumbled
    Salt to taste
  6 jumbo squab
  6 large slices larding pork
½ pound butter, melted
½ pint Cognac

Brown onion lightly in butter, add the chopped mushroom stems and the chicken livers, and sauté for a few minutes until livers are lightly browned but pink inside. Add scrapple and bacon. Crush the livers and scrapple roughly. Pour contents of the pan into a chopping bowl and chop together until livers and scrapple are distributed evenly through the stuffing. Add salt to taste. Stuff the squabs, truss them firmly, and tie the larding pork over their breasts. Brush them with butter and put them close together in a roasting pan. Put mushroom caps over and between them and roast in a 375° F. oven for 1 hour. Baste frequently with remaining butter and Cognac. Deglaze the pan with a little boiling water and strain the juices into a sauceboat.

SUPRÊMES OF PHEASANT
(page 91)

6 suprêmes of pheasant (halved breasts with the first wing joint
    left on)
  Salt and freshly ground black pepper to taste
6 thin pieces of pork fat
½ cup butter
6 greening apples, peeled, cored, and cut into 6 wedges each
1 cup heavy cream
2 pounds cooked sauerkraut

Season the suprêmes and wrap them in pork fat. Tie them loosely, and sauté them in butter in a deep casserole until they are golden on both sides. Reduce the heat, cover tightly, and simmer for about 20 minutes. Add the apple wedges and cook for 10 minutes longer. Remove pork fat, add the cream, and boil for 3 minutes. Correct seasoning, arrange the suprêmes on the hot sauerkraut, surround with the apples, and cover with the sauce. Serve with browned potatoes and celery root salad. Use pheasant legs and carcasses for soup or stew.

WIENER HUHN
Viennese Chicken
(page 142)

   2 large broilers, quartered
     Salt and white pepper to taste
   1 onion
   1 bouquet garni
   1 slice lemon
   6 tablespoons butter
   ½ cup flour
   2 tomatoes, skinned, seeded, and diced
   1 thick slice ham, diced
   1 pimento, diced
   2 tablespoons chopped parsley, seasoned
   1 recipe Risi Pisi, page 279

Place seasoned chicken pieces, onion, bouquet garni, and lemon in a small kettle. Pour boiling water over them to just cover, and simmer, covered, until chicken is tender, about 20 to 25 minutes. Take out the chicken pieces, draw off the skin, loosen the bones, and leave the chicken in very large pieces. Return skin and bones to the kettle and boil rapidly to obtain a stronger broth. Melt butter in a saucepan, stir in the flour, and gradually moisten with 3 cups of the strained broth. Reduce heat, simmer the sauce, stirring occasionally, for 15 minutes. Put chicken pieces and diced tomato into the sauce and cook long enough to reheat the chicken. Serve chicken and sauce in a deep platter, sprinkle with ham and pimento, and surround it with the Risi Pisi.

Meats

Côtelettes de Veau en Papillote
Côtes de Mouton Cyrano
Côtes d'Agneau Lavallière
Faare Frikassée
Filet of Beef with Duxelles
Filet Mignon Opera
Filet Mignon with Rosemary
Grenadins von Kalb
Karlsbader Gulyas
Kasseler Rippchen (Boiled)
Kasseler Rippchen (Roasted)

Langue de Boeuf Mentchikof
Lunzer Gulyas
Münchner Schweinebraten
Polpettini
Pot Roast
Rohes Rindfleisch
Selle d'Agneau Richelieu
Tournedos Rossini
Veal with Cold Sauce Espagnole
Veal Gaston
Züricher Geschnitzeltes

COTELETTES DE VEAU EN PAPILLOTE
Veal Cutlets in Paper
(page 165)

6 thick veal chops (lamb chops may be used instead)
6 tablespoons butter
3 shallots, chopped
6 medium mushrooms, sliced
   Salt and pepper to taste
1 tablespoon chopped parsley
1 tablespoon chopped ripe olives
1 tablespoon chopped chives
6 slices cooked ham, cut to the size of chops

Pan-fry seasoned veal chops in butter until brown on one side and just long enough to whiten the other side. Arrange them on six 12 x 12-inch squares of parchment paper with the brown side up. In the butter left in the pan, sauté the shallots until puffed and golden, add the mushrooms and stir for 3 minutes. Season with salt and pepper. Mix with parsley, olives, and chives, and spread the mixture over the chops. Cover with a slice of ham. Fold the paper and turn the edges under. Arrange the 6 packages on a baking sheet and bake in a 350° F. oven until the paper is brown and brittle, about 40 minutes. Serve in the paper and let every guest open his own. (May be served with a colorful salad of tomato and raw zucchini.)

CÔTES D'AGNEAU LAVALLIÈRE
Lamb Chops with Purée of Asparagus
(page 101)

1 1-pound bunch asparagus, trimmed
8 tablespoons butter
4 tablespoons flour
1 to 1½ cups of the water in which asparagus was boiled
12 small or 6 large cooked artichoke bottoms
   Salt and freshly ground black pepper to taste
½ cup grated Swiss cheese
6 1½-inch-thick loin lamb chops

Prepare the garnish of chopped asparagus in artichoke bottoms before broiling the chops. Trim 1½-inch-long heads from the asparagus spears and cut the stalks across into ¼-inch sections. Discard all tough ends. Boil the asparagus pieces in salted water until they are soft. Blanch the heads in salted water in a second saucepan for about 6 minutes, or until barely tender. Heat the artichoke bottoms in simmering water and have them ready. Melt 4 tablespoons of the butter over low heat, stir in the flour, and moisten with the asparagus water. Stir into a thick white sauce with a wire whisk; season with salt and pepper. Add the cooked asparagus pieces and fill the mixture into the artichoke bottoms. Place the asparagus heads on top of each and sprinkle with Swiss cheese. Brush the chops with part of the melted butter and broil them with their surface about 3 inches from the source of heat, about 16 minutes—for rare— turning them and brushing them with butter once. Dot the artichoke bottoms with the remaining 4 tablespoons of butter and put them in a 450° F. oven until they are brown, or broil them carefully with the chops until the cheese has browned. Arrange chops between the artichoke bottoms and serve at once with Sauce Bordelaise, page 292.

CÔTES DE MOUTON CYRANO
Mutton Chops with Mushroom Tarts
(page 121)

½ recipe Duxelles, page 272
6 baked Tart Shells, page 204
2 tablespoons chopped mint
12 1-inch-thick mutton chops
4 tablespoons hot melted butter
   Salt and freshly ground black pepper to taste

The Duxelles and Tart Shells may be prepared as long as one or two days before they are needed. Warm the shells in a low oven, heat the Duxelles in the top of a double boiler with a little more cream, and chop the mint before broiling the meat. Brush the chops with butter, season them well, and broil them with their surface about 2½ inches from the source of heat for about 8 to 10 minutes on each side, turning them once and brushing them with more butter. Depending on the age of the mutton, decrease or increase broiling time. Serve the chops on a hot platter with the Tart Shells filled with Duxelles and sprinkled with mint. The Duxelles should be kept sufficiently creamy so that no sauce is required.

NOTE: If lamb chops are used, broil them 5 to 6 minutes on each side.

FAARE FRIKASSEE
Norwegian Lamb
(page 164)

4½ to 5 pounds neck and shoulder of lamb, cut for stew
     1½ tablespoons salt, or to taste
      6 white peppercorns
      1 bay leaf
      2 large onions, sliced
      1 sprig fresh dill
18 to 24 small white onions
      ¼ pound butter
      ½ cup flour
      2 tablespoons lemon juice, or to taste
      ¼ cup cut dill
      1 egg yolk
      ¾ cup cream

Place lamb in a casserole on the stove and immediately pour on just enough boiling water to cover. Bring back to boil, skim, and reduce heat to simmer. Add seasonings, bay leaf, onions, and dill. Cover tightly and simmer the stew for about 1½ to 2 hours, or until meat is tender. About 15 minutes before the lamb is done, add small white onions. When meat and onions are done, remove bay leaf and dill, and drain off the broth left in the casserole. Cover it and keep the meat warm in a low oven. Measure the broth and strain 4 cups for the sauce. In a wide pan, melt the butter, stir in flour, and gradually stir in the broth. Add lemon juice and dill. Reduce heat as low as possible. Beat the yolk into the cream and stir it into the hot sauce until it is smooth and creamy. Do not let the sauce boil after the yolk has been added. Pour the sauce over the lamb in the casserole and serve with potatoes boiled in their jackets and shaken in hot butter and salt.

FILET OF BEEF WITH DUXELLES
(page 50)

1 recipe Duxelles, page 272
6 baked Tart Shells, page 204
1 3-pound tenderloin of beef, trimmed and larded
  Salt and freshly ground pepper to taste
¼ cup soft butter
3 large potatoes, cut in thick slices
1 cup Madeira
½ cup dry white wine
2 slices tongue, cut into 6 rounds with a cookie cutter

Prepare Duxelles and Tart Shells. They can both be prepared in advance and heated. Have butcher trim and lard the filet. Season it to taste and brush it generously with soft butter. Lay the meat on the potato slices in an open pan and roast in a 400° F. oven for 20 minutes, basting frequently with the pan juices. Turn the filet, add the Madeira and white wine, and roast it about 10 minutes more. (The filet should always be rare.) Arrange the filet on a hot serving platter while reducing the pan juices over very high heat. Garnish the platter with small Tart Shells filled with Duxelles, and pass the strained juices separately. Place a round of tongue on each Duxelles-filled Tart Shell.

FILET MIGNON OPÉRA
(page 178)

6 ovals made with Duchess Potatoes
1½ cups Sauce Madère, page 293
1 bunch asparagus, tied and trimmed short
6 tablespoons butter
4 tablespoons chopped onion
1 pound chicken livers
  Salt and pepper to taste
6 filet mignon steaks, cut 1 inch thick

Prepare the potatoes and the sauce. Steam the asparagus spears in salted water 20 minutes before serving. Use two pans; heat 3 tablespoons butter in each. Cook the onions in one of them, and as soon as they are golden, add the chicken livers and fry until brown but not done through. In the meantime, season the steaks and pan-fry them in the second pan for 4 minutes on the first side and 3 minutes on the second. Arrange them on a hot platter. Season the chicken livers and arrange them around the steaks. Put the 6 potato ovals around the steaks with a spatula and keep the platter hot in a low oven. Quickly drain the asparagus and divide the spears over the potato ovals. Serve at once with a sauceboat of Sauce Madère.

FILET MIGNON WITH ROSEMARY
(page 176)

6 filet mignon steaks
6 sprigs rosemary (if poor or thin, use 12 or more sprigs)
    Enough butter to cover the filets halfway
    Salt and pepper to taste

Fold 1 or 2 thick sprigs of rosemary around each filet and fry them quickly in butter until brown, turning them once. The pan must be hot enough to fry them deep brown in 5 minutes on each side. (The entire secret of this recipe is to fry the filets in such a small deep pan that they can be crowded into it and the flavor of the rosemary is not dispersed.) Season and serve with the rosemary-flavored pan juices. Serve on very hot plates with sautéed cucumbers and zucchini and Fondant Potatoes (peeled potatoes boiled until half tender in salted water, then browned slowly on all sides in the oven).

GRENADINS VON KALB
Larded Filets of Veal
(page 168)

2 pounds tenderloin of veal, cut into 6 slices
3 slices thick bacon, cut into larding strips
2 tablespoons butter
1 medium onion, sliced thin
1 carrot, sliced thin
    Salt and pepper to taste
1 cup dry white wine
2 cups veal or beef stock
1 pound noodles
1 recipe Purée of Green Peas, page 279

Pound the veal filets lightly and lard them or have them larded by the butcher, with bacon strips cut from 2 slices of the thick bacon. Brown the meat quickly in the butter over high heat. Take out the meat. Lay the remaining bacon, onion, and carrot in an enameled casserole, and arrange the filets on top. Season to taste and add the wine. Cook over high heat until the casserole is nearly dry. Add 1 cup of the stock, and when it has boiled up, cover the casserole, reduce the heat, and braise for about 40 minutes until the veal is tender and the liquid is nearly absorbed. In the meantime, prepare the Purée of Green Peas and cook the noodles. Arrange the filets on a hot platter and strain any sauce left in the pan over them, and keep them hot. Return the pan to the top of the stove, deglaze it with the remaining stock, and stir the sauce for a few minutes. Correct seasoning, and pour the sauce over the filets. Serve them garnished with buttered noodles (which may be enhanced with ½ cup of diced tongue), and pass the Purée of Green Peas separately.

KARLSBADER GULYAS
(A Transylvanian Recipe)
(page 132)

3 onions, finely chopped
½ cup butter
1 tablespoon sweet paprika
3 pounds shoulder of pork, cut into 2-inch cubes
1 bay leaf
2 pounds sauerkraut, precooked for at least 2 hours (retain the juice)
2 teaspoons caraway seeds
  Salt and pepper to taste
2 cups sour cream

In a heavy kettle, sauté onions in 6 tablespoons butter and sprinkle with paprika. Stir until they are transparent and golden, about 7 minutes. Add the meat and turn it until it is lightly browned. Add the bay leaf, cover the kettle, and simmer the meat in its own juice for 1½ hours. If it is very dry, add a little water or stock when necessary. In a second kettle sauté well-drained sauerkraut in remaining butter until it is almost dry, stirring constantly. Add the retained juice and caraway seeds, and simmer it for as long as the meat is cooked. Combine meat and sauerkraut, and season to taste. Continue simmering, adding water only as absolutely necessary, until meat is tender. Stir in sour cream, and cook only long enough to heat thoroughly.

KASSELER RIPPCHEN (BOILED)
Smoked Loin of Pork or Pork Chops
(page 15)

1 3- to 4-pound smoked loin of pork or 8 pork chops
2 onions, quartered
1 carrot, quartered
1 teaspoon caraway seeds or juniper berries
6 peppercorns
1 bay leaf

Boil the loin or chops with the vegetables, spices, and bay leaf until tender, about 1½ hours for the loin and 30 minutes for the chops. Take them out of the water, drain well, and serve on a bed of Brown Sauerkraut, page 268, with apple sauce or stewed prunes and apricots.

KASSELER RIPPCHEN (ROASTED)
Smoked Pork Roast with Sauerkraut
(page 15)

1 3- to 4-pound smoked loin of pork (may have to be ordered from the butcher)
1 cup dried prunes
1 cup dried apricots
½ cup raisins
1 teaspoon marjoram
2 tablespoons flour
½ cup water
1 cup heavy cream
   Salt and pepper to taste

Have the butcher cut the ribs partway through so that they can be folded back and tied. Place dried fruits on the back of the ribs, sprinkle with marjoram, and tie the ends back to cover them. Place the roast, meat side down, in an open roasting pan and add 1½ cups boiling water. Roast the meat for 1 hour in a 400° F. oven, basting frequently and adding more boiling water as needed. Turn the roast and continue basting until crisp and done, about 45 to 60 minutes longer. Place the roast on a hot platter and arrange the fruit around it. Keep it warm while making the sauce. Scrape down the brown particles on the sides of the pan, and bring the pan juices to a boil. Remove from heat and stir in the flour. Add ½ cup water and cream; boil, stirring for 1 minute. Correct seasoning and serve the roast with Brown Sauerkraut, page 268, and steamed potatoes.

LANGUE DE BOEUF MENTCHIKOF
Beef Tongue
(page 101)

1 4- to 5-pound smoked beef tongue
2 onions, stuck with 6 cloves
2 carrots, quartered
4 celery stalks
1 bottle dry white wine
1 bay leaf
1½ cups each: button mushrooms, cucumber dice, small white
   onions, red grapes

Rinse the tongue and let it stand in cold water for 3 hours. Change the water, place it over high heat and bring it to a rapid boil with the vegetables. Cook covered for 1 hour. Take out the tongue and steam it gently in a second kettle with the wine and bay leaf and enough of the strained broth to half cover it. Reduce the remaining broth over high heat until there are 2 cups. Put the broth and the soft vegetables through the blender and season to taste. As soon as the tongue is tender (test on the underside with a fork) take it out and drain it. Cut along the side with a sharp knife and pull off the rough outside skin. Trim off the base and surround the tongue with a mixture of equal quantities of sautéed button mushrooms, sautéed cucumber dice or lozenges, and boiled onions. To this mixture add Malaga or any other red grapes, seeded, just before serving.

LUNZER GULYAS
(page 187)

This can be made well in advance. The longer it simmers or the more often it is reheated, the better.

   3 pounds onions, chopped
   ¾ cup oil
   1 tablespoon sharp paprika
   1 tablespoon sweet paprika
   3 pounds chuck, cut into 2½-inch chunks
   1 garlic clove, crushed
      Salt and freshly ground pepper to taste
   1 lemon, thin outside rind only
   1 tablespoon caraway seeds
   1 bay leaf
   1 sprig rosemary or 1 teaspoon dried
   3 tablespoons flour

   In a heavy skillet, fry onions in oil, stirring constantly until puffed; sprinkle with the paprikas and continue stirring until golden, about 7 minutes. Transfer onions with a slotted spoon to a heavy kettle. Brown the meat on all sides in the oil left in the pan; add oil if necessary. Add the meat and oil in the pan to the kettle with the garlic, seasonings, and lemon rind, crushed with caraway seeds in a mortar, and herbs. Cover and simmer for 1½ hours, adding beef broth only if necessary. Take out the bay leaf, sprinkle gradually with flour, and stir constantly until it is browned and absorbed. Simmer 30 minutes longer, stirring frequently.

MÜNCHNER SCHWEINEBRATEN
Munich Roast Pork
(page 40)

1 10-pound loin roast or leg of pork (fresh ham)
1 teaspoon caraway seeds
1 teaspoon crushed black pepper
1 garlic clove, crushed
  Salt to taste
2 cups dry white wine, heated
4 tablespoons flour
1 recipe Purée of Green Peas, page 279
1 10-ounce jar lingonberries

Pound the roast well with a mallet and rub it with caraway seeds, pepper, and garlic. Put it in a roasting pan and set it aside for 1 hour. Salt the meat to taste, turn it with the fat side down and roast it for 2 hours, basting at first with wine and later with the pan juices, in a 325° F. oven. Turn the meat over with the fat side up. Baste it regularly every 10 minutes until done, in order to make the skin as crisp as possible. (Roast a whole loin for about 35 minutes per pound and a leg for 25 minutes per pound.) When the roast is turned fat side up, the fat may be scored into small triangles with a sharp knife. Take out the meat, pour off all but ½ cup pan juices, stir in the flour until smooth, and then set the pan over low heat. Gradually stir in 2 cups boiling water and stir until it boils. Simmer for 3 minutes, correct seasoning, and serve in a sauceboat. Serve the roast with the Purée of Green Peas and lingonberries. Brown Sauerkraut, page 268, is also a good accompaniment.

SERVES 6 TO 8

POLPETTINI
Miniature Veal Meatballs
(page 114)

1 slice salt pork
1 pound lean veal, ground
4 slices stale white bread
2 cups veal or beef stock
½ onion, finely chopped
4 tablespoons butter
2 tablespoons finely chopped parsley
1 egg, beaten
   Salt and pepper to taste
½ cup flour mixed with 1 teaspoon paprika for dredging

Simmer the pork for 20 minutes; cut it into strips. Grind the veal again with the pork strips and the bread, previously soaked in ½ cup of the stock and pressed out until dry. Fry the onion in 1 tablespoon butter until golden and drain it well. Put the mixture through the finest blade of the meat grinder once more with the onion and parsley. Stir in the egg and season to taste. Shape the mixture into hazelnut-sized meatballs with floured hands and dredge them with prepared flour. Heat the remaining butter in a heavy pan and fry the meatballs over high heat, shaking to brown all sides as quickly as possible. Add the remaining stock, cover the pan and simmer the meatballs gently until done, about 10 minutes. Take them out with a slotted spoon and keep them hot in a low oven. Turn up the heat and reduce the sauce remaining in the pan to 2 cups. Pour it over the meatballs and serve them over a pasta. (The Polpettini may also be added to tomato sauce and served over pasta.)

POT ROAST
(page 150)

1 5-pound bottom round or rump of beef, rolled and tied
  Flour
2 tablespoons each, butter and oil
1 1-pound-4-ounce can tomatoes or 2½ cups stewed tomatoes
2 carrots, quartered
1 onion, stuck with cloves
1 bay leaf
2 sprigs each, parsley and thyme
1 curl lemon peel
1 to 2 tablespoons salt to taste
4 black peppercorns, freshly crushed
1 cup red wine
  Beef bouillon, if necessary
6 tablespoons flour
6 tablespoons butter
18 small white cooked onions, optional

Rub the beef well with flour and brown it in a Dutch oven in the butter and oil. When it is evenly browned on all sides, add tomatoes, carrots, onion, bay leaf, herbs, and lemon peel. Cover tightly and simmer for about 2 hours. Add salt and pepper and a little red wine. Cook 4 hours in all, turning the meat 2 or 3 times, and add a little red wine each time. When the meat is tender, take it out, remove the strings and keep it hot. Depending on how juicy the meat was and how much sauce has cooked away, add enough bouillon to make 4 cups in all. Put the contents of the Dutch oven through the blender, or purée it through a sieve, and correct the seasoning. If a thicker sauce is preferred, stir flour with butter and stir it into the simmering sauce until it thickens. Cooked and drained onions may be added to the sauce. Return the roast to the sauce to reheat, then place it in a deep hot platter. Cut six even slices and lay them in front of the unsliced piece. Pour the sauce over the roast and serve with steamed potatoes and cold bean salad.

SERVES **6** TO **8**

ROHES RINDFLEISCH
Beefsteak Tartare
(page 188)

2 1½-inch-thick slices of top round of beef
3 egg yolks
4 dill pickles, thinly sliced
½ cup minced onion
3 tablespoons smallest capers
3 tablespoons Düsseldorf or Dijon mustard
  Cruets of oil and vinegar
  Small decanter of sherry
  Hot lightly buttered toast triangles

Scrape the beef with the side of a strong silver spoon and place the scraped meat in a bowl with a cover. Turn the slices of beef and scrape them until only the sinews are left (they can be used for soup stock). Shape the beef into 3 rounds. Put them on a serving platter and make a small depression in the center of each. Drop an egg yolk into each. Surround each round with pickle slices and garnish the platter with small mounds of onion, capers, and mustard. Serve the beef with the cruets, seasonings, and sherry. Every two guests will share one of the beef rounds which they season and flavor to their own taste. Pass around salt and pepper. If sherry is added, it should be just a dash.

SELLE D'AGNEAU RICHELIEU
Roast Saddle of Lamb with Filled Mushrooms
(page 177)

1 saddle of lamb weighing about 7 pounds before trimming, or
    4½ pounds trimmed and tied
⅔ cup melted butter
  Salt and freshly ground black pepper to taste
3 cups diced vegetables, carrots, onions, and celery
2 cups brown stock

Brush trimmed and tied saddle generously with butter and season it to taste. Roast it in an open pan in a 475° F. oven for 15 minutes. Reduce heat to 400°, add the vegetables and baste every 10 minutes with the remaining butter. Turn the vegetables, and when they become brown, add 1 cup of the stock to the pan. Roast 20 minutes more for rare, and anywhere from 30 to 40 minutes longer for pink or well-done lamb. A meat thermometer should reach 140° F. Transfer the roast to a serving platter, remove strings, and return it to the oven with heat turned off and door open until the sauce is completed. Place the pan from which the roast was removed over low heat; add remaining stock, and scrape the sides of the pan into it. Simmer for 5 minutes, stirring. Correct the seasoning, strain the sauce into a sauceboat, and serve at once with the lamb garnished with the filled mushrooms.

SERVES 4 TO 6

Mushroom Garnish:

  16 **evenly sized large mushrooms**
  3 **tablespoons butter**
  3 **shallots, chopped**
  ½ to ¾ **cups dried bread crumbs**
  ½ **cup broth or stock**
  2 **tablespoons minced parsley**

Cut stems from mushrooms and chop them fine. Sauté caps in butter only until they are glossy and arrange them, close together, stem side up, in a buttered baking dish. Stir shallots in the butter remaining in the pan for 5 minutes longer, add crumbs and half the parsley and stir until crumbs are lightly browned. Fill the mixture into the mushroom caps, add broth to the pan and bake in a 375° F. oven for 15 minutes. Sprinkle with remaining parsley and use to garnish the lamb.

VARIATION: After lamb is roasted, add 2 cups heavy cream to the pan, stir on top of the stove, and simmer for 3 minutes; season and blend the contents of the pan into a smooth sauce.

TOURNEDOS ROSSINI
(page 6)

6 thick slices white bread, cut into croutons, the size of the tournedos
½ cup butter for frying bread on both sides
6 slices goose-liver pâté, or ¾ cup goose-liver parfait
6 1-inch-thick tournedos (slices cut from tail section of filet of beef),
    weighing about ¼ pound each
1 large peeled truffle, simmered in sherry and cut into 6 slices
  Oil for brushing tournedos
  Salt and pepper to taste
  Sauce Madère, page 293

Fry the bread croutons slowly in the butter in a wide pan, turning them until both sides are golden. Drain and arrange them on a hot platter. Shake the goose-liver pâté slices in the butter for a moment and place them on the bread. If parfait is used, spread it on the warm bread slices. Brush the tournedos with oil and broil them in a very hot broiler for about 3 minutes on each side, or to taste. If pan-fried in butter, fry for 3 to 4 minutes on each side, or to taste. (The meat should be rare.) Place the tournedos on the liver, top with a truffle slice, and serve with Sauce Madère.

VEAL WITH COLD SAUCE ESPAGNOLE
(page 101)

2 envelopes gelatin
½ cup sherry
2 cups bouillon
1 4- to 5-pound rolled roast of veal, roasted for 2 to 2½ hours,
    and cooled, strings removed
6 evenly sized tomatoes, 1½ pounds, peeled, cut in half, and emptied
    of the pulp
2 cups cooked baby green peas
2 cups cooked white pearl corn
1 cup Dick's French Dressing, page 295
½ bunch crisp watercress, cleaned, with thick stems removed

Soften the gelatin in the sherry. Bring the bouillon to a boil, remove from the heat, and stir in the gelatin until it is dissolved. Pour the aspic into a shal-

low pan and chill until it is set. Dice it with a sharp knife. Carve half the
veal and set the remaining roast at the end of a platter; arrange the carved
slices in an overlapping fan in front of the meat, and garnish the platter with
the 12 tomato halves filled wth green pea salad and corn salad, both bound
with Dick's French Dressing. Fill the empty spaces with bunches of watercress
and arrange lines of the minced aspic on the sliced meat. Pipe a rosette or put a
teaspoon of Cold Espagnole Sauce, page 294, on top of the green peas and corn,
and serve the rest of the sauce in a separate bowl.

VEAL GASTON
Stuffed Filet of Veal
(page 96)

Stuffing:

> 10 bread slices, crusts removed
> 1¼ cups milk, heated
> 3 slices bacon, diced
> ½ onion, diced
> 4 sprigs parsley, chopped
> 2 tablespoons salt butter
> 2 egg yolks, beaten
> 4 slices smoked beef tongue, diced
> 3 gherkins, diced
> Salt and pepper to taste

Soak bread in milk for 10 minutes. Press out the milk (a potato ricer does
this well). Sauté bacon, onion, and parsley in the butter until bacon is done.
Pour off the fat, stir in the bread, and remove from heat. Bind with yolks, and
add tongue, gherkins, and seasoning.

The Filets:

> 2 1½- to 2-pound veal filets, larded
> ½ cup hot melted salt butter
> Salt and white pepper to taste
> ½ cup flour
> 2½ cups beef bouillon
> ¾ cup heavy cream

Cut filets down the side to create a pocket. Fill with stuffing and sew them with kitchen string. Place the filets in an open roasting pan. Pour hot butter over them, sprinkle with salt and pepper, and roast in a 400° F. oven for about 20 minutes, or to the desired doneness. Take out the filets, remove the string, and keep them warm. Set the pan over low heat and stir in the flour. Moisten with the bouillon and cream alternately and continue adding them a little at a time, until the sauce is thick and brown. Pour it over the filets and serve with cauliflower and browned potato balls.

ZÜRICHER GESCHNETZELTES
Veal Strips Cooked at the Table
(page 23)

This is an ideal dish to prepare in an electric skillet at the table.

½ cup salt butter
1 small onion, minced
2 pounds veal cutlets, trimmed, lightly pounded, and cut into long
    narrow strips
½ cup brandy, warmed
    Salt and pepper to taste
4 tablespoons flour
¾ cup dry white wine
3 tablespoons finely chopped parsley
1 cup heavy cream (optional)

Heat butter until it smokes, add the onion and stir until it is transparent and lightly browned. Stir in the veal strips with a wooden spoon, and as soon as they are whitened, about 1½ minutes, pour over the warmed brandy and ignite. As soon as the flame subsides, season the meat and shake the flour over it through a fine sieve. Stir for 1 more minute until the flour is brown, then add the wine. Simmer 4 minutes. Sprinkle with parsley. Serve at once, or add the cream, increase heat and boil 1 minute longer. Serve with browned potato cakes, made of a julienne of shredded potatoes, and apple sauce.

Vegetables and Pasta

Aubergines Irma
Brown Sauerkraut
Browned Chestnuts
Chestnut-Stuffed Mushrooms
Chou-Fleur Ignatieff
Choux de Bruxelles aux Marrons
Cold Stuffed Mushrooms
Dilled Potato Ring
Duxelles
Epinard à la Créme
Flan aux Oignons
Gebackener Karfiole
Griess Auflauf

Himmel und Erde
Karfiole mit Dillsosse
Kartoffelpuffer
Lentils à la Stanislas
Pommes de Terre Duchesse
Pommes de Terre Elena Gerhardt
Pommes de Terre Ménagère
Purée de Pois Verts
Risi Pisi
Serbian Asparagus
Spätzle
Tagliatelle alla Genovese
Tarte d'Epinards Pompadour

AUBERGINES IRMA
(page 159)

1 large or 2 small eggplant
¼ cup seasoned flour
   Oil for frying
6 large, solid tomatoes, sliced
2 cups bread crumbs, half white, half whole-wheat bread
¼ cup melted butter

Peel and cut eggplant into ¼-inch slices, dredge them with flour and fry them in oil until golden on both sides. Fry tomato slices for a few minutes and arrange alternating slices in a long heatproof dish. Season and cover them with bread crumbs, sprinkle with butter and bake in a 400° F. oven until the crumbs are browned.

SERVES **4**

BROWN SAUERKRAUT
(page 17)

1 pound sauerkraut
⅓ cup vinegar
1 teaspoon caraway seeds
3 tablespoons butter
1 small onion, thinly sliced
3 tablespoons flour
1 bouillon cube
   Sugar, salt, and pepper to taste

Put sauerkraut into a heavy kettle with vinegar and caraway seeds and 1 cup water, and let it simmer over very low heat for 6 hours, adding a very little water when necessary. Melt butter in a heavy pan and brown onion in it, stirring constantly. When butter is a rich brown, stir in flour and continue to stir until it is browned. Add ⅔ cup hot water and bouillon cube and stir until the sauce is thick. Add any remaining liquid from the sauerkraut—not over ½ cup—and the sauerkraut and stir while it bubbles for about 3 minutes. Add a pinch of sugar and season to taste. Pour the sauerkraut back into the kettle and let it steam, without boiling, until needed. If you prefer a sweeter taste a small lump of sugar may be browned with the butter and the onion before the flour is added.

BROWNED CHESTNUTS

    2 pounds large chestnuts
    2 celery stalks
    1 bay leaf
    4 cups brown stock or beef bouillon
    ½ cup butter
      Salt to taste
    2 teaspoons sugar

With a sharp pointed knife, cut a cross in the flat side of the chestnuts. Put them up in cold water and bring them to a boil. Boil for 2 minutes and remove from heat. Leave the chestnuts in the hot water and peel them, one at a time, holding them in a kitchen towel. Try to remove the outer and the inner skin and leave the chestnuts whole. (Shelled chestnuts are usually dry and unsatisfactory, but if good ones can be obtained, they save a great deal of time.) Put the stubborn nuts, which do not peel easily, back into boiling water for another minute. Boil the shelled nuts with the celery and bay leaf in the stock until tender, about 45 minutes. Do not overcook, as they may fall apart. Glaze the cooked chestnuts in butter with salt and sugar and serve warm with venison. Use half the recipe for Choux de Bruxelles aux Marrons, page 270, and substitute vegetable broth or water for the brown stock.

CHESTNUT-STUFFED MUSHROOMS
(page 25)

    12 very large, evenly sized mushrooms
     1 tablespoon lemon juice
     4 tablespoons butter
     2 shallots, chopped
     2 cups unsweetened chestnut purée or ½ recipe Browned Chestnuts,
         page 269, blended into a purée while hot
     1 recipe Sauce Périgueux, page 294

Trim stem ends and clean the mushrooms with a soft cloth. Simmer them in salted water with lemon juice for 2 minutes, or until they are tender but not flattened out. Take them out, dry them well, and pull out the stems. Chop the stems and sauté them in half the butter with the shallots for about 5 minutes, or until shallots are golden. Stir the mixture into the chestnut purée and stuff the mushroom caps. Place them in a buttered baking dish, dot with the remaining butter and bake in a 375° F. oven for about 10 minutes or until glazed and lightly browned. Serve with Sauce Périgueux.

CHOU-FLEUR IGNATIEFF
Cauliflower Ignatieff
(page 73)

1 large perfect cauliflower
1 cup butter
1½ cups bread crumbs
½ cup ground hazelnuts or filberts

Steam trimmed cauliflower in a little salted water until it is just tender, about 20 to 25 minutes. Drain it well and invert it on a hot platter. Heat the butter in a pan and fry the crumbs and nuts until they are golden. Pour the butter over the cauliflower and spread the crumbs smoothly over the top. Garnish with parsley sprigs, and serve with a muffineer of powdered sugar.

CHOUX DE BRUXELLES AUX MARRONS
Brussels Sprouts with Chestnuts
(page 102)

2 1-quart baskets Brussels sprouts
¼ cup butter
½ recipe Browned Chestnuts, page 269 (substitute vegetable broth or water for brown stock)
   Salt and white pepper to taste

Trim sprouts, wash them in cold water, and boil them in salted water until tender, about 10 minutes. Drain them well and "swing" them in a pan with the butter until they are glossy. Add the hot chestnuts, whole or broken into pieces, and season with salt and freshly ground pepper to taste.

COLD STUFFED MUSHROOMS
(page 91)

18 medium mushrooms
 1 lemon (juice and grate rind)
 1 small onion, finely chopped
 ¾ cup chopped cooked spinach
 1 hard-cooked egg, riced
 1 envelope gelatin
 ¼ cup dry sherry
1¾ cups bouillon
 1 recipe Dick's French Dressing, page 295

Increase amount of spinach if mushrooms are large. Rub mushrooms with a damp cloth and simmer them with 1 tablespoon lemon juice for about 4 minutes. Pull out the stems and chop them. Add onion, spinach, lemon rind, and riced hard-cooked egg, and season to taste. Fill the mushrooms with this mixture, making a dome in the center, and chill them. Soften gelatin in sherry, bring bouillon to boiling and remove from heat. Stir in the gelatin until it dissolves, add remaining lemon juice, cool it and brush a coat over the mushrooms. Put in the refrigerator and continue brushing and chilling until they are heavily glazed. Serve three to a person, and pass Dick's French Dressing separately.

DILLED POTATO RING
(page 91)

1 recipe Pommes de Terre Duchesse, page 278, freshly made and
   still warm
1 4-ounce package cream cheese, at room temperature
¼ cup finely cut dill, or to taste
   Salt and pepper to taste
1 egg, beaten with 1 tablespoon water

Rice cream cheese over potato mixture and stir well. Add dill and season to taste. Pipe the mixture through a pastry bag equipped with the largest tube (made for this purpose) onto an ovenproof platter in the form of a ring. Pipe it in three rows, two at the base and one on top to make a deep ring. Brush it with egg and bake it in a 425° F. oven until lightly browned at the edges. Fill the ring with any fish or shellfish ragout, creamed crab meat, or green vegetable.

DUXELLES
(*Sautéed Mushrooms Used for Flavoring*)

  2 **pounds mushrooms, finely minced**
½ **cup butter**
¼ **cup minced shallots**
½ **cup beef bouillon**
    Salt and pepper to taste
½ **cup heavy cream, several days old if possible**

Twist the mushrooms in a kitchen towel to absorb all liquid. Melt butter in a saucepan, sauté the shallots until soft, add the mushrooms and stir over low heat until the pan is dry. Add the bouillon and cook, uncovered, stirring until the pan is dry again. Season, remove from heat, and stir in the thick cream. Use with Filet of Beef with Duxelles, page 253.

YIELDS ABOUT 3 CUPS

EPINARD À LA CRÊME
Spinach in Cream
(*page 25*)

  2 **pounds spinach (well washed with all coarse stems removed)**
1½ **tablespoons butter**
1½ **tablespoons flour**
½ **cup strong white stock, preferably veal stock**
½ **cup heavy cream, several days old if possible**
    Salt to taste and the smallest possible grinding of nutmeg

Some experts prepare a Sauce Béchamel and combine it with the same amount of thick cream; others chop and season the spinach and add only the heavy cream. Some believe the spinach should be boiled in lots of water for 2 minutes; others believe it should be cooked only in the water that clings to the leaves after washing. Prepare the spinach by either method (Marie used the second), drain it well, press out all liquid and chop it roughly in a wooden bowl. Season it to taste, and either mix with White Sauce made with heavy cream or with plain cream. To make the White Sauce, melt the butter in a heavy saucepan over low heat, stir in the flour and stir, without letting it take on color, for 3 minutes. Gradually stir in the stock and cream and continue to stir until the sauce is smooth and thickened. Reduce heat and let it simmer 15 minutes longer. Combine with the hot spinach and add more cream if preferred.

FLAN AUX OIGNONS
Onion Tart
(page 17)

    3 cups plus 4½ tablespoons flour
    ½ teaspoon salt, or to taste
    6 tablespoons shortening
3 to 4½ tablespoons ice water
    6 medium onions, sliced paper thin
    3 tablespoons salt butter
    4 rashers bacon, fried until crisp, and crumbled
    3 eggs, beaten
    1½ cups heavy cream
      Salt and pepper to taste
    1 tablespoon minced fresh herbs (thyme, parsley, chives, basil)

Sift 3 cups of the flour before measuring, then sift it with the salt into a bowl. Cut in the shortening with a pastry blender, leaving some particles as large as giant peas. Sprinkle ice water over the mixture, a little at a time, and stir with a knife blade until it can be gathered with the fingers. Do not "work" the paste. Place the paste on a canvas-covered pastry board dusted with 3 tablespoons of the flour and roll it out thin. Lift it over to a 10-inch pie pan and trim the edges to within ½ inch outside of the rim. Fold the edge under and flute it attractively. Prick the pie shell thoroughly with a fork and chill it for 1 hour. Bake it for 10 to 12 minutes in a 500° F. oven. Sauté the onion slices in butter until lightly browned. Let them cool, then drain on absorbent paper and combine them with the bacon in the prepared pie shell. Beat the eggs, cream, remaining 1½ tablespoons flour, seasonings, and herbs together, and pour the mixture over the onions. Bake in a 400° F. oven for 15 minutes, reduce heat to 375° and continue baking until the filling is puffed and brown. Serve at once with a crisp green salad.

GEBACKENER KARFIOLE
Cauliflower Casserole
(page 113)

 1 large or 2 medium cauliflowers, about 1¾ to 2 pounds
   Salt and pepper to taste
1½ cups chopped ham and/or tongue
 6 tablespoons butter
 ¼ cup flour
 ¾ cup grated Parmesan cheese
1½ cups light cream
 4 egg yolks

Steam the cauliflower in a little salted water in a covered saucepan until just tender. Take it out, drain it well, and retain the water in which it was steamed. Divide the cauliflower into rosettes and slice the tender part of the stem thinly. Place a layer of cauliflower in a 6-cup buttered casserole, and cover it with a layer of the meat. Top the meat with the remaining cauliflower, cover the casserole and keep it warm. In the top of a double boiler, over boiling water, melt the butter and stir in the flour and half a cup of the cheese. Gradually stir in ½ cup of the water in which the cauliflower was boiled and ½ cup of the cream. Stir the sauce until it is smooth and thickened. Reduce heat to simmer, beat the yolks into the remaining cream, and stir in a little of the hot cheese sauce. Beat the mixture into the sauce, and stir until it is smooth and thick. Pour it over the cauliflower in the casserole and top it with the remaining cheese. Bake in a 375° F. oven for about 15 minutes, then put it under a hot broiler, leaving the oven door open, and brown the top. Watch it carefully and turn the casserole to brown the cheese evenly, about 7 minutes. Serve at once with sliced tomato salad.

GRIESS AUFLAUF
Invalid's Farina
(page 27)

 4 tablespoons farina
1½ cups boiling milk
 1 curl lemon peel
 1 tablespoon butter
 4 lumps sugar
 3 eggs, separated
 ½ jar apricot marmalade
 6 apricots, halved

"Rain" the farina into the boiling milk. Add lemon peel and butter and stir until thick. Add the sugar and stir until it is dissolved. Continue to cook, stirring until all the milk is absorbed. Cool the farina, beat in the yolks and fold in the stiffly beaten egg whites. Spread marmalade in a small buttered porcelain bowl, cover it with the apricot halves and fill with the farina. Bake in a 350° F. oven for 40 minutes. Serve with cinnamon sugar (1 to 2 teaspoons powdered cinnamon stirred into 1 cup granulated sugar). A little apricot brandy may be stirred into the jam.

SERVES 3 INVALIDS

HIMMEL UND ERDE
Heaven and Earth
(page 16)

 2 pounds potatoes
 1 teaspoon salt
 ½ cup hot milk
 2 pounds apples, peeled, cored, and sliced
 2 tablespoons sugar
 1 lemon rind
 6 slices bacon
 2 large onions, sliced
    Salt and freshly ground black pepper to taste
 1 pound pork sausages or frankfurters

Cook potatoes in salted water, draw off the skins, and rice them. Add just enough milk to bind and whip until thick and smooth. Cook the apple slices with sugar and lemon rind in very little water until soft and combine them with the potatoes. Fry the bacon until crisp, drain and crumble it, and fry the onion slices in the bacon fat left in the pan. Add bacon and drained onions to the potato-and-apple-sauce mixture and season it to taste. Arrange it on a platter and surround it with grilled pork sausages or frankfurters.

KARFIOLE MIT DILLSOSSE
Cauliflower with Dill Sauce
(page 145)

1 large cauliflower
1 egg
1 tablespoon dill vinegar
1 lemon, grated rind
¼ teaspoon salt
¼ teaspoon white pepper
¼ teaspoon yellow mustard
1 cup oil
¼ cup snipped dill

Steam trimmed cauliflower in a little salted water until it is just tender, about 20 to 25 minutes. Drain it well and let it cool. When it is cold arrange it in a salad bowl and chill until needed. Put the egg in the blender container with vinegar, lemon rind, seasonings, and mustard, and turn it on for a few seconds; open the top and add oil in a thin stream until all of it has been added. Turn the blender off, scrape down the sides of the container, add ⅔ of the snipped dill, and blend once more for a few seconds. Pour half the sauce over the cauliflower, and sprinkle with the retained dill. Surround the cauliflower with lettuce leaves and serve with the remaining sauce in a china bowl. If a thinner sauce is preferred, blend a little cream into the sauce with the dill.

KARTOFFELPUFFER
Potato and Apple Pancakes
(page 144)

6 medium raw potatoes, peeled, grated, and drained
2 medium apples, peeled, cored, and grated
2 eggs, beaten
   Salt to taste
1 onion, finely chopped
   Flour or potato flour as needed
   Fat (part bacon fat) for frying

Grate potatoes and apple just before preparing the pancakes. Press out all moisture with a kitchen towel. Add eggs, salt, onion, and flour, and stir well. Fry a test pancake in "smoking" hot fat in a pan, and turn it to brown on both sides. If the batter is too dry, add a little cream; if it is too soft, add a little flour. Continue frying the pancakes in the fat, and serve them at once.

LENTILS À LA STANISLAS
(page 17)

2 cups lentils
2 large onions
2 cloves
1 thick slice smoky bacon
3 sprigs parsley
1 sprig thyme
1 bay leaf
1 pinch dried chervil
   Salt and freshly ground black pepper to taste
3 slices bacon, quartered
3 tablespoons butter

Soak lentils overnight in cold water. Next day add enough water to cover again, and add one of the onions spiked with the cloves, the smoky bacon, and herbs. Cook them covered until just soft but not mushy. Discard the herb sprigs, bay leaf, and smoky bacon, and season the lentils with salt and pepper. In a wide pan, fry the second onion, chopped, with the bacon in 2 tablespoons of the butter until brown. Drain the lentils, retaining the liquid, and add them to the pan. Simmer until very hot, stirring well and adding a little of the retained liquid to taste. Remove from heat, stir in the remaining tablespoon of butter, and serve.

POMMES DE TERRE DUCHESSE
Duchess Potatoes
(page 102)

6 large potatoes, peeled, quartered, and boiled in salt water
¼ cup butter
4 egg yolks, beaten
  Salt and white pepper to taste
1 pinch each, sugar and nutmeg
  Approximately ¼ cup heavy cream
1 egg, beaten with 1 tablespoon water

Boil potatoes for about 20 minutes. As soon as they are tender, drain them well. Cover the saucepan with a cloth, and put the potatoes in a low oven for a few minutes to steam. Take them out and rice them, one at a time, into a heavy kettle. Stand the kettle over *very low* heat for a moment and stir the potatoes to dry them out further. Remove from heat and beat in butter, yolks, and seasonings. Beat in the cream, the amount depending on the mealiness of the potatoes, until the mixture is smooth but not too soft to shape. Force it through a pastry tube or shape into ovals with the hands. Brush with beaten egg and put in a 450° F. oven for a few minutes to brown.

POMMES DE TERRE ELENA GERHARDT
(page 27)

1 recipe Duchess Potatoes, above
  Flour for hands and dredging
2 eggs, beaten
¾ cup parched hazelnuts or cashews (obtainable in jars), chopped
  Deep fat for frying

Prepare potato mixture and with floured hands shape into the size of ping-pong balls. Dredge them with flour, dip them in beaten egg, and roll them in the chopped nuts. Fry them in deep fat heated to 370° F. until golden. Serve with poultry, pork, or veal.

POMMES DE TERRE MÉNAGÈRE
(page 102)

Prepare mixture for Duchess Potatoes, page 278, and stir in ½ cup finely diced onions, ½ cup diced ham, and 3 tablespoons chopped parsley. Spread the mixture in a heatproof baking pan and brush it with egg. Brown it in a 450° F. oven and serve at once.

PURÉE DE POIS VERTS
Purée of Green Peas
(page 159)

4 10-ounce packages frozen baby peas or 6 pounds fresh peas
¼ cup heavy cream, or to taste
3 onions
3 tablespoons butter
   Flour for dredging
   Salt and pepper to taste

Cook the peas according to package directions in salted water until soft. Drain well and put them through a blender or a sieve. Stir in cream and season to taste. Mound them in a heatproof dish. Slice onions paper thin, separate them into rings, and dredge them with flour. Fry them in butter until golden and limp, and spread them over the peas. Keep hot in a low oven or over hot water and serve with such meats as roast pork and ham.

RISI PISI
Rice with Peas
(page 142)

2 tablespoons chopped onion
2 tablespoons butter
1 cup long-grained rice
2½ cups boiling beef bouillon or broth
   Salt (depending on whether bouillon is salty enough)
2 cups freshly cooked green peas

Stir the onion into the melted butter in a heavy pan equipped with a lid or a heavy saucepan. Cook over low heat, stirring for about 15 minutes until onion is puffed but not brown. Add the rice and stir until it is glossy and transparent. Add the bouillon or broth and salt, stir well and cover the pan or saucepan tightly. Reduce heat and simmer the rice for about 20 minutes. Test a rice grain and continue to simmer until it is just tender or *al dente*—it should not be soft. Remove from heat, stir in the peas, and serve with Wiener Huhn, page 248.

SERVES 4 TO 6

SERBIAN ASPARAGUS
Cold Asparagus with Egg Sauce
(page 144)

2 pounds asparagus, trimmed
½ cup lightly salted water
4 hard-cooked eggs, separated
2 teaspoons brown mustard, Düsseldorf or Dijon
   Salt and freshly ground black pepper to taste
2 cups oil (½ cup olive oil and 1½ cups salad oil, or all salad oil)
⅔ cup tarragon vinegar
⅔ cup chopped dill pickle, well drained
2 tablespoons smallest capers
2 tablespoons chopped parsley
2 tablespoons chopped chives

Steam the asparagus in the following manner: Trim the lower end of the asparagus stalks and tie them together in bunches with white string. In a very deep saucepan or the bottom part of a double boiler, bring to a boil ½ cup of lightly salted water. Place asparagus upright in pan and steam, tightly covered, for 12 minutes or until tender. Let them cool, then drain well and set in a cool place.

Rice the yolks of the eggs into a bowl and work them with the mustard and salt and pepper until they are smooth. Gradually beat the oil into the yolks, drop by drop, as for Mayonnaise. After the sauce is smooth the oil can be added in a thin stream alternately with additions of vinegar. Chop the egg whites and add half of them and half the well-drained chopped pickle to the sauce. Drain the asparagus again and arrange it on a cold platter. Pour the sauce over it, and garnish the sauce with a strip each of pickle, egg white, capers, and a mixture of parsley and chives.

SERVES 4

SPÄTZLE
Maxim Kopf's Dumplings
(page 83)

3 cups sifted flour
3 teaspoons baking powder
1½ teaspoons salt
3 eggs, beaten
1½ tablespoons melted butter
1½ cups boiling water
3 tablespoons butter

Sift flour, baking powder, and salt into a bowl. Stir in eggs and melted butter and quickly stir in the boiling water. Spread the dough on a small board and hold it over a large kettle of boiling salted water. Cut the dough into slivers and let them fall into the water as they are cut. As soon as all the dough is cut into the water, cover the kettle and let the Spätzle cook for 12 to 15 minutes. Drain them well in a sieve, put them back into the hot empty kettle and swing them with the butter until glossy. Serve at once with Paprika Chicken, Veal Stew, or as other recipes specify.

TAGLIATELLE ALLA GENOVESE
Noodles, Genoese Style
(page 144)

¾ cup julienne of smoked tongue
¾ cup julienne of white turkey meat
2 cups broth
1 pound egg noodles, ¼ inch wide
2 cups grated Parmesan cheese
4 tablespoons butter, at room temperature
½ cup heavy cream, warmed
1 peeled truffle, finely diced

Heat the juliennes of ham and turkey in the broth. Cook the noodles to the *al dente* stage in a large kettle of salted water over high heat. Drain them well.

Spread them on a hot oval platter and sprinkle ¾ cup cheese over them. Dot with the butter and mix with a light hand. Add the hot cream and the drained ham and turkey. Serve with a sprinkling of truffle and more cheese on each portion.

TARTE D'EPINARDS POMPADOUR
Spinach Tart
(page 25)

Crust:

> 2 cups flour
> 1 pinch salt
> ⅔ cup butter
> 1 egg yolk
> 1 teaspoon cold water

Sift flour and salt into a bowl, cut in the butter with a pastry blender until it is evenly distributed. Beat the yolk with the cold water and sprinkle it over the flour mixture. Stir with a knife blade and gather it lightly with the hands. Chill the pastry for 1 hour. Roll it out thinly, line a 10-inch layer-cake pan with it and trim to within ½ inch outside of the edge. Turn under the edge and crimp it evenly. Roll up any remaining dough and refrigerate it for other use.

Filling:

> 1 cup heavy ceam
> 2 eggs, beaten
> 1 tablespoon flour
> ½ cup grated Swiss cheese
> 1 pound spinach, cooked, drained, and chopped, as for Spinach in
>   Cream, page 272
> Salt and pepper to taste
> 1 onion, thinly sliced

Beat cream and eggs with flour, add cheese and the chopped spinach. Season to taste. Fill the pie crust with onion slices, and pour the spinach-and-cream mixture over them. Bake in a 350° F. oven for 45 minutes to 1 hour, or until spinach is puffed and crust is browned. Remove from oven but do not cut for about 10 minutes.

Eggs

Oeufs Héloise
Oeufs Jenny Lind
Oeufs Mozart
Oeufs Offenbach

OEUFS HÉLOISE
Poached Eggs with Sauce and Tomato
(page 61)

10 tablespoons butter
2 tablespoons flour
1 cup chicken consommé, heated
6 thick slices white bread, cut into large rounds
4 tomatoes, peeled, seeded, and diced
6 large eggs
¼ cup heavy cream, whipped
1 egg yolk

Prepare the sauce first. Melt 2 tablespoons of butter in the top of a double boiler, over simmering water. Stir in the flour and gradually stir in the consommé. When the sauce is smooth and thickened, set it aside over the hot water. Fry the bread in remaining butter, and then "melt" the tomatoes in the butter.

Poach the eggs and drain them well. At the last moment whip the cream, beat in the yolk, and fold the mixture into the sauce. Place bread rounds on plates, and cover them with the eggs. Pour the sauce over the eggs and edge with "melted" tomatoes.

OEUFS JENNY LIND
Poached Eggs with Sauce and Cauliflower
(page 61)

1½ cups purée of cooked cauliflower
6 bread rounds fried in butter as for Oeufs Héloise, above
1 recipe Sauce Gribiche, page 298, or Béarnaise Sauce, page 291
6 large eggs, poached

Prepare purée first. Fry the bread slices and then make the sauce. As soon as it is done, poach the eggs. Spread the purée on the bread rounds, place an egg on each, and pour the sauce over the eggs.

OEUFS MOZART
Stuffed Eggs
(page 15)

1 recipe Mayonnaise, page 296
8 hard-cooked eggs
  Anchovy paste to taste
6 tiny gherkins or spiced cherries
3 tablespoons cut chives
3 tomatoes (preferably oval-shaped), peeled, cut in half across and
  hollowed out

Make the Mayonnaise. Cut 2 eggs in half, put the yolks into a bowl and rice the whites. Cut out one-quarter of each remaining egg lengthwise, and take out the yolks with a small spoon. Mash the yolks with anchovy paste and a little of the Mayonnaise, as needed to bind, and stuff or pipe the yolk mixture back into the eggs, filling the cut-out quarter. Decorate the yolk with a gherkin or spiced cherry and sprinkle with cut chives. Set the eggs, cutside up, into the tomato halves. Sprinkle the egg whites over the remaining Mayonnaise and pass it separately.

OEUFS OFFENBACH
Scrambled Eggs with Shrimp
(page 61)

9 eggs
⅓ cup cream
2 tablespoons water
3 anchovies, chopped
1 3-ounce can tuna fish, well drained
  Freshly ground black pepper
  Salt to taste, depending on saltiness of anchovies
12 medium shrimp, cooked
6 slices hot toast, buttered
2 large tomatoes, peeled and seeded, and cut into 6 wide slices,
  with the remaining tomato diced
2 tablespoons chopped parsley

Beat eggs with cream and water, and scramble them in a wide pan. Just before they are done, stir in anchovies and tuna fish and seasonings. Arrange toast slices on hot plates, cover each slice with a tomato slice, and divide the eggs over them. Decorate each portion with 2 shrimp, diced tomato, and parsley.

Salads

Endive Salad Valencia
Green Bean Salad Mimosa
Linzen Salat Leopoldi
Maybelle's Western-Way Salad

ENDIVE SALAD VALENCIA
(page 94)

8 endives, about 3 pounds, all of the same length
6 sweet oranges, completely peeled with a sharp knife and cut into
  sections, free of membrane
2 tablespoons minced capers
1 tablespoon minced pimento
2 tablespoons minced ripe olives
1 tablespoon minced parsley
1 cup Dick's French Dressing, page 295

Trim stems, peel off outside leaves, and cut each endive into quarters, lengthwise. Put them on salad plates; arrange the orange sections evenly over them, and sprinkle with the minced ingredients. Pass Dick's French Dressing in a separate bowl or pour 2½ tablespoons over each salad.

GREEN BEAN SALAD MIMOSA
(page 58)

2 pounds tender young string beans
 Salt to taste
1 pinch baking soda
1 recipe Dick's French Dressing, page 295
2 hard-cooked eggs, separated and riced
1 medium onion, finely chopped
 Summer savory, if available

Snap ends off the beans and arrange them in 6 bunches of even length. Tie them loosely with kitchen string and drop them into a large kettle of rapidly boiling salted water. Add the soda and boil the beans until they are barely tender and still crisp. Drain them well; cool and chill them. Arrange them on a long narrow platter, and pour a little of the dressing over them. Place a row of riced hard-cooked egg yolks along the length of the pile of beans. Arrange a row of riced egg whites on one side of it and a row of chopped onion on the other side. Pass the remaining dressing separately. (If there is an herb garden, and fresh summer savory is available, cook the beans with a sprig, and either blend a sprig into the dressing or add 2 teaspoons minced leaves to the dressing.)

LINZEN SALAT LEOPOLDI
Lentil Salad
(page 130)

2 cups lentils
1 teaspoon salt
1 tablespoon vinegar
3 cold cooked potatoes, cut into large dice
3 dill pickles, 2 diced and 1 sliced
4 thick slices ham, diced
1 onion, chopped
1 tablespoon smallest capers
3 gherkins, finely diced
½ cup Dick's French Dressing, page 295
1 recipe Blender Mustard Mayonnaise, page 297
   Lettuce leaves
3 tablespoons chopped parsley

Soak lentils in water overnight. Drain, add enough water to cover, and boil them with salt and vinegar until they are just tender but not soft, about 15 minutes. Remove from heat and cool them in the liquid in which they boiled. Drain well and set them aside to dry, stirring them occasionally for 2 hours. Combine lentils, potato dice, pickle dice, ham cubes, onion, capers, and gherkins. Stir the salad gently with Dick's French Dressing and chill it again. Just before serving, fold in the Blender Mustard Mayonnaise and transfer the salad to a salad bowl lined with lettuce. Decorate with pickle slices and sprinkle with parsley.

MAYBELLE'S WESTERN-WAY SALAD
(page 162)

1 large clove garlic
1 cup salad oil
2 heads Boston lettuce
2 heads romaine lettuce
1 bunch watercress, coarse stems removed
3 endives, trimmed and sliced across
1 tablespoon Worcestershire sauce
   Salt and freshly grated black pepper to taste
½ cup grated Parmesan cheese
½ cup crumbled Roquefort cheese
1 large egg
3 lemons
1 cup croutons

Cut garlic in half and drop it into ⅓ cup of the oil. Pour remaining oil into a large salad bowl and fill the bowl with the lettuces, watercress, and endives. Add Worcestershire sauce, salt and pepper, and the two cheeses. Break the egg over the greens and squeeze the lemons over the egg. Discard the garlic clove and fry the croutons quickly in the garlic-flavored oil. When they are brown, pour them with the oil over the salad. Toss lightly and serve.

Sauces

Apricot Brandy Sauce
Béarnaise Sauce
The Brown Sauces:
Sauce Bordelaise
Sauce Espagnole
Sauce Madère
Sauce Périgueux
Cold Espagnole Sauce
Dick's French Dressing
Hollandaise Sauce
Mayonnaise
Mother's Sauce of Eggs and Ham for Cold Asparagus
Raspberry Sauce
Sauce Gribiche

APRICOT BRANDY SAUCE

1 jar apricot jam
½ cup syrup from canned apricots (or apricot nectar)
¼ cup slivered scalded almonds
¼ cup apricot brandy

Heat jam and nectar in the top of a double boiler until jam is dissolved. Add more nectar if the sauce is still too thick. Stir in almonds and keep over heat until needed. Add apricot brandy and serve.

YIELDS ABOUT 2 CUPS

BÉARNAISE SAUCE

⅓ cup tarragon vinegar
4 shallots, minced
2 sprigs tarragon, minced
¼ teaspoon roughly ground white pepper
4 egg yolks
2 tablespoons boiling water
1 cup butter, at room temperature
  Salt to taste
  Minced tarragon and chervil (optional)

Prepare the double boiler as for Hollandaise Sauce, page 295. Combine vinegar, shallots, tarragon, and pepper in the upper section and simmer them over direct heat until the vinegar is within ½ tablespoon of being evaporated. Take from heat and set aside until cold, then add yolks and the boiling water and stir until smooth. Set over the simmering water in the undersection and add the butter as for Hollandaise Sauce. When it is incorporated, and the sauce is thick and smooth, take from heat and correct seasoning. Minced fresh herbs may be added to taste.

THE BROWN SAUCES

Sauce Bordelaise

2 cups Sauce Espagnole, below
6 shallots, finely chopped
1 clove garlic, finely chopped
1 cup red wine
  Salt and crushed peppercorns
2 tablespoons brandy
3 tablespoons butter, at room temperature
¼ cup chopped beef marrow, if available, simmered in water for 2
    minutes

Simmer shallots and garlic in wine with seasonings until reduced to half. Add the Sauce Espagnole and bring back to a boil. Remove the sauce from heat, stir in the brandy and butter and, if available, the marrow. Correct the seasoning.

YIELDS ABOUT 2½ CUPS

Sauce Espagnole

1 onion, chopped
3 carrots, chopped
2 leeks, chopped
2 celery stalks, chopped
1 sprig each, parsley and thyme
½ bay leaf
4 tablespoons butter, lard, or poultry fat (use only when sauce is
    intended for poultry)
4 tablespoons flour
4 cups brown stock
1 cup dry white wine, optional
1 pound ripe tomatoes, quartered, or 2 tablespoons tomato paste
  Salt and freshly ground black pepper to taste
1 veal bone, cut into sections
  Wings and neck of a chicken

Sauté the vegetables gently in the butter until they are soft. Sprinkle with the flour and stir until it is browned. Stir in the stock, little by little, and add the wine. When it has come to a boil, add the tomatoes, or tomato paste, and the seasonings. Add the veal bone and chicken wings and neck and bring the sauce to a slow boil. Skim it and simmer, covered, for 1 hour. Uncover it and increase heat slightly and cook until it is reduced to the desired amount, approximately 2½ to 3 cups. Pour the sauce through a strainer and again through a strainer lined with triple cheesecloth. If there is time, make this sauce in larger quantity and simmer it at least 4 hours.

YIELDS 2½ TO 3 CUPS

A Quicker Method:

- 1 carrot, sliced
- 1 onion, chopped
- 1 stalk celery, chopped
  Pinch of thyme
- ½ bay leaf
- 4 tablespoons butter
- 4 tablespoons flour
- 2 cups brown stock
  Salt and pepper to taste

Cook vegetables in butter until they are soft and onion is brown. Stir in the flour, moisten gradually with stock, and simmer until thickened. Strain **and** season.

YIELDS ABOUT 2½ CUPS

NOTE: Espagnole is the base for Sauce Bordelaise (page 292) and Sauce Madère (below).

Sauce Madère

- 2 cups Sauce Espagnole, page 292
- ¼ cup Madeira
- 6 tablespoons butter, at room temperature

Heat Sauce Espagnole to boiling and stir in the Madeira. Remove from heat and add the butter, little by little, stirring it until the sauce is thickened and smooth. Serve at once.

YIELDS ABOUT 2½ CUPS

Sauce Périgueux
(page 25)

2 cups Sauce Espagnole, page 292
¼ cup Madeira
2 tablespoons liquid from simmered truffles
2 tablespoons chopped truffles

Follow directions for making Sauce Madère. Add truffle liquid and truffles with the Madeira, and simmer until reduced and smooth.

YIELDS ABOUT 2¼ CUPS

COLD ESPAGNOLE SAUCE

1 egg
1 teaspoon salt
2 peppercorns
¼ teaspoon English mustard
1 tablespoon tarragon vinegar
¾ cup peanut oil
¼ cup olive oil
1 garlic clove, crushed
2 tablespoons brown mustard
½ cup finely chopped ham
Paprika
2 tablespoons finely cut chives

Place egg, salt, peppercorns, English mustard, and vinegar in blender container. Whirl and add the combined oils in a thin stream. Turn off the blender and stir the oil in the center. Add garlic and mustard, and whirl once more. Transfer the sauce to a bowl and fold in the chopped ham. Chill the sauce until needed. Before serving, transfer it to a crystal bowl and sprinkle the top with paprika and chives.

YIELDS 1½ CUPS

DICK'S FRENCH DRESSING

  1 clove garlic
1½ tablespoons salt
  1 tablespoon peppercorns, ground
 ½ tablespoon dry mustard
  1 cup salad oil
 ¼ cup tarragon vinegar
  1 tablespoon dry oregano
  1 teaspoon Maggi or other similar seasoning

Slice the garlic into the container of a blender. Add dry ingredients and blend for a few seconds. Add oil and blend for half a minute. Add vinegar, oregano, and Maggi seasoning and blend for one minute longer.

YIELDS ABOUT 1½ CUPS

HOLLANDAISE SAUCE

4 egg yolks
2 tablespoons boiling water
1 cup butter, at room temperature
1 teaspoon lemon juice, or to taste
  Salt to taste

Prepare a double boiler carefully with just enough water in the lower section to create steam. The water must not come high enough to touch the upper section of the double boiler. Set the lower section over medium heat. Stir egg yolks in the upper section with 1 tablespoon boiling water with a wooden spoon until light. Set them over the lower section and reduce heat so that the water barely simmers. Have the butter at hand and stir it in, a spoonful at a time, until it is absorbed and the sauce starts to thicken. Lift the upper section once or twice to allow steam to escape. Continue stirring in the butter until all of it has been incorporated and the sauce is smooth. Stir in lemon juice and salt. Add the remaining spoon of boiling water if a lighter sauce is wanted. Add boiling water, off the heat, if the sauce shows an inclination to curdle.

YIELDS ABOUT 2 CUPS

MAYONNAISE

Make Mayonnaise with an electric beater or in a blender.

Beater Mayonnaise

4 large egg yolks
½ teaspoon salt
2 tablespoons tarragon vinegar
2 cups oil, half olive and half peanut or any preferred proportion, or all peanut oil
2 teaspoons lemon juice
1 teaspoon boiling water (2 tablespoons more if necessary)
1 teaspoon English mustard, optional

Beat yolks at low speed (or with a French wire whisk) with salt and vinegar. Continue beating while adding the oil drop by drop. As soon as the sauce starts to thicken, add the oil in a very thin stream. Finish the Mayonnaise with lemon juice and boiling water. Chill until needed. If the Mayonnaise seems to be separating, beat boiling water into it until it coheres again. If oil is too cold or if Mayonnaise is overbeaten it may separate or curdle. English mustard may be added with the salt.

YIELDS ABOUT 2⅔ CUPS

Blender Mustard Mayonnaise

1 whole egg
1 tablespoon tarragon vinegar
½ teaspoon salt
¼ teaspoon English mustard
1 cup oil (peanut, olive, or vegetable, or any combination)

Place all ingredients except oil in the blender container and blend at full speed for 2 seconds. Open the top and add oil in a thin stream. Stir the Mayonnaise, and blend 6 seconds longer. Chill.

YIELDS ABOUT 1¼ CUPS

Blender Lemon Mayonnaise

1 whole egg
1 tablespoon lemon juice
½ teaspoon salt
   Grated rind of 1 whole lemon
1 cup oil (peanut, olive, or vegetable, or any combination)

Blend egg, lemon juice, salt, and rind for 2 seconds at high speed. Add the oil in a thin stream. Stir the Mayonnaise, and blend 6 seconds longer. Chill.

YIELDS ABOUT 1¼ CUPS

MOTHER'S SAUCE OF EGGS AND HAM FOR COLD ASPARAGUS
(page 20)

Almost all of Mother's recipes have to be read to the end and through all the variations before a menu can be properly prepared.

2 large egg yolks
2 teaspoons French olive oil
1 tablespoon smallest capers, drained
¼ to ½ teaspoon salt, depending on saltiness of last additions
½ teaspoon English mustard
   Juice of ¼ lemon, about 1 teaspoon
3 tablespoons Mayonnaise, page 296, or more to taste
2 tablespoons chopped Virginia or Westphalian ham (or minced smoked salmon or caviar)

Stir the yolks in a shallow bowl with a fork. Add the olive oil, drop by drop, while stirring constantly. Stir in the capers, salt, and mustard, and add the lemon juice, drop by drop. Stir the Mayonnaise into the mixture, and just before serving, stir in the ham. Serve with cold cooked asparagus.

YIELDS 1½ CUPS

RASPBERRY SAUCE
(page 125)

1 lemon peel
1 short piece cinnamon
1 cup water
1 tablespoon sugar
1 tablespoon cornstarch, stirred with a little cold water
1 cup fresh raspberry juice or raspberry syrup

Boil lemon peel, cinnamon, water, and sugar for 5 minutes. Add cornstarch and boil 1 minute, until thickened and clear. Add raspberry juice and serve warm or cold.

YIELDS ENOUGH SAUCE FOR 6 SERVINGS QUEEN'S PUDDING, PAGE 335

SAUCE GRIBICHE
(page 20)

3 hard-cooked eggs, separated
1 teaspoon prepared mustard
⅓ cup tarragon vinegar
1 cup olive or salad oil
½ teaspoon salt
1 pinch pepper
1 tablespoon finely chopped capers
2 tablespoons finely chopped gherkins
2 teaspoons minced parsley
1 teaspoon minced fresh or scalded dried tarragon

Crush the yolks to a smooth paste with the mustard and a little of the vinegar until smooth. Add oil, drop by drop, stirring constantly. When the sauce thickens, add 1 teaspoon vinegar, and continue stirring in the oil in a fine stream. Finish with the remaining vinegar, season, and add the chopped ingredients with the chopped egg whites. (Increase oil and vinegar, in proportion, if a thinner sauce is preferred.) Serve with cold asparagus or cold boiled beef, fish or shellfish.

YIELDS 2 TO 2½ CUPS

Bowles
and Drinks

Blue Blazes
Kalte Ente I
Kalte Ente II
May Wine
Pfirsichbowle

BLUE BLAZES
(page 122)

2½ jiggers blended whiskey
2½ jiggers boiling water
  1 teaspoon confectioners' sugar
  1 shaving of lemon peel

Pour whiskey and boiling water into two different mugs. Ignite the whiskey and let it blaze, then pour on it the boiling water, sugar, and lemon. (Actually, the flaming whiskey should be poured into the boiling water, but Father never got around to doing it that way.)

KALTE ENTE I
Cold Duck
(page 143)

(A Cold Duck is really a guest who dines in a restaurant and only drinks water.)

  2 bottles Moselle wine, chilled
    Juice of 1 lemon
  1 thinly sliced lemon
  8 lumps sugar, grated against the rind of a lemon
  5 drops Angostura Bitters
  1 bottle dry champagne, chilled

Combine and serve cold in small glasses.

KALTE ENTE II
(page 143)

To 1 bottle each of Rhine wine and dry champagne add ½ cup burgundy and 8 lumps of sugar saturated in the juice of 2 lemons. Serve cold.

MAY WINE
Maibowle
(page 19)

Assemble on the day before serving:

1 pint strawberries, hulled
⅓ cup sugar, or to taste
1½ cups loosely packed dried woodruff (*Waldmeister*) obtainable
    at pharmacies or herb shops (Use one-day-old wilted woodruff
    if an herb garden is available.)
1 bottle light Moselle wine

Assemble on the day the *Bowle* will be served:

1 quart fresh strawberries, hulled
3 bottles light Moselle wine, chilled
1 bottle dry champagne, chilled
    Shaved or crushed ice

Put strawberries in a bowl and add sugar. Steep the woodruff in 2 cups wine and set it aside at room temperature. Pour remaining wine over the sugared strawberries and set them in the refrigerator. On the following day, clean the fresh strawberries and chill them. Chill the punch bowl. Just before serving the May wine, strain into the cold punch bowl the wine in which the woodruff was steeped. Strain the wine from the sugared strawberries into the punch bowl, and discard the woodruff and strawberries. Add the fresh strawberries and the remaining Moselle wine and champagne, and pack the punch bowl in shaved ice. Each glass of May wine should contain a few strawberries. Chill glasses if possible.

Red May Wine

1 cup dried or fresh woodruff
1 bottle red wine, chilled
2 bottles dry white wine, chilled
    Sugar to taste
1 quart strawberries, hulled and chilled
    Juice of 1 orange
1 bottle dry champagne, chilled

Prepare the May wine on the day it is to be served. Steep the woodruff in 2 cups of the wine for 1 hour, and strain the wine into the chilled punch bowl with the other ingredients.

PFIRSICHBOWLE
Peach Bowl
(page 19)

6 ripe peaches
¼ cup sugar
1 jigger anisette
1 bottle dry Moselle wine
1 bottle Rhine wine
1 bottle dry champagne

Scald, peel, and halve peaches, and slice them thin. Sprinkle them with sugar, add the anisette, add ½ bottle Moselle. Let them "draw" for a few hours on ice. Pour them into a punch bowl, add ice, and fill with the remaining Moselle and the other wines.

Desserts and Baking

Abricots Créole
Almond Pudding
Almond Soufflé
Alt Wiener Apfelstrudel
Ananas Créole
Ananas Helena
Apricot Raisin Pie
Apricot Sugar Syrup
Apricot Turnovers
Baba au Rhum
Bavarian Cream
Biscuit Torte
Caffè Granita
Caruso Torte
Chocolate Butter Cream
Crème Anglaise
Crêpes Copenhagen
Fig Pudding
Fraises Sarah Bernhardt
Frozen Hazelnut Soufflé
Gelatina all' Arancia
Gelée Voltaire
Griesspudding

Gugelhopf
Haustorte
Hazelnut Pralinée
Heidesand
Husarengebäck
Kirschenkuchen
Kossuth Blitztorte
Latticed Apple Cake
Linzer Augen
Malteserritter Reis
Marie's Rice Pudding
Metternich Pudding
Miniature Fritters
Montblanc
Nusshörnchen
Orange Slices in Syrup
Pastry Cream
Pêches Ninette
Poires Petit Duc
Pumpernickel Pudding
Queen's Pudding
Salzburger Schneenockerl
Sevastopol Schnitten
Soufflé Camargo
Tarte au Sucre
Trifle
Trude Hudler's Kaiserschmarren
Vacherin
Vanilla Haselnuss Kipferl

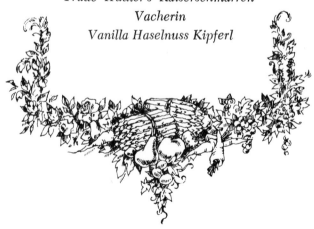

ABRICOTS CRÉOLE
Apricots with Vanilla Rice
(page 9)

½ recipe cold vanilla rice as for Maltese Rice, page 327
1 cup chopped candied fruit and angelica (as prepared for fruit cakes)
1 1-pound-4-ounce can apricot halves
  Apricot Brandy Sauce, page 291

When the vanilla rice is cool, stir in the candied fruit before folding in the whipped cream. Pour the mixture into a rinsed wide pan, which it will fill about 1½ inches deep. Chill until it is set. Cut the rice into rounds with a rinsed cookie cutter and place 1 round on each dessert plate. Cover the rice with apricot halves, cut side down, and serve with hot Apricot Brandy Sauce.

ALMOND PUDDING
(page 188)

1½ cups blanched almonds
1 cup butter
¾ cup sugar
5 eggs, separated
1 lemon, grated rind only

Grind almonds through the nut grinder and set them aside. Cream the butter well, add the sugar gradually until light and fluffy. Beat in the egg yolks and lemon rind. Beat the egg whites until stiff and fold them into the batter with the ground almonds. Pour into a buttered pudding mold with a close-fitting lid. Put the mold into a kettle of boiling water, with the water reaching about halfway up the sides of the mold. Cover the kettle and steam the pudding for 1 hour. Invert on a serving platter, and serve with vanilla sauce or 1 pint soft vanilla ice cream whipped with 3 tablespoons rum.

ALMOND SOUFFLÉ
(page 125)

2 cups cold milk
2 tablespoons butter
1 cup flour
8 eggs, separated
6 tablespoons sugar
½ cup scalded almonds, ground
    Confectioners' sugar, for sprinkling

Bring 1 cup milk to a boil with half the butter. Stir the second cup of milk into the flour, and when it is smooth, stir it into the boiling milk. Continue stirring until the paste leaves the sides of the saucepan. Remove from heat, cool slightly, and beat in 2 egg yolks. Cream the remaining tablespoon of butter and add. Also add, one at a time, 6 tablespoons sugar and 6 egg yolks. Alternate the sugar and yolks and after each yolk beat in one-sixth of the cooled flour-and-milk paste. When all the ingredients are smoothly blended, add the almonds and fold in the stiffly beaten egg whites. Pour the soufflé mixture into a buttered and crumbed soufflé pan and bake it in a 375° F. oven for 45 minutes. Sprinkle with confectioners' sugar and serve at once with raspberry or apricot sauce.

ALT WIENER APFELSTRUDEL
Old-Fashioned Apple Strudel
(page 31)

Dough:

> 2¼ cups sifted flour
> 1 pinch salt
> 1 large egg
> ¼ to ⅓ cup lukewarm water
> 1½ tablespoons oil

Filling:

> ⅔ cup melted butter
> 1½ pounds cooking apples, peeled, cored, and thinly sliced
> 1 cup dry bread crumbs
> ½ teaspoon ground cinnamon
> ½ cup sugar
> ⅓ cup raisins
> ⅔ cup heavy cream, whipped
> ¾ cup roughly chopped walnuts
> Confectioners' sugar, enough for sprinkling

Sift flour and salt into a bowl and make a well in the center. Beat the egg with ¼ cup water and the oil, and pour it into the well. Stir it with a kitchen spoon until the flour is moistened, adding a little water if necessary. Invert the dough onto a lightly floured pastry board and work it with the hands and beat it against the board until it is silky and shows small bubbles. It will leave hands and board clean. Flour a corner of the board lightly, put the dough on it, cover it with a bowl, heated in hot water and dried, and let it rest for 1 hour. Roll out the dough on a lightly floured cloth spread on a 3 x 3-foot or larger table. When the dough has been rolled as thin as possible in all directions, pull it out by placing the backs of the hands under the dough and easing it toward the edge of the table. Go around and around the table, drawing the dough toward you with the backs of your hands until it has been drawn out as thin as it will go and hangs down over the sides of the table.

Sprinkle the dough with about 3 tablespoons butter and spread the apples evenly over two-thirds of the dough. Fry the bread crumbs in about 4 tablespoons of the butter and sprinkle them over the apples with cinnamon, sugar, and raisins. Sprinkle with whipped cream and walnuts. Trim the thick edges off with kitchen scissors. Grasp the table cover with two hands and carefully start the strudel rolling toward the *unfilled* side. When it reaches the last third of the dough, brush the strudel with butter and let the plain dough make the last wrapping. Fold the ends under and bend it into a very heavily buttered baking pan, brush it with the remaining butter, and bake it in a 375° F. oven for about 40 minutes. Continue to bake the strudel until it is brown and crisp (depending on the size of the oven and the weight of the pan this can take from 5 to 15 minutes longer). Slide out the strudel with the help of a spatula, and serve it warm, heavily sprinkled with confectioners' sugar.

ANANAS CRÉOLE
(page 33)

Prepare ½ recipe for cold rice as for Maltese Rice, page 327, with candied fruits. Invert the layer of rice onto a dessert platter, cover it with slices of fresh ripe pineapple, or cut individual tarts of rice as large as the pineapple slices. Serve with a sauce of pineapple conserve or jam, thinned with pineapple juice and kirsch to taste. If pineapple conserve is not available, use apricot jam.

ANANAS HELENA
Pineapple with Bavarian Cream
(page 173)

    1 ripe pineapple
      Bavarian Cream, page 312
    ½ pint large strawberries

Cut pineapple in half lengthwise through the leaves. Cut out the meat and cut it into large dice. Scrape the half shells and chill them. Prepare the Bavarian Cream, stir the pineapple dice into it and mound it into the 2 half shells. Put them in the freezer for 30 minutes, then place them in the refrigerator for at least 2 hours. Before serving, cover the Bavarian Cream with a border of half strawberries and arrange the 2 pineapple halves facing in opposite directions on a platter.

APRICOT RAISIN PIE
(*page 77*)

Crust:

2 cups flour
2 tablespoons sugar
1 pinch salt
10 tablespoons butter
1 teaspoon grated lemon rind
1 egg yolk
1 teaspoon ice water if necessary

Sift flour, sugar, and salt, and work in the butter with a pastry blender until it is evenly cut into the flour. Stir the lemon rind into the egg yolk. Sprinkle the mixture over the flour and stir with the blade of a knife. Add a very little ice water if necessary, to gather the paste. Shape the paste into a ball and chill for at least 1 hour. Roll it out on a lightly floured pastry board ⅛ inch thick. Press it into a 9-inch layer-cake pan. Trim the edges to within ½ inch of the pan, turn it under and crimp it with the fingers. Prick the bottom of the pie shell frequently with the tines of a fork and put a round of waxed paper in the bottom of it. Fill with dried beans or cherry pits and bake in a 400° F. oven for 15 minutes, or until golden and dry. If necessary, reduce oven to 350° F. and leave it in a little longer. Cool the pie shell and remove the beans.

Filling:

1 recipe Pastry Cream, page 332
2 tablespoons apricot brandy
1 1-pound can apricot halves, drained
½ cup raisins
2 egg whites
2 tablespoons sugar

Stir the brandy into the Pastry Cream and fill half of the mixture into the pie shell. Top with the drained apricots, cut side down, and sprinkle them with the raisins. Cover with the remaining Pastry Cream and smooth it with a spatula. Beat egg whites until just stiff, and beat in the sugar little by little. Pipe the meringue, through a pastry tube, in a latticework over the Pastry Cream. Brown it in a 300° F. oven for about 15 to 20 minutes.

APRICOT SUGAR SYRUP

8 ounces lump sugar or 1 cup granulated sugar
1½ cups water
1 10-ounce jar apricot jam
¼ cup rum

Boil sugar and water together until sugar is dissolved. Remove from heat and stir in jam until it is also dissolved. Add the rum and keep the syrup hot in the top of a double boiler over simmering water. Use for Baba au Rhum, page 311.

YIELDS ABOUT 2 CUPS

APRICOT TURNOVERS
(page 157)

1 8-ounce package cream cheese, at room temperature
1 cup cold butter
2 cups flour
¼ teaspoon vanilla
1 egg yolk
1 cup thick apricot jam
Confectioners' sugar, enough for sprinkling

In a bowl, cut cheese and butter into flour with a pastry blender. Beat vanilla with the egg yolk, pour it over the flour mixture, and work it quickly into a smooth dough. Chill it for 3 hours. Roll the dough out on a lightly floured board to ⅕ of an inch thickness and cut it into 4-inch squares with a knife or fluted pastry wheel. Put a teaspoon of jam in the center of each square, bend up the four corners, pinch them together and pinch the four seams together. Bake on a very lightly buttered pastry sheet in a 350° F. oven for 15 to 20 minutes, or until golden. Some of the turnovers may open, but it doesn't matter. Sprinkle while hot with confectioners' sugar and serve warm.

Cocktail Turnovers
(page 94)

Make the same pastry as for Apricot Turnovers and cut it into 2-inch squares instead of 4-inch squares. Fill with a mixture of ground meat, chopped onion, pickle relish, and mustard. Bake in the same way and serve warm.

BABA AU RHUM
(page 121)

    1 cake yeast
    2 cups flour
    ½ cup butter, creamed
    ½ cup sugar
    ¼ cup milk, scalded and cooled to lukewarm
    3 eggs, at room temperature
    ½ cup raisins
    3 cups Apricot Sugar Syrup, page 310
    3 tablespoons chopped pistachio nuts

In a bowl, soften the yeast in ¼ cup lukewarm water. Stir in ½ cup of the flour, cover the bowl with a kitchen towel, and set it in a warm place until it has doubled in bulk, about 1 hour. In the large bowl of an electric beater cream the butter, add the sugar and beat until light. Alternately add a little of the milk and a little of the remaining 1½ cups of flour until all the flour is added. Beat in the eggs one at a time, beating well before the next is added. Beat in the yeast dough and the raisins, and continue to beat until the dough is smooth and light. Cover the bowl again and let the dough rise in a warm place until doubled in bulk, about 1 hour. Beat it down and half-fill 8 well-buttered individual Baba molds. Depending on the size of the molds it may be possible to half-fill more than 8. Cover the molds and let the Babas rise in the same warm place until they come over the tops of the little molds. Bake them in a 375° F. oven for 25 minutes. Dip them into Apricot Sugar Syrup and sprinkle the tops with pistachio nuts. Either serve them at once, in which case they can be saturated with syrup, or cool them after dipping. Before serving reheat them gently in the remaining syrup and serve them with Vanilla Ice Cream Sauce (1 pint vanilla ice cream, softened in the refrigerator and beaten until creamy and smooth in the electric beater).

BAVARIAN CREAM
(page 173)

    1 envelope gelatin
    ¼ cup cold milk
    1 cup milk, scalded
    2 egg yolks
    2 tablespoons granulated sugar
    1 cup heavy cream
    ¼ cup confectioners' sugar
    1 teaspoon vanilla

Stir gelatin into the ¼ cup cold milk and set it aside. In the top of a double boiler, off the heat, beat scalded milk gradually into the egg yolks, beaten until light with the granulated sugar. Set over lower section of double boiler over simmering water, and stir constantly until the mixture thickens. Remove from heat and stir in the gelatin until it dissolves completely. Set the top of the double boiler into a bowl of ice cubes and beat mixture until cold. Fold in the cream whipped with the confectioners' sugar and vanilla and then the pineapple dice. Mound the mixture of Bavarian Cream into the pineapple shells and chill.

BISCUIT TORTE

    ⅔ cup unsalted butter
    4 large eggs, separated
    2 tablespoons confectioners' sugar
    ⅔ cup granulated sugar
    1 teaspoon grated lemon rind
    1⅓ cups flour, sifted twice

Melt the butter in an enameled saucepan in a low oven. Turn off the oven and keep the butter lukewarm. Butter an 11 x 17-inch chocolate-roll pan or a cookie pan with a 1-inch-high rim, and line the bottom with a piece of brown paper. Butter the brown paper and sides of the pan generously. Beat the egg whites until almost stiff, then gradually add the confectioners' sugar, while continuing to beat, until they are stiff. In a second bowl, beat the yolks with the granulated sugar until pale and thick. Test a drop of the mixture between thumb and fingertip, and if it feels granulated, continue to beat only until all sugar is dissolved. Add lemon rind, gently fold in the egg whites, adding the flour very gradually. Fold in the warm melted butter—do not overmix, the batter must retain as much air as possible. Spread the batter in the prepared pan and bake it in a 350° F. oven for about 12 minutes, or until the cake layer is golden and springs back when lightly pressed. Invert it carefully onto a pastry board, draw off the brown paper and let the cake cool. When it is cold, cut two 8-inch-diameter rounds out of the cake with the tip of a sharp knife. Use an 8-inch dinner plate as a guide. Split the rounds across with a long sharp knife to make 4 trim layers or leave it as 2 layers. Cut the remaining base into squares to ice for tea cakes or dry them out and grind them for cake crumbs.

NOTE: This may be used as biscuit base for Caruso Torte, p. 314.

CAFFÈ GRANITA
Coffee Ice
(page 107)

2 cups superfine sugar
1½ cups water
2 cups very strong black coffee
1 cup ice water
2 cups heavy cream
2 tablespoons rum
2 tablespoons grated bitter chocolate

Start this recipe early in the day. Boil the sugar and water in an enamel saucepan for 5 minutes, or until the syrup spins a fine thread when dropped from the end of a spoon. Remove from heat and cool partially. Combine with coffee and ice water. Turn temperature of freezer or refrigerator to lowest point. Pour the coffee mixture into ice trays in the freezing compartment of the refrigerator or into a bowl and put it into the freezer. Let it freeze almost solid, then chop it into pieces and put them through the blender until they resemble crushed ice. Freeze the Granita again for 1 hour and crush it again in the same way. Repeat this once more. Chill tall glasses and the cream. Whip the cream and flavor it with rum. Pour a little Granita into the glasses, add cream, put in another layer of Granita, and continue until they are full, ending with cream. Top with a little grated chocolate and put the glasses in the freezer until needed.

CARUSO TORTE
(page 33)

Bake 1 recipe Biscuit Torte, page 312, and cut into 2 cake layers 8 inches in diameter (an 8-inch plate can be used for this purpose). Arrange a paper doily on a cake plate. Put two pieces of waxed paper over them to exactly meet in the center, and put one of the cake layers on one piece of the paper in the position where it will remain. Prepare 1 recipe Chocolate Butter Cream, below, without the chocolate. Divide the mixture in half, and mix one-half with 1 square semisweet chocolate, melted. Mix the second half with 1 tablespoon coffee essence (if unobtainable, stir 2 tablespoons instant coffee into only enough boiling water to dissolve it completely). When the egg-and-sugar mixture is cold, divide it in half and fold one-half into the chocolate butter cream and one-half into the coffee butter cream. Chill the two creams until they are of spreading consistency. Sprinkle the cake layer forming the base with a few drops of maraschino, and spread with a thin layer of the chocolate butter cream. Cover with the second layer of cake and sprinkle again with maraschino. Spread completely across the top and sides with the coffee butter cream and chill for a few minutes. Cover the sides of the cake gently with shaved and toasted scalded almonds and chill for 2 hours. Hold the remaining chocolate butter cream at room temperature. Fill a pastry bag with it and pipe rosettes through a ½-inch fluted tube around the edge of the cake. Pull out the two pieces of wax paper, and pipe a row of tiny rosettes around the base through a ¼-inch tube. Center each rosette on top of the cake with 1 toasted hazelnut.

CHOCOLATE BUTTER CREAM
(For Caruso Torte)

3 tablespoons coconut oil
1 pound butter, at room temperature
¾ cup confectioners' sugar, sifted
2 squares semisweet chocolate melted over hot water
3 eggs
1½ cups sugar
1 teaspoon vanilla

Warm the coconut oil slightly, beat in the butter and confectioners' sugar, and stir in the cooled melted chocolate. Set in a cool place. Beat eggs, sugar, and vanilla in the top of a double boiler over simmering water, with an electric beater, until thick and creamy. Remove from heat and beat until entirely cold (cooling can be speeded by setting the top of the double boiler over a bowl of ice cubes). Fold the cold egg cream into the chocolate cream and chill to spreading consistency.

CRÈME ANGLAISE
Custard Cream

4 cups milk
1 piece vanilla bean, or 1 teaspoon vanilla extract
1 cup sugar, or to taste
7 egg yolks
   Additional liqueur flavoring (optional)

Scald the milk with the piece of vanilla bean; or scald the milk, remove from heat, and stir in the vanilla extract. Beat the sugar with the egg yolks until light and creamy. Pour the mixture into the top of a double boiler over simmering water and stir in the hot milk in a thin stream. Continue to stir constantly with a wooden spoon; cook the custard over the simmering water until the surface is smooth and free of bubbles and the custard will coat the back of a spoon. Remove from heat, set it over a bowl of ice cubes, and continue to stir until it is cold. Flavor it with a liqueur, and pour it over the sponge cake fingers for Trifle (p. 339) or use it as a sauce for desserts.

CRÊPES COPENHAGEN
(page 36)

In Copenhagen they fill these pancakes with liqueured pastry cream, cover them with hot chocolate sauce, a small scoop of vanilla ice cream, and some whipped cream and toasted nuts.

1½ cups sifted flour
  1 pinch salt
  3 eggs, lightly beaten
  2 tablespoons melted butter or salad oil
1½ cups milk
  2 tablespoons mild brandy or any other preferred liqueur
     Melted butter for pan
  1 recipe Pastry Cream, page 332

Sift flour with salt into a bowl, stir in the eggs until smooth. Gradually stir in the butter (or salad oil) and milk. Refrigerate for 2 hours. Stir in brandy and add a little water if batter is too thick to flow easily. Brush pan lightly with melted butter and pour batter from a serving spoon or sauce ladle. Use just enough batter so that it can be spread to cover the pan and go a little way up the sides. Tilt the pan to spread the batter. Cook over moderate heat until edges brown lightly and the surface of the pancake is dry. Turn with the fingers or a spatula and cook the other side in the same way. The amount of batter and the cooking time can be determined after the first pancake. As they are completed, pile them on each other with the first side that was browned on top. Either keep them warm in a casserole in a very low oven or fold a warm napkin over them and serve them as soon as possible with the Pastry Cream (which usually rewarms them).

FIG PUDDING
(page 52)

½ pound moist dried figs, about 1⅓ cups packed
6 canned Kadota figs
¼ cup syrup from the can of figs
1 cup dry bread crumbs sifted with 1 teaspoon baking powder
⅔ cup sugar
¾ cup light cream
2 eggs, separated
2 tablespoons brandy
1 orange, grated rind only
  Confectioners' sugar to taste

Put the dried and canned figs through the meat grinder and moisten the mixture with the syrup. Add bread crumbs, sugar, cream, yolks, brandy, and rind, and stir until smooth. Fold in the stiffly beaten egg whites and pour the mixture into a well-buttered pudding form with a close-fitting lid. Place pudding in a kettle of boiling water, with the water reaching about halfway up the mold. Cover the kettle and steam the pudding about 2½ hours, replacing water as it steams away. Depending on the dryness of the figs, the pudding may have to steam for as long as 3 hours. Invert pudding onto a hot platter and serve it with whipped cream flavored with vanilla and sweetened with confectioners' sugar to taste.

FRAISES SARAH BERNHARDT
Strawberry Meringues
(page 177)

½ recipe meringue for Vacherin, page 340
1 quart strawberries, hulled
  Maraschino to taste

Prepare the meringue and sprinkle strawberries with maraschino. Pipe 6 small circles of the meringue through a large fluted pastry tube onto a brown paper-lined baking sheet. Set a few strawberries on each, and build 6 pyramids of strawberries on them. Pipe more meringue over the strawberries and bake them in a 200° F. oven for about 1½ hours, or until they are crisp and faintly cream-colored. Watch them carefully. If they do not loosen from the paper, slide the paper onto a wet surface to moisten it. Serve the meringues immediately.

FROZEN HAZELNUT SOUFFLÉ
(page 27)

6 egg yolks
⅔ cup sugar
3 tablespoons liqueur
2½ cups heavy cream, whipped
2 egg whites, beaten stiff
1 cup crushed Hazelnut Pralinée, page 322

In the top of a double boiler over (but not touching) simmering water, beat egg yolks with sugar until they are thick and creamy. Remove from heat and continue to beat the mixture until cold. (Cooling can be speeded by beating it over a bowl of ice.) Flavor with a preferred liqueur and fold in the whipped cream, stiff egg whites, and pralinée. Pour the mixture into a 1-quart soufflé dish tied with a 2-inch waxed-paper cuff, and chill for at least 4 hours in the freezer. To serve, take off the paper cuff and smooth the sides of the soufflé with a warm knife. Sprinkle the top with more pralinée. The mixture can be poured into a 2-quart soufflé dish and served a little "softer" than the soufflé.

GELATINA ALL' ARANCIA
Orange Gelatin
(page 101)

    2 envelopes gelatin
    ¼ cup sherry
    ½ cup flat ginger ale
    2 cups orange juice
 2½ cups sugar
    1 lemon
    4 eating oranges
    ¼ cup Cointreau

Stir gelatin into the sherry and set aside for 10 minutes. Heat ginger ale to boiling, remove from heat, and stir in gelatine until it dissolves. Add orange juice and ½ cup of the sugar and continue stirring until the sugar has dissolved. Cut the outside rind from the lemon with a potato parer and set it aside. Juice the lemon and add it to the orange-jelly mixture. Stir once more and pour the jelly into a wide crystal dessert bowl. Chill it until set. Cut the outside peel from the oranges and cut the lemon and orange peel into slivers with kitchen scissors or a sharp knife. Boil them for 1 minute in water to cover. Drain and boil them again, with the remaining sugar and ⅔ cup water, for 10 minutes. Stir in the Cointreau. Peel the 4 oranges with a sharp knife, removing all white membrane. Slice the oranges and arrange them in a circle on the jelly in the bowl. Cool the syrup and pour it with the slivered orange and lemon rind over the orange slices. Chill until needed.

GELÉE VOLTAIRE
Chilled Coffee Ring with Whipped Cream
(page 126)

    3 envelopes gelatin (in summer use 4 envelopes)
    ½ cup brandy
    1 cup sugar
 1½ cups water
    4 cups strong black coffee
 1½ cups heavy cream, whipped
    ½ teaspoon vanilla
    3 tablespoons powdered sugar
    ½ cup Hazelnut Pralinée, page 322

Stir gelatin into brandy and set it aside. Boil sugar with water for 5 minutes, remove from heat, stir in coffee and gelatin until gelatine is dissolved. Pour the mixture into a rinsed 1½-quart ring mold and chill for at least 3 hours until set. Unmold on a cold platter and fill the center with whipped cream flavored with vanilla and sweetened with powdered sugar. Sprinkle the whipped cream with pralinée powder or blended Hopjes Coffee Candies.

GRIESSPUDDING
Farina Pudding
(page 27)

    1 cup milk
    1 tablespoon butter
    ¼ cup sugar
    1 lemon, grated rind only
    1 cup heavy cream
      Salt to taste
    3 eggs, separated
    6 tablespoons farina
    ¼ cup slivered almonds
    1 teaspoon vanilla

Bring the milk, butter, sugar, grated lemon rind, half the cream, and salt to a boil in a large saucepan. Stir together the egg yolks, the remaining cream, and the farina until thick and smooth and add the almonds. Stir this mixture into the boiling flavored milk, reduce heat immediately and continue to stir. (A trivet or asbestos plate helps to maintain a low heat while cooking.) Continue stirring until the mixture no longer gains in volume or thickness. Remove from heat and cool; stir in the vanilla. Beat the egg whites stiff with a pinch of salt and fold them into the mixture after it has cooled. Pour the pudding into individual dessert dishes or a crystal bowl and let it set in the refrigerator. Serve with fresh fruit or a fruit sauce.

GUGELHUPF
Tube Cake
(page 155)

  5 tablespoons confectioners' sugar
  7 eggs, separated
    Grated rind of lemon
½ cup granulated sugar
1¼ cups sifted flour
1½ tablespoons melted butter

Beat confectioners' sugar with egg yolks and lemon rind until light. Whip the egg whites until just stiff. Continue to whip while sprinkling in the granulated sugar. Fold the stiff whites into the yolks while adding the flour. Mix the warm butter in lightly. Butter and flour a tube pan well, shake out the superfluous flour and turn the batter into the pan. Bake in a 390° F. oven until golden, about 45 minutes. Cool the cake in the mold, invert it, and sieve confectioners' sugar over it.

SERVES 6 OR MORE

HAUSTORTE
Lofer Chocolate Cake
(page 44)

  5 eggs, separated
 10 tablespoons sugar
  1 teaspoon vanilla
  2 teaspoons rum
¼ cup bitter chocolate, melted over hot water
⅓ cup flour
  1 scant cup unscalded brown almonds, ground
  1 recipe Chocolate Butter Cream, page 314

Beat egg yolks with 2 tablespoons of the sugar, vanilla, and rum until light and creamy. Stir in the melted chocolate. Whip egg whites until stiff, continue to whip while adding the remaining sugar, little by little. Fold the whites into the yolk mixture. Stir flour and almonds and fold them in very carefully. Pour the batter into 2 buttered layer-cake pans and bake them in a 325° F. oven until done (a toothpick, inserted, will come out clean), about 40 minutes. Cool, then fill and ice with Chocolate Butter Cream.

SERVES 6 OR MORE

HAZELNUT PRALINÉE

1 cup sugar
⅓ teaspoon cream of tartar
5 tablespoons water
¾ cup toasted hazelnuts (if unobtainable, toast until brown in a
    300° F. oven and rub off the skins)

Boil sugar, cream of tartar, and water in a heavy metal pan until the sugar
is dissolved. Add the nuts and cook until the syrup turns brown—do not stir.
Pour the syrup onto a piece of buttered foil in a wide pan and cool until it is
hard and brittle. Break it into a plastic bag and crush it with a wooden mallet
or blend it to the desired fineness. Store the leftover pralinée powder tightly
covered. Use for Frozen Hazelnut Soufflé, page 318.

HEIDESAND
Heath Sand
(page 154)

¾ cup butter
½ cup powdered sugar
½ teaspoon vanilla
2¼ cups sifted flour
1 egg white, beaten
½ cup crystal sugar
3 tablespoons apricot or raspberry jam

Cream the butter with the sugar and vanilla until light, add the flour
gradually, and work into a smooth dough. Shape it into a roll 16 inches long
and 1½ inches in diameter and brush it with the egg white. Roll it in crystal
sugar until the surface is covered and chill for at least 1 hour. Cut the roll into
⅓ inch slices and place them, 1 inch apart, on a lightly buttered pastry sheet.
Make an identation in the center of each slice with the floured end of a wooden
kitchen spoon. Fill the hollows with jam and bake in a 375° F. oven until golden,
about 20 minutes.

MAKES 48

HUSARENGEBÄCK
Hussar Cookies
(page 33)

⅔ cup butter
6 tablespoons granulated sugar
2 egg yolks
½ teaspoon vanilla
2¼ cups flour
¼ cup strawberry jam
1 egg white, beaten
3 tablespoons chopped scalded almonds
2 tablespoons crystal sugar

Cream the butter with the granulated sugar and beat in the egg yolks until light and foamy. Add vanilla and work in the flour until smooth. Chill the dough for 1 hour. Shape it into 44 walnut-sized balls and arrange them on a slightly buttered pastry sheet. Dip the handle of a woden kitchen spoon into milk and make a deep hollow in the top of each ball, going about halfway down. Fill the hollow with jam. Paint the edge around the jam with egg white, sprinkle with almonds and sugar and bake in a 350° F. oven until golden, about 20 to 25 minutes.

MAKES 44 COOKIES

KIRSCHENKUCHEN
Cherry Cake
(page 41)

1 cup butter, at room temperature
1½ cups sugar
5 eggs, separated
1 pinch salt
Grated rind of 1 lemon
1 teaspoon vanilla
2⅓ cups cake flour
¾ pound black cherries, stemmed but not pitted
Confectioners' sugar

Cream butter with half the sugar, beat in the egg yolks, one by one, until foamy. Add salt and flavorings. Whip the egg whites until just stiff, then add the remaining sugar gradually while continuing to beat until stiff. Fold egg whites into yolk mixture while adding flour, little by little. Pour the batter into a buttered spring form or deep cake pan and cover the entire surface with cherries. Bake in a 375° F. oven for about 50 minutes or until cake is brown and has risen around the cherries. Sprinkle with confectioners' sugar and cool. Sprinkle again before serving.

SERVES 6 OR MORE

KOSSUTH BLITZTORTE
Lightning Cake
(page 83)

    9 tablespoons butter
   10 tablespoons sugar
    3 eggs
    1 cup and 2 tablespoons flour, sifted
       Grated rind of 1 lemon
    1 cup shaved or slivered almonds

Cream butter with sugar, beat in the eggs, alternating with the flour, mixed with the grated lemon rind. Spread the batter ⅓ inch thick on a buttered 10 x 17-inch jelly-roll tin lined with buttered paper. Sprinkle it with the shaved almonds and bake in a medium 375° F. oven until golden. Cool a few minutes and cut into diamond shapes with a sharp knife. Loosen them at once from the paper with a spatula and serve while still warm.

MAKES 24 OR MORE

NOTE: Butter, sugar, flour, and almonds all weigh about the same, namely, 4½ ounces.

LATTICED APPLE CAKE
(page 85)

  2 cups cake flour
10 tablespoons sugar
  ¼ cup butter
  ¼ cup vegetable shortening
  1 egg yolk
  2 tablespoons brandy
3 to 4 tablespoons ice water
5 or 6 sweet apples

Sift flour with 2 tablespoons of the sugar and salt into a bowl; cut in the butter and shortening until the mixture resembles bread crumbs. Beat the egg yolk and brandy into 3 tablespoons of the ice water and sprinkle over the flour. Stir in with a knife and gather the dough rapidly into a smooth ball. Use the last tablespoon of water if there are any dry crumbs in the bottom of the bowl. Chill the dough for 15 minutes. Roll it out thin on a lightly floured pastry board and transfer it to a Pyrex or metal 9-inch layer-cake pan. Line the pan carefully without stretching the dough, draw it over the rim and trim off the superfluous dough. Sprinkle the base with 1 tablespoon flour and 1 tablespoon sugar. Peel, core, and slice the apples into the shell and arrange the top with overlapping circles of slices. Sprinkle remaining sugar on arranged apple slices. Roll out the dough scraps, cut them into 12 strips with a fluted pastry wheel and interweave the strips, 5 in each direction, across the apples. Press down the ends and use the last 2 strips to make an edge around the cake. Bake in a 350° F. oven until the lattice top and edges are golden, about 40 minutes. Serve warm with clotted cream.

LINZER AUGEN
Linzer Tarts
(page 62)

3½ cups flour
1 pinch salt
1 cup and 2 tablespoons butter
1 cup confectioners' sugar
¾ cup scalded almonds, finely ground
3 small or 2 very large egg yolks, beaten
Grated rind of 1 lemon
1 teaspoon vanilla
2 egg yolks, beaten with 2 tablespoons water
½ cup shaved scalded almonds
1 10-ounce jar raspberry jam, strained

Sift flour and salt onto a pastry board, spread sliced butter over it and add the sugar and ground almonds. Make a well in the center and add yolks with lemon rind and vanilla. Work the ingredients quickly into a smooth paste with the hands. Chill it for 1 hour. Roll it out thin and cut it into 12 large rounds with a fluted cookie cutter. Bake half the rounds on a buttered cookie sheet in a 375° F. oven for about 20 minutes, or until golden. Let them cool slightly and transfer them to a piece of waxed paper with a pancake turner. Butter the sheet as soon as it is cool. Cut the centers out of the second half of the rounds with a small cookie cutter and bake the rings for 5 minutes. Take them out and brush them with the egg yolk. Sprinkle them densely with the shaved almonds and continue baking until the almonds are golden, about 18 minutes. After rounds and rings are cool, spread the rounds with raspberry jam and cover them with the rings. Fill a little more jam into the "eye" in the center.

MAKES 6 TARTS

MALTESERRITTER REIS
Maltese Rice
(page 54)

1 cup rice
2 cups milk
2 envelopes gelatin
1 orange (grated rind only)
1 cup sugar
1 teaspoon vanilla
½ cup confectioners' sugar, or to taste (optional)
1 cup heavy cream, whipped
6 oranges

"Rain" the rice into rapidly boiling water and let it boil for 5 minutes. Drain it well and cook it in the top of a double boiler with 1¾ cups of the milk, stirring once or twice, until it is tender but not soft, about 15 minutes. Soften gelatin in the remaining milk. As soon as the rice is tender, remove from heat and stir in the gelatin until it is completely dissolved. Add orange rind, sugar, and vanilla and cool. When it is cold but before it sets, fold in the whipped cream. Confectioners' sugar may be added to the whipped cream if desired. Pour the mixture into a rinsed ring mold and chill for at least 2 hours until it is set. Unmold on a serving platter and fill the ring with Orange Slices in Syrup, page 331, and covered with slivered orange peel.

MARIE'S RICE PUDDING
(page 28)

1½ cups long-grain rice
1 quart milk
½ teaspoon salt
6 tablespoons butter
½ cup sugar, or to taste
1 lemon, grated rind only
6 eggs, separated
½ cup slivered almonds
3 tablespoons small white raisins or diced citron

Boil rice for 15 minutes in water, drain well, and add it to boiling milk. Add the salt, and boil until tender (test it after 10 minutes). Remove from heat, stir in the butter, sugar, and lemon rind and cool the rice. Beat in the egg yolks, almonds, and raisins and fold in the stiffly beaten egg whites. Pour the mixture into a buttered baking dish, smooth the top with a spatula and bake in a 375° F. oven until golden and until a knife comes out clean, about 1 hour. Serve with Raspberry Sauce, page 298.

METTERNICH PUDDING
Chestnut Pudding
(page 113)

1½ pounds peeled chestnuts
  3 cups milk
  1 cup water
  1 teaspoon vanilla
  ¼ cup sugar, or to taste
  3 tablespoons butter
  4 eggs, separated
  2 teaspoons cocoa powder, or to taste
  ¼ cup finely chopped candied orange peel
  6 marrons glacés
    Hot chocolate sauce

Boil the peeled chestnuts in 2 cups of the milk and 1 cup water until they are very soft and crumbled. Drain them well and press them through a potato ricer. Stir vanilla and sugar into them. Heat butter in a heavy pan, add the chestnut mixture and the remaining milk and stir over medium heat until it is thick and dry. Remove it from heat and beat in the egg yolks, cocoa, and orange peel. Fold in the stiffly beaten egg whites and pour the batter to half-fill a well-buttered pudding mold. Cover and steam in a kettle of simmering water for about 1¼ hours. Unmold the pudding on a hot platter and decorate it with the marrons glacés. Serve with hot chocolate sauce.

MINIATURE FRITTERS
(page 162)

Batter:
  2 cups and 2 tablespoons flour
  1 cup dry white wine
  2 tablespoons and 2 teaspoons salad oil
  2 eggs, separated
  1 pinch salt
  2 tablespoons and 2 teaspoons sugar

Beat flour, wine, oil, and egg yolks into a smooth batter. Just before using, whip the egg whites until stiff, add salt, and gradually whip in the sugar. Fold the whites into the batter.

Fruit:
  Bananas, peeled and cut into ½-inch slices
  Apples, peeled and cored and cut into 12 wedges each. Wedges cut across in half
  Small strawberries, hulled

Dry small pieces of fruit, dip them in batter, and fry them in vegetable shortening or oil (not in butter or margarine) heated to 360° F. until golden. Drain them on blotting paper and roll banana fritters in powdered sugar, apple fritters in cinnamon sugar (1 teaspoon powdered cinnamon stirred into ½ cup granulated sugar), strawberry fritters in vanilla sugar (powdered sugar stored with a vanilla bean in a small canister).

MONTBLANC
Chestnut Rice
(page 38)

2 pounds chestnuts, according to recipe for Browned Chestnuts,
    page 269
1¾ cups confectioners' sugar
  2 teaspoons heavy rum, or to taste
  ½ teaspoon vanilla
1½ cups heavy cream, whipped and sweetened to taste
  3 marrons glacés

Mash the soft cooked chestnuts and work them into a smooth purée with
sugar and flavorings. Mound half the whipped cream onto a crystal dessert
platter and rice the chestnut purée over it. Through a wide fluted tube, pipe
the remaining cream into 6 rosettes at the base of the mound. Decorate the
rosettes with halves of marrons glacés or candied violets.

NUSSHÖRNCHEN
Nut-Filled Crescents
(page 92)

2¾ cups sifted flour
 ⅓ cup confectioners' sugar
  1 cup cold butter (take out enough to butter the baking sheet)
  2 large egg yolks, chilled
  1 lemon (grated rind and 1 teaspoon of the juice)
    Nut filling (recipe below)
    Powdered sugar for sprinkling

Sift flour onto a pastry board, sprinkle sugar over it, and cut the butter
into thin slices and spread them over the sugar. Make a well in the center and
drop in the 2 beaten egg yolks, the lemon juice, and the rind. Stir flour into the
well while working the butter into the flour with fingertips. Work quickly into
a smooth paste and chill it for 1½ hours. Cut off a slice of the paste and roll
it out thin on lightly floured pastry canvas with a floured rolling pin. Cut it
into 4-inch squares and place a tablespoon of Nut Filling on each square. Turn
one corner of the square over the filling and roll it up to the opposite corner.
Turn so that the corner tip is on the underside, and bend the two ends around

to shape the little rolls into crescents. Pinch the two ends firmly. Continue to use the paste, a slice at a time, until a buttered baking sheet is filled. Bake the crescents in a 375° F. oven for 18 to 20 minutes or until lightly browned and firm. (Note that size of oven and baking sheet can make a difference in the baking time. Watch the crescents after about 12 minutes.) Let them cool for a minute and then move them with a spatula to a sheet of waxed paper. Sprinkle them generously with powdered sugar in which a vanilla bean has been stored.

MAKES ABOUT 30 CRESCENTS

Nut Filling:

　　6 tablespoons sugar
　　3 tablespoons water
　1¼ cups nuts (almonds, walnuts, and hazelnuts), grated
　　2 egg yolks

Cook sugar and water for 5 minutes, remove from heat, and stir in nuts. Stir in the egg yolks to obtain a rather dry, crumbly filling. If too moist, add more nuts.

ORANGE SLICES IN SYRUP

　6 large navel oranges
　1 cup sugar
　2 tablespoons Curaçao

Cut thin outside peel from oranges in one long wide strip from the center with a potato peeler. Peel the rest of the oranges and retain the peel. Cut the white membrane from the oranges with a very sharp knife. (Do this over a bowl to retain the orange juice.) Scrape any remaining white pulp from the back of the wide strips of peel and cut them diagonally into long thin slivers with sharp kitchen scissors or a sharp knife. Boil slivers with the retained peel and sugar in 1 cup water until the slivers are limp. Take out the peel. Slice the oranges, add the juice to the syrup, and boil it a few minutes longer. Add Curaçao to the syrup and pour it over the orange slices. When they are cold, place them in a Maltese Rice ring and top with the slivered peel.

PASTRY CREAM

2 cups milk
6 egg yolks
½ cup sugar
6 tablespoons sifted flour
1 pinch salt
1 teaspoon vanilla

Scald milk. Beat egg yolks and sugar, flour, and salt in the top of a double boiler until pale and creamy. Set the mixture over simmering water and stir in the hot milk in a thin stream. Stir constantly until the mixture is thick and smooth. Do not allow the water in the double boiler to come to a high boil. Remove from heat, stir in the vanilla, and pour into a bowl. Cover and refrigerate. May be flavored with liqueur to taste. Can also be used for Apricot Raisin Pie, page 309.

PÊCHES NINETTE
Cold Poached Peaches
(page 10)

When peaches are ripe and beautiful, poach them in sugar syrup and dress them on a base of macaroons drenched in maraschino. Serve with vanilla sauce as for Baba au Rhum, page 311.

2 cups sugar
2 cups water
6 large peaches, scalded, skinned, and halved
1 slice lemon
12 macaroons
¼ cup maraschino
3 tablespoons shaved scalded almonds
2 tablespoons butter

Boil sugar and water for exactly 5 minutes or until candy thermometer reaches 219° F. Pour the syrup over peach halves arranged in an enamel saucepan. Add lemon, cover and simmer until peaches are tender but not pulpy.

Take them out with a slotted spoon and drain them well. If large macaroons are available, drench them from the bottom (which is more absorbent) with maraschino and arrange 1 peach half on each. Sprinkle the peaches with shaved almonds, browned in butter and drained, and serve. If small macaroons are used, allow 2 or 3 to each peach half.

POIRES PETIT DUC
Poached Pears on Pineapple
(page 17)

4 large ripe pears
2 cups water
1 cup sugar
1 12-ounce jar red currant jelly (preferably red currant jam)
¼ cup maraschino
¼ cup kirsch
1 ripe pineapple, peeled, cored, and sliced
1 pint vanilla ice cream, slightly softened
¼ cup chopped pistachio nuts

Peel pears, cut them in half and scoop out the seed area. Poach the pear halves gently in water previously boiled for 5 minutes with the sugar. If pears are ripe this will take only a few minutes. Take them out, let them drain and reduce the syrup in which they boiled to 1 cup. Add the jelly and stir until dissolved. Remove from heat and stir in maraschino and kirsch. Dip the pineapple slices into this syrup and arrange them in a crystal dessert bowl. Cover pineapple with ice cream and pear halves, cut side down, and serve sprinkled with pistachio nuts. Serve the current syrup sauce separately.

PUMPERNICKEL PUDDING
(page 15)

  1 pound pumpernickel, grated or blended into crumbs
½ cup almonds, ground
⅔ cup butter
  6 eggs
¾ cup sugar
¼ teaspoon each, ground cloves and cinnamon, or to taste
  1 tablespoon finely chopped citron
  3 tablespoons raisins
  3 tablespoons brandy
  1 tablespoon lemon juice
  1 cup heavy cream
    Butter and bread crumbs for pudding mold

Combine pumpernickel crumbs, almonds, and butter over very low heat and stir until mixed. Remove from heat and cool. Beat 3 whole eggs and 3 yolks with the sugar, spices, and citron and add them to the mixture. Add raisins soaked in brandy and lemon juice. Beat the 3 egg whites until stiff and whip the cream. Fold both into the pudding mixture and pour it into a pudding mold, well buttered and crumbed, which is large enough to allow for expansion. Close the mold firmly and set. Cook it in a kettle of boiling water for 1¼ hours. The water should not come higher than three-quarters up the sides of the mold. Take kettle from heat and let the pudding stand for 15 minutes before inverting it onto a hot platter. If necessary loosen it from the mold by running a knife along the edge until it slips out easily. Serve with Spiced Red Cherry Sauce (recipe below) or sweetened whipped cream.

Spiced Red Cherry Sauce

Heat 1 jar cherry conserve with ¼ cup kirsch. Stir in ground cloves and cinnamon to taste, and cook the sauce, uncovered, in a double boiler over simmering water until slightly reduced.

YIELDS ABOUT 3 CUPS

QUEEN'S PUDDING
(page 153)

    4 slices stale bread, cubed
    6 tablespoons red raisins
    6 tablespoons white currants
    3 tablespoons finely diced candied peel
2¼ cups milk
    ¼ cup sugar, or to taste
    3 eggs
    3 egg yolks
    1 10-ounce jar red raspberry jam
    ½ cup raspberry juice

Butter a 2-quart pudding mold and put in bread cubes, raisins, currants, and candied peel. Bring milk to a boil. Beat sugar with eggs and yolks until light. Stir in the milk in a thin stream, and when it is smooth and slightly thickened, pour it over the ingredients in the mold. Stir well, cover the mold and steam it very gently in a kettle of hot water for 45 minutes. The water should extend three-quarters up the sides of the mold. Unmold the pudding and serve it at once with Raspberry Sauce, page 298.

SALZBURGER SCHNEENOCKERL
Salzburg Meringue Soufflé
(page 38)

    3 large egg yolks
    ¾ cup granulated sugar
    2 tablespoons flour
    1 teaspoon vanilla
       Milk
    3 tablespoons butter
    6 large egg whites
    1 tablespoon confectioners' sugar

Beat the egg yolks with 3 tablespoons of the granulated sugar until almost white, add the flour gradually and beat in half the vanilla. Set the mixture aside. In a shallow baking pan, preferably an oval 9-inch cocotte, bring ¾ inch of milk to the simmering point with 3 tablespoons of the sugar, the rest of the vanilla, and the butter. When the butter is melted, hold it at just under simmering. Beat the egg whites until half stiff, gradually add the remaining sugar and continue to beat until glossy and "solid." Fold about a cup of the meringue into the yolk mixture until smooth. Increase heat under the milk to simmer, and fold the remaining meringue carefully into the yolk mixture. Take the simmering milk from the stove, scoop the meringue up in 3 large portions and set them on the milk. They should completely cover the milk and stand about 4 inches high. Smooth the surfaces quickly with a spatula. Sprinkle the meringues with confectioners' sugar through a hair sieve and bake them in a 450° F. oven for about 8 to 10 minutes, or until they are faintly browned but not until a tough surface has formed. Serve at once.

MAKES 3 LARGE MERINGUES

SEVASTOPOL SCHNITTEN
Almond Slices
(page 165)

6 tablespoons butter
¼ cup and 14 tablespoons sugar
1 large egg yolk
  Grated rind of ½ lemon
½ teaspoon vanilla
1⅓ cups flour
2 tablespoons cold heavy cream
¾ cup shaved almonds
4 large egg whites
1 pinch ground cinnamon

Cream butter, gradually beat in ¼ cup of the sugar, egg yolk, lemon rind, and vanilla until the mixture is light and creamy. Gradually add the flour and work into a smooth paste with the cream. Press the paste into a buttered 10 x 17-inch baking dish—it will just make a thin base. Prick it with a fork and bake it in a 375° F. oven until faintly browned and half baked, about 12 minutes. Let it cool. In the meantime bring the remaining sugar to a boil with the almonds, egg whites, and cinnamon, stirring constantly, as the sugar burns easily. (If the pan is heavy the sugar will turn to a pale gold color.) Let it boil for less than a minute, take it off and spread it evenly over the half-baked paste in the pan. Return it to the 375° F. oven and bake it until it is golden and the surface is crackled, about 20 to 25 minutes. Remove from heat, mark it with a sharp knife into 2 long lines and 10 cross lines making 33 slices measuring about 3½ x 1½ inches. Set the pan aside until the next day, then cut the slices with a sharp knife and lift them out with a spatula. They can be kept for 4 or 5 days.

YIELDS 33 SLICES

SOUFFLE CAMARGO
(page 165)

4 slices sponge cake ½ inch thick, cut into triangles
3 tablespoons Grand Marnier
1 tablespoon maraschino
2 tablespoons butter
2 tablespoons flour
⅓ cup sugar, or to taste
1 cup light cream
⅔ cup finely chopped, toasted scalded almonds
1 tablespoon grated orange rind
6 eggs, separated
⅔ cup well-drained orange sections, free of white membranes
1 cup heavy cream, whipped

Arrange the cake triangles in the bottom of a buttered and sugared 1½-quart soufflé dish. Sprinkle with Grand Marnier and maraschino. Cream butter and flour until smooth and stir with sugar and cream. Cook the mixture until thickened over low heat, about 5 minutes, stirring constantly. Take from heat, cool and beat with the almonds, the orange rind, and egg yolks. Stir in gently the drained orange sections and fold in the stiffly beaten egg whites. Pour the batter into the prepared soufflé dish and bake in a 375° F. oven for about 35 to 40 minutes, or until puffed and brown. Serve with lightly sweetened whipped cream flavored with Grand Marnier to taste.

TARTE AU SUCRE
Sugar Custard Tart
(page 86)

    2 cups flour
    10 tablespoons unsalted butter
    1 egg
    3 tablespoons heavy cream, chilled
    1 pinch salt

Sift flour into a bowl, slice the butter over it. Make a well in the center and pour in the egg beaten with cream and salt. Work the butter into the flour with your fingertips and quickly work in the moist ingredients. Knead into a smooth paste and chill for 2 hours before using. Roll it out to a little less than ¼ inch thick on floured pastry canvas with a stockinette-covered rolling pin. Cut it out a little larger than the pie pan and transfer it to the pan, or invert the pan on it and turn the paste—canvas and all—onto the pan. Take away the canvas and fit the paste loosely into the pan. Trim and pinch the edge into a standing border. Chill the tart shell for 1 hour, then prick the bottom with the tines of a fork and bake it in a 350° F. oven for 16 minutes.

While the shell is baking, prepare the filling.

Filling:

    4 egg yolks
    ½ cup sugar
    ⅓ cup butter, at room temperature
    ⅓ cup flour
    1 whole egg
    1 teaspoon vanilla
    2 cups milk
    ⅔ cup crushed macaroons
    ¼ cup Hazelnut Pralinée, page 322

Beat egg yolks and sugar until pale and thick. Beat in the butter, flour, the egg, and vanilla. Beat in the milk gradually and add the macaroon crumbs. Pour the mixture into the tart shell and bake in a 325° F. oven for about 30 minutes or until set. Cool, sprinkle with pralinée or with more macaroon crumbs, and serve.

TRIFLE
(page 93)

1 stale sponge cake cut into slices ½ inch thick and each slice cut
    into 3 strips
1 cup sherry
¼ cup brandy or apricot brandy
1 cup apricot jam
1 recipe Crème Anglaise, page 315
1 cup heavy cream
2 tablespoons confectioners' sugar
1 teaspoon vanilla
¼ cup shaved and toasted almonds
    Angelica cut in the shape of leaves
    Fresh raspberries for decoration

Soak the sponge strips in a combination of sherry and brandy. Spread them
with apricot jam, and transfer them carefully with a spatula to a deep crystal
dish. Pour the Crème Anglaise over them to completely submerge the cake.
Chill. Before serving, whip the heavy cream and gradually stir in sugar and
vanilla. Pipe the whipped cream around the edge of the dish and make rosettes
along the sides and in the center. Decorate the outer edge of the cream with
shaved almonds and garnish the surface of the custard with angelica leaves
and raspberries.

TRUDE HUDLER'S KAISERSCHMARREN
Emperor's Pancakes
(page 142)

1 cup flour
1 cup milk
4 eggs, separated
1 pinch salt
1 tablespoon sugar
1 apple, peeled and thinly sliced
6 tablespoons butter
    Confectioners' sugar, enough for sprinkling

Beat flour into milk, add yolks, salt, and sugar and beat until smooth. Stir in apple slices and fold in the stiffly beaten egg whites. Melt half the butter in a heavy frying pan, pour in the batter and bake in a 400° F. oven until puffed and brown, for 10 or 12 minutes. Place pan over medium heat, tear the pancakes into pieces with two forks and add the remaining butter to the pan. Stir until the pieces are lightly fried and glossy. Invert over a hot platter and sieve confectioners' sugar over them. Serve at once with plum or other conserves.

VACHERIN
Meringue Layers
(page 153)

8 **egg whites**
½ **teaspoon salt**
1 **teaspoon lemon juice**
1¾ **cups superfine sugar**

Sprinkle flour on a well-buttered baking sheet and shake to cover evenly. Draw four 8-inch circles in the flour. Beat the egg whites with salt and lemon juice in the beater or in a bowl with a French wire whisk. When the eggs are half stiff, gradually add the sugar, continuing to beat until the sugar has been incorporated and the meringue is smooth and glossy. Spread the meringue with a spatula, or pipe it around and around, into the four marked 8-inch circles. They should be at least ⅓ inch thick. Choose one of the circles for the top of the cake. Pipe a border through a fluted tube, and pipe rosettes along the border and in the center. Use up all the meringue and make the top very elaborate. Bake the layers in a 175° F. oven. If your oven dial does not go as low as 175°, bake the Vacherin layers at 200° or the lowest point on the dial for as long as possible—for half the day if you can spare the oven—until they are crisp and cream-colored. Loosen them carefully from the baking sheet with a spatula and dry them further on a cake rack. Chill the layers for 2 hours.

Filling:

Fill the 3 layers to your taste with whipped cream mixed with Hazelnut Pralinée, page 322, or with sweetened whipped cream and sliced strawberries, or with riced chestnuts and sweetened whipped cream. Adjust the layers evenly and top with the elaborate one. Smooth the sides with more cream and serve.

VANILLA HASELNUSS KIPFERL
Vanilla Hazelnut Horns
(page 78)

¾ cup hazelnuts or filberts
2 cups flour
1 pinch double-acting baking powder
¾ cup butter
9 tablespoons sugar
1 cup confectioners sugar, stored with a vanilla bean
1 tablespoon vanilla

Toast the nuts in an open pan in a 200° F. oven, shaking them frequently, for about 30 minutes until the brown skins are brittle and can be rubbed off with a rough kitchen towel. They will never rub off completely, but at least half of them should be removed. (If vacuum-packed parched hazelnuts can be obtained, wash them well to remove all salt. Dry them completely and use in place of the fresh hazelnut kernels.) Grind the nuts finely in a nut grater and combine them with the flour and less than ⅛ teaspoon baking powder. Cream the butter, beat in the sugar and vanilla, and gradually work in the flour mixture to obtain a smooth paste. Chill it for 30 minutes. On lightly floured pastry canvas roll it into rolls of the thickness of a little finger. Cut the rolls into 2½-inch lengths and bend them into little horns on a well-buttered baking sheet. Bake them in a 350° F. oven for about 20 minutes, watching them after 15 minutes. They should be creamy in color, dry and firm but not browned. Take them from the oven and move at once to a platter sprinkled with vanilla-flavored sugar. Sprinkle the remaining sugar over the warm horns through a fine sieve.

MAKES ABOUT 70 HORNS

Indexes

Index to Part I

Note: Recipes for those dishes appearing in boldface type may be found in Part II of this volume.

Index to Part II

Note: Page numbers appearing in boldface type refer to the author's mention of the dishes in Part I of this volume.